GOOD TASTE

Southern Recipes and Traditions
by Annette Sanderson

For my family

GOOD TASTE

Southern Recipes and Traditions

Copyright© 2000 Annette Sanderson
107 Woodland Terrace
Moulton, Alabama 35650
256-974-0311
anniels@bellsouth.net

Library of Congress Catalog Number: 202-707-6372
ISBN: 0-9679414-0-7

Editor: Dianne Norwood
Computer Specialist: Larry Smith
Typist: Patsy Suggs

Printed in the United States of America
by

Jumbo Jack's Cookbooks
1-800-798-2635

FIRST EDITION
First Printing: 2000
Second Printing: 2000
SECOND EDITION
First Printing: 2006

All rights reserved. No part of this book may be reproduced or transmitted in any form or by any means, electronic or mechanical, including photocopying, recording, or by any information storage and retrieval system, without prior written permission from the publisher.

Contents

Acknowledgements 4

Introduction 5

Menus 6

Appetizers and Beverages 11

Soups, Salads and Sandwiches 43

Breads, Breakfasts and Brunches 87

Entrées 127

Vegetables and Side Dishes 175

Desserts 215

Condiments and Basics/Charts 299

Appendix 341

Index 342

Credits and Purpose 350

Order Information 353

Acknowledgments

To my husband Ott, who supported me in every way and endured the most; to Scott, Cathy and Laura Lee who were guinea pigs for a long, long time; and to Bart and Kate who supported this effort long-distance.

Artists

Cover Design: Jane McCullough

Jane is an artist from Moulton, Alabama. Her work includes oils, acrylics and watercolors recognized throughout the South. She is a signature member of the Watercolor Society of Alabama, and her work is permanently exhibited at the Loretta Goodwin Gallery in Birmingham, Alabama.

Watercolor Illustrations: Bart Sanderson

Bart, my younger son, is an architect in Seattle, Washington, where he lives with his wife, Kate. He has a Bachelor of Architecture degree from Auburn University and a Master of Architecture degree from The University of Arizona.

Technical Assistance: Robert Rhyne, Pete Wolverton, Scott Sanderson and Ott Sanderson.

Menu and Recipe Development: Betty Mitchell Sims, Caryl Ward Littrell, Syble Murphy and Marlynn Rhyne

Architectural Research: Mary Morris and Melissa Beasley, Pond Spring (Wheeler Plantation); Lawrence County Historical Commission and Archives; Jane Cowart; Lillie Hogue; and Joan Lang, Administrator, Lawrence County Commission.

Proofreaders: Marlynn Rhyne, Christy Wright, Marie Jeffreys and Ott Sanderson.

Recipe Testers: Marlynn Rhyne, Betty Mitchell Sims, Caryl Ward Littrell, Syble Murphy, Jane McCullough, Patsy Terry, Annie Frances Proctor and Virginia Johnson.

A special thanks to Dianne Norwood, Patsy Suggs, Larry Smith and to Marlynn Rhyne for countless hours. Also to Christy Wright for her contribution. To all others who shared their time and support in any way, including Anna Little.

Introduction

GOOD TASTE is the result of many, many volunteer hours of research, writing, editing, proofreading, testing and food-related decisions. It began over 3 years ago as a collection of personal favorite recipes compiled into one easy-to-use book. Most are not originals but simply favorites that have withstood the test of time and that cause grown children to call home for. All recipes have been tested to ensure good results for the reader.

Producing a cookbook eventually becomes a consuming passion. We finally admit to ourselves that our lives have become food-obsessed. But there's no turning back! We read cookbooks as if they were novels; we gain extra pounds and fall into sinking spells. We put the book aside for life events, then come up for air and continue the ongoing search for the very best hush puppy recipe.

With that in the past, let me express my heartfelt appreciation to all who shared wonderful recipes, ideas and support and to all volunteers who worked willingly and enthusiastically on this project, some from the beginning and others who were lights of joy when they were most needed. Each of you will stay in my heart forever.

So we wish you *GOOD TASTE*, good traditions and good times. Hopefully, this cookbook will encourage many celebrations and memories that will lead to your new traditions.

GOOD TASTE MENUS

New Year's Day Ballgame

Rosy Wassail
Black-Eyed Pea Dip with Corn Chips
Lela Phillip's Seafood Gumbo over Rice
Crunchy Chicken Wings
Fresh Turnip Greens
Waldorf Salad
Corn Muffins
Deep Chocolate Cake
Lemon-Almond Buttermilk Loaf with Balsamic Strawberries

Caryl Ward Littrell

Classic Easter Luncheon

Baked Easter Ham
Pineapple Casserole
The Ultimate Macaroni and Cheese
Company Potatoes
Marinated Asparagus
Advent Bazaar Rolls
Strawberry Trifle
Coconut Cream Pie

All-American Summer Cookout

Auburn Lemonade
July 4th Hamburgers or Onion-Stuffed Burgers
Grilled Corn in Husk with Basil Butter
Best Baked Beans
Crunchy Cabbage Slaw
Party Relish Tray
Lettuce and Tomato
Onion Buns
Marion's Dishpan Cookies
Praline Thumbprint Cookies
Watermelon Quarters

Fish Fry Down On the Farm

Catfish Stew
Clara's 3-Week Slaw
Best Stuffed Eggs
Pickles, Sliced Vidalia Onions, Sliced Tomatoes
Summer Potato Salad
Deep-Fried Catfish
Hush Puppies and Tartar Sauce
Peach Ice Cream
The Ultimate Sugar Cookies

Syble Murphy

Before The Game

Spinach Dip with crackers
Marinated Pork Tenderloin with Mustard Sauce
Marinated Vegetable Salad with Dijon Dressing
Sweet Potato Salad with Rosemary-Honey Vinaigrette
Betty's Famous Pimento Cheese Sandwiches
German Chocolate Chess Squares
Commercial rolls

Syble Murphy

Taste of Tradition Holiday Gathering

Roast Turkey
Southern Corn Bread Dressing with Giblet Gravy
Baked Plantation Country Ham
Green Beans, Southern Style
Macaroni and Cheese
Sweet Potato-Praline Casserole with Marshmallows
Cranberry Ring Mold and Old Fashioned Mayonnaise with Pansies
Party Relish Tray
Best Stuffed Eggs
Sweet Potato Muffins
Mattie B's Fabulous Fresh Coconut Cake
Fruitcake Cookies
Southern Pecan Pie

Caryl Ward Littrell

Home for the Holidays

Leg of Lamb Roast with Lemon or Saffron Sauce
Cornish Game Hens
Toasted Walnut Salad
Garlic Mashed Potatoes
Steamed Asparagus with Lemon Butter
Ginger and Honey-Glazed Carrots
Ice Cream Tortoni
Caramelized Pumpkin Custards

Caryl Ward Littrell

Holiday Brunch

Coffee, Boiled Custard and Brandy Slush
Asparagus Quiche
Creamy Grits with Mushroom Sauce
Baked Plantation Country Ham
Cream Biscuits
Blackberry Jam
Fresh Fruit Salad with Citrus Sauce
Skillet Coffee Cake
Short and Sweet Caramel Bubble Ring

Betty Mitchell Sims

Family Brunch

Canadian Egg Casserole
Stove-top Potatoes
Baked Tomatoes
Hot Sherried Fruit
Quick and Easy Biscuits
Honey-Orange Butter
Orange Marmalade Spread
Simple Orange Rolls

Betty Mitchell Sims

Sunny Side Up

Creamy Scrambled Eggs with Chives
Country Ham with Red-Eye Gravy
Bacon or Sausage
Creamy Grits
Spiced Fruit in Light Syrup
Peppery White Cheddar Biscuit Squares
or
Sweet Potato Biscuits
Blackberry Coffee Cake

Southern Afternoon Tea

French Mint Tea
Raspberry Sherbet Punch
Pecan Chicken Salad in Toast Cups
Tomato-Basil Sandwiches
Cucumber Sandwiches
Turkey Tea Sandwiches
Toasted Pecans
Fresh Fruit Tray with Dip
Lime Tartlets
Amaretto Brownies
Mini Cheesecake Fruit Tarts

Betty Mitchell Sims

Appetizers and Beverages

Entrance to Sherrod Home, a two-story 1830's Federal-style house.
Pond Spring (Wheeler Plantation) Hillsboro, Alabama

Appetizers and Beverages

Pecan Chicken Salad in Toast Cups

4 cups finely chopped cooked chicken (white meat)
3/4 cup mayonnaise
1/4 cup sour cream
1/2 cup finely diced celery
1/2 cup finely chopped pecans
Salt and black pepper to taste
Toast Cups (page 321)

Combine all ingredients in a large mixing bowl. Spoon into Toast Cups.

Makes filling for 24 Toast Cups

Betty Mitchell Sims

Crunchy Chicken Wings

1/2 cup melted butter
1/4 teaspoon garlic powder
1 teaspoon cayenne pepper
1/2 cup finely chopped pecans
1 cup finely crushed pretzels
1/4 teaspoon black pepper
2 pounds chicken wings
Chutney Pecan Sauce or Gourmet Hot Mustard (*recipes follow*)

Chutney Pecan Sauce:
1/4 cup butter, room temperature
1/3 cup chutney
1/4 cup honey
1/4 cup pecan halves

Gourmet Hot Mustard:
1 cup sugar
1 cup vinegar
3 eggs
1 (1-ounce) can dry mustard
1/2 teaspoon salt

Wings: Preheat oven to 350 degrees. Combine butter, garlic powder and cayenne pepper in a bowl; set aside. Combine pecans, pretzels and pepper; set aside. Rinse chicken wings and pat dry. Cut wings into 2 pieces at the joint, discarding the tips. Dip wings into butter mixture. Roll in the pecan mixture to coat. Place on greased baking sheet. Bake for 50 to 60 minutes or until golden brown. Serve with Chutney Pecan Sauce or Gourmet Hot Mustard. Makes about 16 to 20 chicken pieces
    Chutney Pecan Sauce: Combine butter, chutney, honey and pecan halves in a food processor. Process until pecans are a chunky consistency.
    Gourmet Hot Mustard: Combine the sugar, vinegar, eggs, mustard and salt in a blender. Process for 3 minutes. Cook in a double boiler until thickened. Cover and store in refrigerator.

Caryl Ward Littrell

Appetizers and Beverages

Hot Crab Dip

2 (8- ounce) packages cream cheese, room temperature
2 1/3 cups chopped onions
1 pound fresh crab meat or 2 (6-ounce) cans
1 teaspoon prepared horseradish
1/4 cup milk
Salt to taste

Preheat oven to 350 degrees. In a large bowl, mix all ingredients except milk together. Put into 1 1/2-quart greased baking dish. Pour milk over top and bake 1 hour.

Note: Can be made 1 day ahead. If so, bring to room temperature and pour milk over top just before baking.

Betty Mitchell Sims

Magnificent Mushrooms

1 stick butter
1 small onion, minced
1 pound whole fresh mushrooms
1 teaspoon dried basil
1 teaspoon dried oregano
1/2 teaspoon garlic salt
1/2 teaspoon thyme
1/2 teaspoon Tabasco
2 tablespoons fresh lime juice
1/2 teaspoon salt
1/4 cup dry sherry

Melt butter in a large saucepan or skillet. Sauté onion in butter until soft. Add mushrooms and coat well with the butter-onion mixture. Add basil, oregano, garlic salt, thyme, Tabasco, lime juice, salt and sherry. Mix well; cover and simmer until dry. Serve with toothpicks.

Lynn Littrell

Citrus-Shrimp Salad

Wonderful prepare-ahead dish. Can be dressed up or down for a buffet

3 quarts water
4 pounds unpeeled, medium-size fresh shrimp
1/4 cup Italian salad dressing
3 tablespoons finely chopped shallots
2 tablespoons red wine vinegar
2 tablespoons plain yogurt
2 tablespoons orange juice
1 1/2 tablespoons Dijon mustard
1 tablespoon honey
1/8 teaspoon pepper
4 cups coarsely chopped hearts of romaine lettuce
2 cups pink grapefruit sections
2 cups orange sections
1/4 cup chopped fresh chives

In pot, bring water to a boil; add shrimp. Cook shrimp 3 to 5 minutes. Drain and rinse with cold water. Peel and devein shrimp; chill.

In bowl, combine salad dressing, shallots, vinegar, yogurt, orange juice, mustard, honey and pepper in a large bowl, and stir well. Add shrimp, and stir.

Line a large platter with chopped lettuce. Spoon shrimp mixture into center of platter; arrange grapefruit and orange sections around salad. Sprinkle with chives.

Note: Can be done 1 to 2 days ahead. Cook, peel and chill shrimp. Peel and section oranges and grapefruit; make dressing. Store in separate containers and assemble 1 to 2 hours before serving. Cover with plastic and chill.

Serves 8 to 10

Cheese Ball

2 (8-ounce) packages cream cheese, room temperature
2 cups mild shredded Cheddar cheese
2 tablespoons chopped pimento
2 tablespoons chopped green pepper
2 tablespoons chopped onion
2 tablespoons Worcestershire sauce
1 tablespoon lemon juice
1/4 teaspoon seasoned salt
1 cup pecans, finely chopped

In medium bowl, mix well, roll into a ball and then roll ball in pecans. Can be frozen.

Cathy Flory

Blue Cheese Ball

2 (8-ounce) packages cream cheese, room temperature
1 (5-ounce) jar Kraft Old English Cheese
1 (4-ounce) package blue cheese
1/4 pound Cheddar cheese, shredded
2 tablespoons onion juice
3/4 tablespoon horseradish
1/4 teaspoon Worcestershire sauce
1/2 cup chopped parsley
1/2 cup chopped pecans

In large bowl, mix all ingredients, except parsley and pecans, together. Shape into ball and roll in parsley and pecans.

Note: If Kraft Old English Cheese is not available, use 9 tablespoons of Cheese Whiz.

Betty Mitchell Sims

Appetizers and Beverages

Cheddar Cheese Ring

16 ounces extra-sharp Cheddar cheese, shredded
16 ounces medium Cheddar cheese, shredded
1 small onion, grated
1 cup mayonnaise
1 teaspoon red pepper
1 cup chopped pecans
Parsley
1 cup strawberry preserves

In large bowl, combine all ingredients except strawberry preserves and mix well. Put in 7-cup ring mold, which has been lightly oiled. Chill thoroughly. (Mixture will form together when chilled). Unmold and fill center with preserves.

Note: Use Ritz crackers with this combination.

Anne Littrell

Cheese Rolls

16 ounces Cheddar cheese, shredded
1/3 cup mayonnaise
2 tablespoons milk
1 tablespoon dried parsley
3 green onions, finely chopped (with green tops)
2 teaspoons Worcestershire sauce
1/2 teaspoon Tabasco
1/4 teaspoon onion powder
1/2 teaspoon seasoned salt
1/2 teaspoon black pepper
1/2 teaspoon cayenne pepper
1 loaf sliced white bread, crusts removed
1/2 cup unsalted butter, melted

Preheat oven to 375 degrees. In a bowl, combine all ingredients except bread and melted butter. For each roll, flatten one slice of bread with a rolling pin and spread with cheese mixture. Roll bread diagonally and secure with a toothpick. Place rolls on cookie sheet and brush with melted butter. Bake until cheese is melted and bread is golden brown, 10 to 12 minutes.

Makes 24 rolls

Appetizers and Beverages

Fabulous Pimento Cheese Spread

1 (8-ounce) loaf process cheese spread, cubed
1 (8-ounce) package shredded three-cheese gourmet Cheddar cheese blend
1 (8-ounce) package shredded sharp Cheddar cheese
1 1/2 tablespoons sugar
1/4 teaspoon salt
1/4 teaspoon pepper
1 (4-ounce) jar diced pimento, drained
1 cup mayonnaise

Process half of cheese in a food processor until smooth, stopping to scrape down sides. Transfer to a bowl. Process remaining cheese, sugar, salt and pepper in food processor until smooth, stopping to scrape down sides. Stir this into cheese mixture in bowl; stir in pimento and mayonnaise.

Makes 1 quart spread

Cheese Straws

16 ounces New York State sharp or extra-sharp cheese,
   shredded and room temperature
1 stick margarine, room temperature
2 cups all purpose flour
1 teaspoon salt
1/2 teaspoon red pepper
1 teaspoon baking powder
Paprika

Secret of success: let cheese and margarine sit out overnight to soften. Next morning, preheat oven to 375 degrees. In large bowl, mix all ingredients except paprika; knead by hand (or with mixer fitted with paddle attachment) to blend well. Place in cookie press, use small star design and press onto ungreased cookie sheet. Bake 12 minutes and sprinkle with paprika after baking.

Makes 200 straws

Lynn Littrell

Hot Bean Dip

1 (9-ounce) can bean dip
1 (8-ounce) package cream cheese, room temperature
1/2 (1-ounce) package taco seasoning mix
1 cup chopped green onions (include green tops)
1/2 cup shredded Monterey Jack cheese
1/2 cup shredded Cheddar cheese
1 (8-ounce) container sour cream
20 drops Tabasco sauce

Preheat oven to 350 degrees. In bowl, mix all ingredients together and bake for 20 minutes. Serve hot with tortilla chips or corn chips.

Note: Also good wrapped in a flour tortilla like a burrito.

Alicia Johnson Nails

Texas Caviar

2 (11-ounce) cans shoe peg corn, drained
2 (15-ounce) cans black-eyed peas, rinsed and drained
1 (28-ounce) can tomatoes, chopped and drained
12 green onions, chopped (include green tops)
1 large bell pepper, chopped
2 (10-ounce) cans Rotel tomatoes, chopped
1 (16-ounce) bottle Italian salad dressing
Salt and pepper to taste

In bowl, mix all ingredients together. Chill before serving with tortilla chips.

Verna White

Appetizers and Beverages

Mississippi Sin

1 round loaf (16-ounce) Hawaiian bread
  (Cut top off and take out middle of bread; leave loaf in aluminum pan.)
1(8-ounce) package cream cheese
2 cups Cheddar cheese, grated

Add:
1 (12-ounce) package ham, chopped
1 1/2 cups sour cream
1 small bunch green onions, chopped (with green tops)
1 (4 1/2-ounce) can green chilies, chopped

Preheat oven to 350 degrees. Soften cream cheese and Cheddar cheese in a bowl in microwave. Mix all ingredients together in a large bowl and place mixture inside bread. Put top back on bread. Cover with aluminum foil and bake for 1 hour. Serve with bread pieces, crackers or corn chips.

Lynn Littrell

Marinated Vidalia Onions

2/3 cup water
1/3 cup sugar
3 tablespoons white vinegar
2 Vidalia onions, thinly sliced
1/2 cup (or to taste) Miracle Whip or mayonnaise
2 tablespoons poppy seeds
Salt and pepper to taste

In pot, boil water, sugar and vinegar. Pour over thinly sliced onions and refrigerate overnight. Drain well and mix to taste with mayonnaise, poppy seeds, salt and pepper.

Note: The marinated onions will keep 2 weeks or more in the refrigerator before being mixed with other ingredients. Spoon these onions on your favorite cracker.

Kathy Slaton

Vidalia Onion Soufflé

3 to 4 cups finely chopped Vidalia onions
1 tablespoon butter
3 (8-ounce) packages cream cheese, room temperature
2 cups grated Parmesan cheese
1/2 cup mayonnaise

Preheat oven to 425 degrees. Sauté onions in butter. Mix all ingredients in a large mixing bowl. Bake in a 9x13x2-inch-baking dish for 15 minutes. Jumbo corn chips are great for dipping this!

Suzanne Terry Cunningham

Black-Eyed Pea Dip

1 (15-ounce) can black-eyed peas, drained
1 (14-ounce) can artichoke hearts, drained
2 tablespoons grated Parmesan cheese
1/2 cup mayonnaise
1/2 cup sour cream
1 (.4-ounce) package Hidden Valley Ranch Salad Dressing Mix
1 cup shredded mozzarella cheese

Preheat oven to 350 degrees. Mix all ingredients together, except mozzarella cheese, and put in a 10-inch baking dish. Top with cheese and bake for 20 minutes.

Note: Serve hot with large corn chips.

Makes 4 cups dip

Carol Rollins

Peanuty Dip

This dip is good with Grilled Lemon Chicken, (page 145) cut and used on cocktail skewers as an appetizer

2 tablespoons olive oil
2/3 cup red onion, diced very small
1 1/2 teaspoons (2 cloves) garlic, minced
1 1/2 teaspoons fresh ginger root, minced
1/4 teaspoon crushed red pepper flakes
2 tablespoons red wine vinegar
1/4 cup light brown sugar, packed
2 tablespoons soy sauce
1/4 cup smooth peanut butter
1/4 cup ketchup
1 1/2 teaspoons freshly squeezed lime juice

Cook the olive oil, red onion, garlic, ginger root and red pepper flakes in a small heavy-bottomed pot on medium heat until the onion is transparent, 10 to 15 minutes. Whisk in the vinegar, sugar, soy sauce, peanut butter, ketchup and lime juice; cook for 1 more minute. Cool and use.

Note: Dip will keep 4 weeks refrigerated.

Makes 1 1/2 cups dip

Black Bean Salsa

1 (15-ounce) can black beans, drained and rinsed
1 1/2 cups cooked fresh corn kernels (3 cobs)
2 medium tomatoes, diced 1/4 inch
1 green bell pepper, diced
1 red bell pepper, diced
1/2 cup diced red onion
1 to 2 fresh green serrano peppers, thinly sliced
1/3 cup fresh lime juice
1/3 cup olive oil
1/3 cup fresh cilantro
1 teaspoon salt
1/2 teaspoon ground cumin
1/2 teaspoon pure ground red chili pepper or a pinch of cayenne pepper

Combine all ingredients in a bowl and mix well. Make a day ahead and bring to room temperature for serving. Serve with large corn chips.

Makes 5 cups salsa

Serve homemade salsa in individual cabbage cups and place near each serving plate.

Appetizers and Beverages 23

Buckaroo Bean and Bacon Salsa

Vegetable cooking spray
1 cup chopped onion
2 garlic cloves, minced
1 (15-ounce) can black-eyed peas, rinsed and drained
1 (15-ounce) can black beans, rinsed and drained
1 (15-ounce) can pinquito or pinto beans, rinsed and drained
1 (14.5-ounce) can salsa with chipotle peppers
1 (14.5-ounce) can salsa with cilantro
4 bacon slices, cooked, drained and crumbled
2 tablespoons fresh chopped cilantro

Coat a large nonstick skillet with cooking spray; place over medium heat. Add onions; sauté 5 minutes or until tender. Add garlic; sauté 1 minute. Add peas, beans, salsas and bacon; cover and cook until thoroughly heated. Remove from heat; stir in cilantro.

Note: Serve warm with tortilla chips.
Variation: If the salsas listed are not available, just substitute a good salsa. A 4-ounce can of chopped black olives can also be added.

Makes 7 cups salsa

Lynn Littrell

Seviche

1 pound fresh fish fillets, uncooked and cut into bite-size pieces
Juice of 4 lemons (or limes)
1 small garlic clove, crushed (optional)
2 medium tomatoes, peeled, seeded and cubed
2 green chilies, chopped
3 tablespoons olive oil
1/2 teaspoon dried oregano
1 teaspoon salt
Freshly ground black pepper to taste
Garlic to taste
2 tablespoons coarsely chopped fresh cilantro
Sliced avocado and sweet onions for garnish

Place fish in glass bowl; cover with lemon juice and small clove of crushed garlic if desired. Allow to stand in refrigerator for 4 hours, stirring occasionally. Drain and combine fish with other ingredients. Garnish and serve.

Note: Fresh whiting, speckled trout, small peeled and cleaned shrimp or any similar fish will do. Serve with tortilla chips or as a salad course on mixed greens or as a filling for tomato or avocado halves. Will keep overnight refrigerated, but flavor will be stronger.

Makes 1 1/2 cups seviche

Pam Norwood

Appetizers and Beverages 25

Spinach Dip

1 (16-ounce) container sour cream
1 (1.4-ounce) package Knorr vegetable recipe mix
2 (10-ounce) packages frozen chopped spinach, thawed and drained until no moisture remains
2 small onions, finely chopped
2 (4-ounce) cans water chestnuts, finely chopped
2 cups mayonnaise

In bowl, mix all ingredients together and refrigerate overnight. Serve in pumpernickel or rye bread that has been hollowed-out or use a cabbage as a container.

Note: Sour cream and Knorr vegetable recipe mix make a good dip without any other ingredients.

Makes 3 cups dip

Betty Mitchell Sims

Baked Mexican Spinach Dip

1 cup finely chopped onion
2 tablespoons cooking oil
3 medium tomatoes, chopped
2 to 4 tablespoons chopped jalapeño peppers
1 (10-ounce) package frozen chopped spinach, thawed and drained until no moisture remains
2 1/2 cups shredded Monterey Jack cheese
1 (3-ounce) package cream cheese, cut into 1/2-inch cubes
1 cup half-and-half
1/2 cup sliced black olives
1 tablespoon red wine vinegar
Salt and pepper to taste

Preheat oven to 400 degrees. In large pot, cook onion in oil until tender. Add 2/3 cup tomatoes and all jalapeño peppers, and cook 2 minutes more. Transfer to a large mixing bowl and add spinach, 2 cups Monterey Jack cheese, cream cheese cubes, half-and-half, olives, vinegar, salt and pepper. Spoon into 9x13x2-inch greased baking dish. Top with remaining cheese and tomatoes. Bake for 35 minutes. Serve with crackers.

Makes 6 1/2 cups dip

Suzanne Terry Cunningham

Toasted Pecans

1/2 cup butter
1 quart pecan halves
Salt

Preheat oven to 325 degrees. In a heavy skillet, melt butter. Add pecans and stir until warm and coated with butter. Spread on a large baking sheet and toast 10 to 15 minutes. Place on paper towels to drain. Salt while hot.

Makes 1 quart

Betty Mitchell Sims

Cucumber Sandwiches

1/3 cup mayonnaise
1 (8-ounce) package cream cheese, room temperature
1 medium cucumber, peeled, seeded and finely chopped
1/4 teaspoon garlic salt
1/2 teaspoon chopped fresh dill
20 thin white bread slices
20 thin wheat bread slices

Put mayonnaise and cream cheese in blender or food processor and blend until smooth, stopping once to scrape down sides.
    Combine cream cheese mixture, cucumber, garlic salt and dill.
    Spread cucumber mixture evenly onto white bread slices, and top with wheat bread. Using a 2 to 3-inch round cutter, cut sandwiches, discarding edges.
    Store cucumber sandwiches in an airtight container for up to 1 hour before serving.

Note: Crusts may be cut from bread and discarded. Sandwiches can then be cut in quarters.

Makes 20 rounds or 80 quarters

Betty Mitchell Sims

Appetizers and Beverages

Party Cucumber Sandwiches

1 (8-ounce) package cream cheese, room temperature
1/4 cup mayonnaise
1 seedless cucumber, unpeeled
1 loaf fresh sandwich bread (white or whole wheat)
1 (4-ounce) can whole shrimp, rinsed and drained

In bowl, mix cream cheese and mayonnaise thoroughly and set aside. Wash cucumber and remove ends. Make rows of indentations on outside of cucumber with fork tines and then slice cucumber. Cut bread with biscuit cutter. Spread cream cheese mixture on bread rounds and top with a cucumber. Garnish each with a shrimp. Chill until ready to serve.

Makes forty 1 1/2-inch sandwiches

Betty Mitchell Sims

Tomato-Basil Sandwiches

1 (3-ounce) package cream cheese, cubed and at room temperature
1/3 cup dried tomatoes in oil, drained well and minced
2 tablespoons finely chopped walnuts
2 tablespoons shredded Parmesan cheese
12 very thin wheat sandwich bread slices
12 very thin white sandwich bread slices
3/4 cup Basil Butter
Crushed walnuts for sandwich sides, if desired

Basil Butter:
1/2 cup butter, room temperature
1/2 cup loosely packed fresh basil leaves, chopped
1/4 teaspoon sugar
1/2 teaspoon lemon juice

In bowl, beat first 4 ingredients to blend. Spread cheese mixture evenly on 1 side of wheat bread slices. Spread 1 side of white bread slices evenly with Basil Butter which has been well blended and chilled.

Press together spread sides of 1 wheat slice and 1 white slice. Repeat procedure with remaining bread slices.

Trim crusts from sandwiches. Cut sandwiches with a 2-inch round cutter or cut into 4 squares. Roll crust sides in crushed walnuts if desired.

Makes 24 (2-inch) sandwiches

Betty Mitchell Sims

Cherry Tomato Tea Sandwich

Spread miniature bread rounds with mayonnaise. Add a very thin slice of unpeeled cherry tomato. Top with a sliver of green bell pepper. Sprinkle lightly with salt just before serving.

Note: Rounds may be cut the night before and wrapped tightly, but sandwiches should be made the day of serving.

Betty Mitchell Sims

Appetizers and Beverages

Turkey Tea Sandwiches

1 loaf wheat bread (remove crusts and cut into squares or rounds)
1 pound thinly sliced turkey, cut in squares or rounds to fit bread
1 (4-ounce) box alfalfa or broccoli sprouts

Spread bread evenly with Honey-Mustard Butter Spread or Cranberry-Butter Spread. Place turkey on bread, then sprouts. Top with another bread slice.

Makes 24 sandwiches

Honey-Mustard Butter Spread:
1/2 cup butter or margarine, room temperature
1/4 cup honey
2 tablespoons prepared mustard

Mix ingredients well.

Makes 3/4 cup spread

Cranberry-Butter Spread:
1 cup sugar
1/2 cup water
1 1/4 cups fresh cranberries
1/2 cup butter, room temperature
1 tablespoon confectioners' sugar

Bring sugar and water to a boil in a small saucepan over medium heat, stirring until sugar dissolves. Stir in cranberries and bring to a boil. Reduce heat and simmer, stirring occasionally, 10 to 15 minutes or until thick. Remove from heat and cool completely.

Press cranberry mixture through a fine strainer, discarding hulls.

In electric mixer bowl, beat butter at medium speed until light and fluffy. Add confectioners' sugar and cranberry mixture. Beat until well blended.

Makes 1 cup spread

Betty Mitchell Sims

Apricot-Pecan Tea Sandwich Spread

2 (8-ounce) packages cream cheese, room temperature
16 ounces dried apricots, soaked in 2 cups boiling water for 10 minutes, drained and chopped
1 cup chopped pecans
1/2 cup honey (Orange Blossom preferred)
Wheat bread

In bowl, mix ingredients well and spread on wheat bread from which crust has been removed.

Makes 4 cups spread

Cream Cheese-Olive Spread

6 ounces cream cheese, room temperature
2 tablespoons mayonnaise
1/8 teaspoon pepper
4 small green onions, finely chopped (include green tops)
1/2 cup pimento-stuffed olives, chopped

In bowl, combine cream cheese, mayonnaise and pepper; beat until smooth. Stir in onions and olives.
Mixture may be used to stuff celery or tomatoes or as a sandwich spread.

Makes 1 1/4 cups spread

Betty Mitchell Sims

Appetizers and Beverages   31

Fillings for Yeast Rolls

Beef Tenderloin Filling:
1 cup sour cream
1/4 to 1/3 cup prepared horseradish
1/4 teaspoon salt
1 tablespoon lemon juice
24 thin slices beef tenderloin

In bowl, combine sour cream, horseradish, salt and lemon juice. Spread small amount in center of roll and place slice of tenderloin on top. Cover until ready to heat. Bake, covered, at 350 degrees for 15 to 20 minutes.

Makes 24 rolls

Turkey Filling:
4 ounces orange marmalade
12 thin slices roasted or smoked turkey

Spread small amount of orange marmalade in center of rolls and place slice of turkey on top. Cover until ready to bake. Bake, covered, at 350 degrees for 15 to 20 minutes.

Makes 12 rolls

Pineapple-Cream Cheese Spread

1 (8-ounce) package cream cheese, room temperature
1/4 cup diced pineapple, drained
2 tablespoons finely chopped pecans
1 teaspoon vanilla extract

In bowl, combine all ingredients; mix well. Serve on date-nut or whole wheat bread.

Makes 1 cup spread

Apple Julep

3 quarts orange juice
1 gallon apple cider
3 quarts pineapple juice
1 cup lemon juice

In large container, mix, chill and serve.

Note: Serve over crushed ice and garnish with a sprig of mint.

Makes 2 1/2 gallons julep

Frannie Adair
Classical Fruits
Moulton, AL

Brandy Slush

4 cups water
2 cups sugar
4 green tea bags
1 (12-ounce) can frozen lemonade
1 (12-ounce) can frozen orange juice
2 cups peach brandy
7-Up
Orange slices and maraschino cherries for garnish on each glass

Mix sugar and water and boil until dissolved. Soak 4 green tea bags in water and sugar mixture.
   In a large plastic container, mix 5 1/2 cups cold water, frozen lemonade, frozen orange juice and 2 cups peach brandy.
   Combine water and sugar mixture with juice mixture and freeze for 48 hours. To serve, spoon 2 tablespoons frozen mixture into an 8-ounce glass; fill with 7-Up and stir. Garnish each glass with orange slices and maraschino cherry.

Makes about 1 gallon slush

Syble Murphy

Appetizers and Beverages

Boiled Custard

1 quart milk
4 large eggs
3/4 cup sugar
2 tablespoons all-purpose flour
2 teaspoons vanilla extract

Heat milk in medium-size heavy non-aluminum saucepan (to avoid discoloring) over medium heat 10 minutes or until hot.

Combine eggs, sugar, flour and vanilla in a small bowl, stirring with a wire whisk until blended. Gradually stir 1 cup hot milk into egg mixture; then add this to remaining hot milk, stirring constantly.

Cook over medium heat, stirring constantly, 6 to 8 minutes or until mixture begins to thicken and thermometer registers 180 degrees (do not boil mixture).

Remove from heat and pour mixture through a strainer into a pitcher or bowl and place heavy plastic wrap directly on surface of custard (to keep skin from forming) and chill.

Note: Above recipe is drinkable. To make a spoonable custard, cook mixture, stirring constantly, 9 to 10 minutes or until mixture thickens.

Makes 1 quart custard

Betty Mitchell Sims

Cathy's Party Punch

1 (2-ounce) container Crystal Light lemonade mix
1 teaspoon coconut extract
1 teaspoon almond extract
1 teaspoon vanilla extract
1 (46-ounce) can pineapple juice
1 (67-ounce) bottle ginger ale

Use enough lemonade mix to make 1 gallon. To this 1 gallon, add flavorings, pineapple juice and ginger ale. Pour over ice ring (page 36).

Makes 30 (8-ounce) cups

Cathy Flory

Mock Champagne Punch

3 cups sugar
3 cups water
2 (6-ounce) cans frozen lemon juice
2 (2-liter) bottles ginger ale
1/2 cup sparkling white grape juice

In large pan, boil sugar and water and let cool. Add lemon juice, ginger ale and white grape juice. Pour over ice ring (page 36).

Note: Nice to serve at very special occasions.

Serves 30 to 35

French Mint Tea

3 lemons, juice reserved
10 cups water, divided
2 cups sugar
1 1/2 teaspoons almond extract
1 1/2 teaspoons vanilla extract
6 individual-size tea bags
2 (46-ounce) cans pineapple juice
Fresh mint

In large pan, add lemon rinds to 6 cups water and sugar. Boil 5 minutes. Discard the rinds and add extracts and lemon juice. Steep tea bags in 4 cups boiling water for 15 minutes. Remove tea bags and add tea to the mixture. Add the pineapple juice and chill. Serve over ice and garnish with fresh mint.

Makes 1 1/2 gallons tea

Syble Murphy

Grape Juice Punch

When in doubt, use this! Very quick, very easy and not too sweet!

4 (25-ounce) bottles white grape juice
3 (33-ounce) bottles ginger ale
1 ice ring (recipe follows)

Chill juice and ginger ale in bottles. Place ice ring in punch bowl and pour chilled grape juice and ginger ale into bowl.

Note: To increase amount, add more grape juice and ginger ale in approximate amounts.

Makes 1 1/2 gallons punch

Fruited Ice Ring

Thin lemon slices
Thin lime slices
Thin orange slices

Select a large gelatin mold. Pour enough water into mold to cover the bottom. Cut citrus slices and arrange a layer of fruit in mold. Freeze until firm. Continue to add thin layers of water and fruit in mold, freezing each layer before adding the next. Store in freezer until needed. Ice ring can be prepared several days in advance. When ready to use, dip the bottom of the mold in warm water and invert ice ring into the punch bowl.

Makes 1 ice ring

Frozen Ice Rounds

1 orange, halved and sliced into half-moons
1 cup fresh cranberries
12 large mint leaves, plus 2 for garnish

Using a 6-cup muffin tin, arrange orange slices, cranberries and mint leaves in each cup. Cover with water and freeze.
       When ready to serve punch, fill punch bowl. Remove ice rounds from freezer; place in punch bowl with mint sprigs.

Icy Tea Punch

3 lemons (reserve peel)
2 oranges (reserve peel)
9 (family-size) tea bags
1 cup fresh chopped mint
3 cups sugar
1/4 cup maraschino cherry juice

Squeeze the juice of lemons and oranges into a bowl and chill, reserving peel. Place tea bags, mint and the reserved citrus peel in 2 quarts boiling water. Steep for 30 minutes; strain.

Add sugar, stirring until dissolved. Chill for up to 24 hours. Stir in the lemon and orange juice mixture, maraschino cherry juice mixture and 1 1/2 quarts of cold water. Freeze in a 1-gallon container until of a slushy consistency, about 1 1/2 hours. Garnish each serving with a mint sprig and maraschino cherry.

Note: This punch freezes solid in about 4 to 5 hours. Best frozen in plastic or cardboard containers that can be cut or peeled off. Frozen punch takes 2 to 3 hours to become slushy.

Makes 1 gallon punch

Raspberry Sherbet Punch

1 (12-ounce) can frozen pink lemonade concentrate, thawed and undiluted
1 quart raspberry sherbet, softened
1 (2-liter) bottle raspberry ginger ale (or regular ginger ale), chilled

Combine lemonade concentrate and sherbet in a punch bowl. Stir in ginger ale and break up sherbet. Serve immediately.

Makes 12 cups punch

Betty Mitchell Sims

Cube Art

Turn ordinary summer beverages into spectacular refreshments with the addition of herbal or floral ice cubes.

Snip fresh mint or any edible flower blossom (page 326). Place them in an ice cube tray compartment. Fill compartments halfway, or enough to cover blossoms with boiled water (to make ice clear) or ginger ale. Freeze until firm. Fill remainder with water or ginger ale and freeze again.

Try mint cubes in iced tea and pansy cubes in lemonade or use in punch bowl.

Appetizers and Beverages

Auburn Lemonade

Freshly-squeezed lemonade is an Auburn University tradition, but only if it's served at Toomer's Corner, on a hot fall day and most importantly, after a victorious ballgame. The fact that everything in sight has been "rolled," I think, contributes to the delicious taste!

1 pint lemon juice, freshly squeezed
2 pints simple syrup (page 321)

Pour 1 pint lemon juice and 2 pints simple syrup into a gallon container. Finish filling container with water. Stir well. Pour over ice in glasses. Garnish with lemon slices.

Makes 1 gallon lemonade

Just 1 Lemonade

Juice of 1 lemon
4 ounces simple syrup (page 321)

To make a single serving lemonade, squeeze the juice of 1 lemon into a 16-ounce glass. Add 4 ounces simple syrup and fill remainder of glass with water. Stir well and add ice.

Note: Substitute limes for lemons for the same good taste.

Makes 1 serving of lemonade

Cold, clear pitchers of lemonade can look elegant with lemon halves, whole stemmed strawberries and mint peeping out from the crushed ice. Add the same in the bottom of clear glasses; fill with ice and lemonade.

Quick Iced Tea

5 (family-size) tea bags
4 cups water
1 1/4 cups sugar
1 quart ice

Heat tea bags and water in a nonreactive saucepan over medium heat until small bubbles form on sides of pan, but not to boiling (10 to 15 minutes).
    Remove from heat, cover pan and steep for 3 minutes. Remove tea bags; pour tea into pitcher. Stir in sugar until it dissolves; stir in ice until melted. Serve in ice-filled glasses.

Makes 1 1/2 quarts tea

Hot Chocolate

On a cold winter day, who doesn't love hot chocolate? This drink receives great depth of flavor from really good chocolate and a bit of coffee. Serve it as dessert or surprise those Christmas carolers!

2 1/2 cups whole milk
2 cups half-and-half
4 ounces bittersweet chocolate, chopped
6 ounces milk chocolate, chopped
1 1/2 tablespoons sugar
1 1/2 teaspoons vanilla extract
1 teaspoon instant coffee powder, or espresso powder, or to taste
Vanilla beans or cinnamon sticks, for stirring
Whipped cream for garnish

Heat milk and half-and-half in a saucepan over medium heat to just below the simmering point. Remove from heat and add chocolate.
    When chocolate is melted, add sugar, vanilla and coffee powder. Whisk vigorously.
    Reheat gently and serve immediately.

Makes 5 cups hot chocolate

To get more juice from each lemon, microwave for 15 seconds on high and then with palm of hand, roll the lemon on the counter top.

Appetizers and Beverages

Hot White Chocolate

2 ounces top-quality white chocolate, chopped
1/3 cup brewed coffee
1 1/2 cups half-and-half or milk
1/2 teaspoon vanilla
Ground nutmeg

In a small heavy saucepan melt baking bar over low heat. Stir in coffee; heat until smooth (use whisk). Add half-and-half; cook over medium heat until hot (do not boil). Remove from heat; stir in vanilla. Return to heat and cook 5 minutes and place in blender container. Blend until frothy. Pour into 2 mugs; sprinkle lightly with nutmeg. Serve immediately.

Makes 2 servings

Spiced Tea

4 sticks cinnamon
4 tablespoons whole cloves
6 (family-size) tea bags
2 cups sugar
1 (46-ounce) can unsweetened pineapple juice
1 cup orange juice (made from frozen concentrate)
Juice of 3 lemons

In large pan, boil cinnamon and cloves in 4 cups water for 4 minutes. Add tea bags and steep, covered, for 4 minutes. Add 2 cups sugar, pineapple juice, orange juice and lemon juice. Add enough water to make 1 gallon. Remove cinnamon and cloves before serving. Heat to serve.

Makes 1 gallon tea

Syble Murphy

Rosy Wassail

1 pint cranberry juice cocktail
1 (6-ounce) can frozen orange juice concentrate, thawed
2 cups water
1 tablespoon sugar
1/4 teaspoon allspice
3 1/2 cups white wine
Few drops of red food coloring (optional)

Combine all ingredients in a large saucepan. Bring to a simmer. Do not boil.

Serves 12 to 14

Caryl Ward Littrell

Iced tea, like ice cubes, made with spring water has a fresh, clean, clear look and taste.

Notes

Soups, Salads and Sandwiches

Limestone carvings atop Lawrence County Courthouse columns, 1936
Moulton, Alabama

Soups, Salads and Sandwiches

Mean Beans

School days often call for one-dish meals. Mean Beans is a hearty, quick meal. Corn bread is a must!

1 pound ground chuck
1 large onion, chopped
Salt and pepper to taste
2 medium potatoes, chopped
1 cup water
1 (15-ounce) can cream corn
1 (15-ounce) can pinto beans
1 (15-ounce) can Great Northern beans
1 small head cabbage, chopped

Brown ground chuck and onion; add salt and pepper. Add potatoes and put in large pot with 1 cup water. Add corn, beans and cabbage. Cook until tender, 20 to 30 minutes. Refrigerate and warm as needed.

Serves 6

Helen Holland Sanderson

Ballgame Chili

2 1/2 pounds ground chuck
1 large onion, chopped
1 (1 3/4-ounce) package French's Chili-O-Mix seasoning
1/2 to 1 teaspoon chili powder, or to taste
1 or 2 (15-ounce) cans Van Camp chili beans
1 (28-ounce) can whole tomatoes, slightly crushed
1 (15-ounce) can tomatoes, whole, or tomato juice
1 small green pepper, diced
Salt and pepper to taste

In large Dutch oven, sauté ground chuck and onion in 2 tablespoons oil until onion is translucent and chuck is beginning to brown. Add all other ingredients and simmer until sauce is thickened, about 1 hour. Stir occasionally to prevent sticking.

Serves 8

Chicken and Dumplings

1 large (3 to 3 1/2-pound) chicken
Water to cover
3 cups sifted all-purpose flour
1 teaspoon salt
1/2 cup shortening
Ice water (start with 1/2 cup and add more if necessary by the tablespoon)
1/2 cup margarine
1 teaspoon black pepper

In a large Dutch oven, cover chicken with water (3 1/2 quarts) and cook until tender, about 45 minutes. Remove chicken from broth. When cool, skin and debone chicken and pull into bite-size pieces. Set chicken and broth aside. There should be at least 3 quarts broth.

In a medium bowl, mix flour and salt. Add shortening and cut into flour until it resembles coarse crumbs. Add ice water to make dough come together. Knead 3 or 4 times and roll into a disc. Refrigerate for 1 hour or overnight.

Place chilled dough on floured surface and roll out as thinly as possible. Cut into strips about 1 1/2 by 6-inches long. Add 1/2 cup margarine and black pepper to reserved broth and bring to a boil. Drop some dumplings into broth, but do not stir. Let dumplings cook and toughen. Add remaining dumplings and repeat process. Be careful and gently try to keep them from sticking together as they cook.

Reduce heat to medium low or low and simmer, covered, about 8 to 10 minutes. Stir occasionally very gently. When dumplings are done, add chicken. Salt and pepper to taste. Ladle into bowls.

Serves 6 to 8

Berlin Sanderson

Soups, Salads and Sandwiches

Texas-Style Chili

1 1/2 pounds boneless beef stew meat, cut into 1-inch cubes
1 1/2 pounds boneless pork shoulder, cut into 1-inch cubes
2 tablespoons vegetable oil
3 tablespoons all-purpose flour
3 tablespoons chili powder
2 teaspoons ground cumin
1/2 teaspoon crushed, dried oregano
3 cloves garlic, minced
1/2 teaspoon red pepper
1/4 teaspoon black pepper
1 (10-ounce) can condensed beef broth
4 to 6 cups cooked pinto beans
Sour cream
Lime wedges
Parsley

In Dutch oven, brown meat cubes, 1/2 at a time in hot oil. Return all meat to pan. Stir in flour, chili powder, cumin, oregano, garlic and peppers. Add broth and enough water to cover meat. Simmer, covered, about 1 1/2 hours or until tender, stirring occasionally. Serve meat over pinto beans. Dollop with sour cream and a squeeze of lime juice. Garnish with parsley.

Note: Serve this with grilled cheese sandwiches, slaw and a simple dessert—a good cold-weather meal.

Serves 6 to 8

Caryl Ward Littrell

Cold Cucumber Mint Gazpacho

3 cucumbers, peeled, seeded and chopped, plus 1 cup peeled, seeded and finely diced cucumber
1 cup plain yogurt
2/3 cup sour cream
1/2 teaspoon dry mustard, or to taste
1/4 cup tiny mint leaves
Cucumber slices and mint sprigs for garnish

In a blender, purée chopped cucumbers, yogurt, sour cream, mustard, salt and pepper to taste until smooth.
    Transfer to a bowl. Chill gazpacho at least 6 hours or overnight.
    Stir in finely diced cucumber and tiny mint leaves and garnish gazpacho with cucumber slices and a sprig of mint.

Note: Very good with salmon.

Makes 4 1/2 cups gazpacho

Gazpacho

5 slices French bread, large loaf; crust removed, torn and lightly toasted
1 quart buttermilk
2 cucumbers, peeled, seeded and roughly chopped
1 rib celery, roughly chopped
1 red pepper, seeded and roughly chopped
1 onion, roughly chopped
2 cloves garlic, peeled
2 tablespoons champagne vinegar (may use apple cider vinegar)
2 tablespoons fresh lemon juice
1/4 teaspoon Worcestershire
Dash of Tabasco
1/4 cup extra-virgin olive oil
Kosher salt and freshly ground black pepper

In a bowl, soak the bread in buttermilk. In batches, blend the cucumber, celery, red pepper, onion and garlic with the buttermilk and bread. Combine the blender batches in a bowl. Stir in the vinegar, lemon juice, Worcestershire, Tabasco and extra-virgin olive oil. Season to taste with salt and pepper. Chill and serve cold.

Note: Garnish each bowl with diced red pepper and cilantro.

Serves 8

Lela Phillips' Seafood Gumbo Over Rice

Gumbos are thickened by the addition of either okra or filé powder. Gumbo gets better with time, so make it a day or two in advance.

4 (14-ounce) cans chicken broth
2 quarts water
4 (28-ounce) cans chopped tomatoes
1 (12-ounce) can tomato paste
6 bay leaves
4 large onions, chopped
4 large green bell peppers, chopped
1 cup chopped celery
1 cup chopped fresh parsley
1 tablespoon chives
1 tablespoon basil
Dash Tabasco
1 cup olive oil
2 (16-ounce) packages frozen sliced okra, thawed
2 cups chopped ham
1 pound smoked sausage, cubed and sautéed
4 to 5 pounds peeled shrimp, (uncooked and tailed removed) floured
1 pound flaked crab
1 teaspoon filé powder, (optional)
Hot cooked rice

Combine chicken broth, water, chopped tomatoes, tomato paste and bay leaves in a large 12-or 15-quart pot. Place on stove over high heat and cover.

Mix chopped onions, green peppers and celery with parsley, chives, basil and Tabasco. Sauté in olive oil until partially cooked. Add okra and cook 10 minutes.

Add cooked vegetables to pot and cook slowly for 1 hour. Add ham and sausage to pot and cook for 1 1/2 hours over low heat.

Flour shrimp generously and fry a few at a time until slightly brown. Add shrimp the last 30 minutes, stirring often. Add crab and cook for 10 minutes. Remove from heat. Remove bay leaves and serve over hot, cooked rice. If filé is used, sprinkle sparingly over each serving and stir.

Note: Freezes well if filé powder isn't added to entire recipe.

Makes 3 gallons gumbo

Syble Murphy

Filé Powder

Filé powder, the classic thickener of Creole gumbos, is derived from the leaves of the sassafras tree. Besides adding thickness, it lends an earthy, somewhat musty flavor, making it unsuitable as a universal thickening agent. It is rarely found in any dish besides gumbo.

Okra

The viscous sap given off when okra is sliced will thicken the liquid in which it is cooked. Select firm, brightly colored pods under 4 inches in length. Store unwashed okra in a plastic bag in the refrigerator for up to 3 days.

Broccoli Cheese Soup

1 stick margarine
1 onion, minced
2 tablespoons flour
2 tablespoons water
2 quarts chicken broth
1 bunch fresh broccoli, cut in florets
Lemon-pepper seasoning, to taste
5 cups cooked egg noodles, or wide ribbons, drained
16 ounces Velveeta cheese, cubed

In a large Dutch oven, melt margarine, add onion and sauté. Make a paste of flour and 2 tablespoons water. Dilute with small amount of chicken broth and add to onion mixture. Add remaining broth, broccoli florets and lemon-pepper seasoning. Cook gently until broccoli is tender, approximately 6 minutes.

Add cooked and drained noodles. Stir in cheese. Heat, but do not boil.

Variation: Add cooked chicken for a hearty main dish.

Serves 6 to 8

Virginia Johnson

Soups, Salads and Sandwiches

Cold-Weather Cheese Soup

1/2 cup margarine
1 cup minced carrots
1 cup minced yellow onion
1 cup minced celery
1/2 cup all-purpose flour
3 cups chicken broth
3 cups half-and-half
32 ounces Velveeta cheese, cubed
1 tablespoon finely chopped fresh parsley
Chopped tomatoes
Minced jalapeños

Heat margarine in a stockpot until melted. Add carrots, onion and celery. Sauté until vegetables are tender but not brown. Add flour, stirring until mixed. Cook until mixture turns a light brown, stirring constantly. Add chicken broth gradually and mix well after each addition. Cook over medium heat until thickened, whisking constantly.

Add half-and-half and mix well. Stir in cheese. Cook just until cheese melts and soup is heated through, stirring frequently; do not boil. Add parsley just before serving. Ladle into soup bowls. Top each serving with chopped tomatoes and minced jalapeños.

Serves 12

Soups, Salads and Sandwiches 51

Dieter's Soup

1 cup shredded cabbage
2 ribs of celery, diced
2 carrots, diced
1 medium onion, chopped
1 (15-ounce) can whole tomatoes
1 (4.5-ounce) can mushrooms
1 (1-ounce) package Hidden Valley Ranch Dressing Mix (optional)
1 (15-ounce) can green beans
2 bouillon cubes, chicken

In a large Dutch oven, cook cabbage, celery, carrots and onion in a small amount of water until tender. Add remaining ingredients and bring to a boil. Simmer several minutes.

Serves 6 to 8

Chunky Italian Soup

1 pound lean ground beef
1 medium onion, chopped
2 (14-ounce) cans Italian tomatoes
1 (10-ounce) can tomato soup with basil, undiluted
4 cups water
2 cloves of garlic, minced
2 teaspoons dried basil
2 teaspoons dried oregano
1 teaspoon salt
1/2 teaspoon pepper
1 tablespoon chili powder (optional)
1 (16-ounce) can kidney beans, drained
1 (16-ounce) can Italian green beans, drained
1 carrot, chopped
1 zucchini, chopped
8 ounces rotini noodles, cooked
Parmesan cheese, grated

Cook beef and onion in Dutch oven over medium heat, stirring until beef crumbles and is no longer pink; drain. Return mixture to pan. Stir in tomatoes, soup, water, garlic, basil, oregano, salt, pepper and, if desired, chili powder; bring to a boil. Reduce heat; simmer, stirring occasionally, 30 minutes. Stir in kidney beans, green beans, carrots, and zucchini; simmer, stirring occasionally, 15 minutes. Stir in noodles. Sprinkle each serving with cheese.

Makes 10 cups soup

Marlynn Rhyne

Chicken Stock

Homemade stock adds a rich, deep flavor to soups, stews and sauces. Make and freeze in amounts you often use. Stocks are quite flexible, so experiment or use what you have on hand. One good trick: 1 pound of solids to 1 pint liquid makes a stock which will not be too weak.

Onion Soup

This is an old family recipe Philip Reich shared. It was one of his father's favorites and a classic served at the Reich Hotel in Gadsden, Alabama. It freezes well.

12 onions, thinly sliced
4 tablespoons butter
14 cups beef bouillon (better with beef stock)
1 teaspoon Worcestershire sauce
1/4 teaspoon Tabasco sauce
1 teaspoon Kitchen Bouquet
Freshly ground black pepper
Salt
6 slices French bread, 1-inch thick
6 tablespoons grated Parmesan cheese

Sauté onions in butter in a large saucepan for 15 minutes or until golden brown. Add bouillon, Worcestershire, Tabasco, Kitchen Bouquet, pepper and salt if needed. Bring to a boil, reduce heat, cover and simmer for approximately 4 hours (6 to 8 hours are better). Preheat oven to 350 degrees. Toast French bread until brown on both sides. Sprinkle top side with 1 tablespoon Parmesan cheese and place soup in oven-ready bowls. "Float" bread with cheese and broil only long enough to melt cheese. Serve immediately.

Serves 6

Baked Potato Soup

8 slices bacon
1 cup diced yellow onion
2/3 cup all-purpose flour
6 cups hot chicken broth
4 or 5 cups, peeled and sliced baked potatoes (5 medium-large)
2 cups half-and-half
1/4 cup chopped fresh parsley
1 1/2 teaspoons minced garlic
1 1/2 teaspoons dried basil
1 teaspoon salt
1 teaspoon coarsely ground black pepper
1/2 teaspoon Tabasco
1 cup grated Cheddar cheese
1/4 cup sliced green onions (include green tops)
Garnishes: cooked, crumbled bacon; grated Cheddar cheese; chopped fresh parsley

In Dutch oven, cook bacon until crisp; remove bacon, reserve drippings. Crumble bacon and set aside. Cook onion in reserved drippings over medium-high heat about 3 minutes or until transparent. Add flour, whisking until smooth or until mixture just begins to turn golden. Add chicken broth gradually, whisking until liquid thickens. Add potatoes and next 7 ingredients. Reduce heat and simmer 10 minutes. (Do not allow soup to boil.) Add grated cheese and scallions. Heat until cheese melts completely.

Garnish each serving with bacon, Cheddar cheese and parsley.

Serves 8

Easy Potato Soup

1 (16-ounce) bag frozen diced hash brown potatoes
1 cup chopped onion
1 (14-ounce) can chicken broth
2 cups water
1 (10-ounce) can cream of celery soup, undiluted
1 (10-ounce) can cream of chicken soup, undiluted
2 cups milk
Garnishes: shredded Cheddar cheese or cooked bacon

Combine potatoes, onion, chicken broth and water in a Dutch oven; bring to a boil. Cover, reduce heat and simmer 30 minutes. Stir in soups and milk which have been whisked together until very smooth. Heat thoroughly. Garnish if desired.

Makes 2 1/2 quarts soup

Betty Mitchell Sims

Santa Fe Soup

2 pounds ground round
1 medium onion, chopped
2 (1-ounce) packages taco seasoning
2 (1-ounce) packages Hidden Valley Ranch Dressing mix
2 cups water
1 (28-ounce) can diced tomatoes
1 (10-ounce) can Rotel tomatoes
2 (15-ounce) cans whole kernel corn, drained
2 (15-ounce) cans black beans, undrained
1 (14 ounce) can pinto beans, undrained
1 (14 ounce) can kidney beans, undrained
1 (14 ounce) can white kidney beans, undrained
Tabasco, to taste
Salt and pepper, to taste
Garlic powder, to taste
Cheddar cheese, green onion or sour cream for garnish

In a large Dutch oven, sauté meat and onion. Drain off fat and sprinkle taco seasoning over meat. Mix Ranch Dressing mix in 2 cups water. Add to meat mixture along with remaining ingredients. Add Tabasco, salt, pepper and garlic powder to taste. Simmer gently and serve. Garnish as desired.

Serves 8 to 10

Marlo Johnson Greene

Soups, Salads and Sandwiches

Tomato and White Bean Soup

2 teaspoons olive oil
1 cup chopped onion
3 garlic cloves, crushed
2 (14-ounce) cans whole tomatoes, undrained and chopped
2 (16-ounce) cans navy beans, drained
1 (14-ounce) can chicken broth
1 tablespoon chopped fresh parsley
3/4 teaspoon dried oregano
1/4 teaspoon pepper
1/4 cup grated Parmesan cheese

Heat oil in large saucepan over medium heat. Add onion and garlic and sauté 4 minutes or until tender. Add tomatoes and next 5 ingredients; bring to a boil. Reduce heat, and simmer 10 minutes. Ladle into bowls and sprinkle with cheese.

Serves 4 or 6

Catfish Stew

2 pounds catfish fillets
2 cups water
1 (28-ounce) can crushed tomatoes
1 (16-ounce) can tomato juice
4 large potatoes, peeled, cubed and cooked until tender
1 large onion, chopped
1 (16-ounce) package frozen shoe peg corn, thawed
2 bay leaves
1 tablespoon salt
1 teaspoon black pepper
20 saltine crackers, crushed

In large pot, cook catfish in 2 cups water until just flaky (15 to 20 minutes). Add all other ingredients except crackers. Cook 30 minutes over medium heat. Add crackers and cook for 30 minutes until thickened and flavors have blended. Remove bay leaves.

Note: Serve with hush puppies and slaw.

Serves 4

Bobby Murphy

Remove Bay Leaf

When cooking with bay leaves, always remove from dish before serving. They do not soften during cooking and cannot be eaten.

Chicken Stew

Make this stew when you are home for a few hours to stir, stir, stir!

1 large chicken (about 4 pounds)
Salt and pepper to taste
3 large Idaho potatoes, peeled and cubed
2 medium onions, finely chopped
1 1/2 cups large elbow macaroni, cooked separately
1 3/4 cups white sweet corn (frozen or one 15-ounce can Pride of Illinois corn)
1 (28-ounce) can tomato juice or canned tomatoes
1 tablespoon salt
1 tablespoon pepper
1 stick butter

In a Dutch oven, cover chicken with water. Add salt and pepper and cover. Bring to a boil; lower heat. Cook until chicken is tender, about 45 minutes to 1 hour. Remove chicken from broth, cool and debone.

While chicken cools, add potatoes and onions to broth and cook over medium heat until tender. Remove some of the potatoes and mash with a fork. Return to broth. Add chicken to broth along with cooked macaroni. Add corn, tomato juice, salt and pepper. Stir well. Add butter. Cook over low heat and stir often for 3 to 4 hours.

Serves 6 to 8

Berlin Sanderson

Cranberry Ring Mold and Old-Fashioned Mayonnaise with Pansies

Cranberry Mold:
1 (3-ounce) package raspberry gelatin
1 cup hot water and 1/2 cup cold water
2 teaspoons lemon juice
1 cup whole cranberry sauce
1/2 cup drained, canned, crushed pineapple
1/2 cup diced celery

Old-Fashioned Mayonnaise:
1 tablespoon sugar
1 tablespoon plain flour
1/2 teaspoon dry mustard
1/2 teaspoon salt
1/2 cup vinegar
1/2 cup water
2 tablespoons butter
2 eggs, beaten
1/2 cup milk
1/2 cup chopped nuts
Pansies (optional)

Cranberry Mold: Dissolve gelatin in 1 cup hot water. Add 1/2 cup of cold water and lemon juice. Chill until slightly thickened and fold in cranberry sauce, pineapple and celery. Pour into mold; chill until firm. Unmold and garnish with mayonnaise and pansies.

Old Fashioned Mayonnaise: Combine sugar, flour, mustard, salt, vinegar and water; bring to boil, over low heat, stirring constantly. Add butter, eggs and milk; cook about 3 minutes. Remove from heat, beat and let cool. Serve with Cranberry Ring Mold and garnish with nuts and pansies, if using.

Serves 6

Caryl Ward Littrell

Soups, Salads and Sandwiches

Frozen Frosted Fruit Salad

This salad is a tongue-twister, but it will surely delight the taste buds.

1 (8-ounce) package cream cheese, room temperature
3/4 cup sugar
1 (8-ounce) can pineapple tidbits, drained
1 (16-ounce) can blueberries, drained and rinsed
1 (8-ounce) box frozen strawberries
2 bananas, sliced
1/2 cup chopped pecans
1 (16-ounce) carton whipped topping

In a large mixing bowl of electric mixer, cream cheese and sugar together. Add pineapple, blueberries, strawberries, bananas and pecans. Mix until blended. Fold in whipped topping. Pour into a 9 x 13 x 2-inch baking dish. Cover tightly and freeze overnight. Soften in refrigerator 45 minutes before serving.

Note: Can be frozen in paper baking cups.

Serves 9 to 12

Annie Frances Proctor

Magnolia Salad

2 eggs, beaten
1 1/2 tablespoons vinegar
1/2 teaspoon dry mustard
1 tablespoon flour
1/2 cup milk
3 cups miniature marshmallows
1 cup chopped pecans
1 (8-ounce) can crushed pineapple, drained
1 (12-ounce) container whipped topping, room temperature

Mix together eggs, vinegar, mustard, flour and milk in a saucepan. Blend well and bring to a boil. Stirring constantly, cook until consistency of pudding.

In a large bowl, place pudding mixture, marshmallows, pecans and pineapple. Mix to blend. When cool, fold in whipped topping and pour into an 11 x 14 x 2-inch baking dish. Cool several hours.

Note: To serve, spoon individual servings into lettuce-leaf cups. Delicious with chicken and dressing or ham.

Serves 6

Patsy Terry

Strawberry Pretzel Salad

An old favorite that remains just that—a favorite.

2 1/2 cups crushed pretzels (food processor works well)
3/4 cup melted margarine
3 tablespoons sugar
1 cup sugar
1 (8-ounce) package cream cheese, room temperature
1 (8-ounce) container whipped topping, thawed
1 (6-ounce) package strawberry gelatin
2 cups boiling water
1 (16-ounce) package frozen strawberries, slightly broken up

Preheat oven to 375 degrees. Mix pretzels, margarine and 3 tablespoons sugar together and press into a 9 x 13 x 2-inch baking dish. Bake for 8 to 9 minutes. Cool completely.

In a mixer bowl, cream 1 cup sugar and cream cheese together well. Fold the whipped topping into sugar and cream cheese mixture and spread over cooled pretzel crust.

Combine the strawberry gelatin and boiling water until dissolved. Add frozen strawberries. Chill until it thickens and pour over the cream cheese layer. Refrigerate overnight. Cut into squares and serve.

Serves 10 to 12

Waldorf Salad

1 Red Delicious apple, unpeeled and chopped
1 Granny Smith apple, unpeeled and chopped
1 pear, unpeeled and chopped
1 tablespoon lemon juice
1/4 cup golden raisins
1 rib celery, diagonally sliced
1 (8-ounce) carton plain yogurt
1 tablespoon honey
1 teaspoon grated orange rind
1/4 cup slivered almonds, toasted

Combine first 3 ingredients in a medium bowl. Sprinkle lemon juice over fruit mixture and toss gently. Stir in raisins and celery.
　　Combine yogurt, honey and orange rind; stir well. Add 1/4 cup yogurt mixture to fruit mixture. Spoon into serving bowl. Sprinkle with almonds. Serve remaining yogurt dressing separately.

Serves 6

Caryl Ward Littrell

Fresh Lettuce

The best way to prolong the freshness of bulk or bagged lettuce greens is to soak the leaves for 5 to 10 minutes in cold water right after you buy them, then dry thoroughly by using a salad spinner or rolling the leaves between cotton towels. When the leaves are dry, wrap them loosely with 1 or 2 paper towels, and seal them in a plastic bag.
Finally, always store lettuce greens in the most humid part of the refrigerator, which is generally the crisper. The lettuce should stay fresh for 4 to 5 days.

Delightful Green Salad with
Poppy Seed Dressing

1 pound assorted lettuces, (red-leaf, spring mix, etc.)
1 pound fresh spinach, tough stems removed
1 medium avocado, peeled and sliced
1 pint fresh strawberries, halved
1 cantaloupe, scooped into balls
1 pint cherry tomatoes, halved
2 cucumbers, unpeeled and thinly sliced
8 ounces fresh mushrooms, sliced

Poppy Seed Dressing:
1 cup vegetable oil
1/2 cup tarragon vinegar
1/2 cup sugar
1 tablespoon poppy seeds
1 teaspoon salt
1 teaspoon dry mustard
1 teaspoon grated onion
3/4 teaspoon onion salt

Salad: Tear lettuces and spinach into pieces. Add remaining ingredients and toss in large bowl with Poppy Seed Dressing just before serving.

   Dressing: Combine all ingredients in a covered jar; shake well. Refrigerate until ready to use. This may be prepared ahead.

Serves 8 to 10

Mandarin Orange Salad

This salad has withstood the test of time. Still a favorite after so many years!

3 3/4 ounces slivered almonds, candied
2 tablespoons sugar
1 (11-ounce) can mandarin oranges, drained
1 head of lettuce or a mixture of lettuce, torn into bite-size pieces
1/2 cup finely chopped green onions (include green tops)
1/2 cup finely chopped celery

Dressing:
1/4 cup wine vinegar
1 tablespoon sugar
1/2 cup salad oil
2 to 3 drops Tabasco
Salt and pepper to taste

To candy almonds: Place almonds in skillet; add sugar and stir over moderate heat until sugar melts and coats almonds. Remove almonds and set aside. (This burns easily; so watch carefully.) Cool.

Mix together all dressing ingredients and chill. Combine all salad ingredients and toss in large bowl with dressing just before serving.

Serves 4

Spinach Dill Salad

Salad:
2 pounds fresh spinach, torn and coarse stems discarded
1/2 bunch green onions, chopped (include green tops)
1/2 cup slivered almonds, toasted
1 pint fresh strawberries, sliced
1 banana, sliced and dipped in pineapple juice
1/8 cup chopped fresh dill

Dressing:
1/2 cup extra-virgin olive oil
1/4 cup red wine vinegar
1/4 cup sugar
1 clove garlic, minced
1/4 teaspoon salt
1/4 teaspoon freshly ground pepper
1/4 teaspoon dry mustard
1/4 teaspoon onion powder

Whisk oil, vinegar, sugar, garlic, salt, pepper, mustard and onion powder until blended. Cover and chill.

Toss spinach, green onions, almonds, strawberries, banana and dill in a salad bowl. Just before serving, pour dressing over salad and toss.

Serves 6

Toasted Walnut Salad

Walnut Dressing:
2/3 cup walnut oil
1/3 cup fresh lemon juice
1/2 teaspoon Dijon mustard
3/4 teaspoon sugar
Salt
Freshly ground pepper

Salad:
4 heads Boston lettuce, torn into bite size pieces
1 cup toasted walnuts, coarsely chopped
2 ounces blue cheese, crumbled (1/2 cup)
1 pear, peeled, cored and thinly sliced

Walnut Dressing: Combine walnut oil, lemon juice, mustard, sugar, salt and pepper in a covered jar. Shake well and refrigerate.

Salad: Toss lettuce, walnuts, blue cheese and pear in a salad bowl. Add dressing, toss and serve immediately.

Note: Dressing may be made up to 4 days in advance and kept covered in refrigerator. Store walnut oil in refrigerator as it turns rancid quickly.

Serves 8

Caryl Ward Littrell

Poppy Seed Dressing

3/4 cup sugar
1 teaspoon dry mustard
1/3 cup vinegar
1 teaspoon salt
1 tablespoon onion juice
1 cup vegetable oil
1 tablespoon poppy seeds

In bowl, mix sugar, mustard, vinegar and salt. Add onion juice and mix. Add oil very slowly, beating constantly until dressing thickens. Add poppy seeds and beat until blended.

Note: This mixes best in blender or mixer.

Makes 1 1/2 cups dressing

Ranch Dressing

1 cup mayonnaise
1 1/2 teaspoons dried onion flakes
1 teaspoon Accent
1/4 teaspoon minced garlic
1 cup buttermilk
1 tablespoon dried parsley
1 teaspoon onion salt
1/4 teaspoon salt

In bowl, mix all ingredients together and store in refrigerator until ready to use. May prepare ahead.

Makes 2 cups dressing

Roquefort Dressing

3/4 cup buttermilk
1 tablespoon Worcestershire sauce
1/2 teaspoon garlic powder
1 cup mayonnaise
2 to 4 ounces Roquefort or blue cheese, crumbled

Blend thoroughly but gently so that there will be tasty bites of cheese. Keep in a tightly covered jar in refrigerator.
    May prepare ahead.

Makes 2 cups dressing

Thousand Island Dressing

1 cup mayonnaise
2 tablespoons commercial chili sauce, or to taste
1 cup whipped cream
2 tablespoons sweet pickle relish

Combine ingredients in order given. Blend well. Refrigerate in covered container until needed.

Makes about 1 2/3 cups dressing

Broccoli Salad

An exceptional recipe with boring broccoli. Chances are, President Bush never tasted this!

2 bunches broccoli
4 ounces shredded Swiss cheese
3 green onions, chopped (include green tops)
1 cup mayonnaise
1/2 cup sugar
2 tablespoons apple cider vinegar
3/4 cup raisins
3/4 cup walnuts

Wash broccoli and cut the tops into bite-size florets. Discard stems for another use. Combine broccoli in a bowl with Swiss cheese and green onions.

In a small bowl, stir together the mayonnaise, sugar and vinegar to make a dressing. Add it to the broccoli mixture. Let the salad marinate overnight. Just before serving, stir in raisins and walnuts.

Variation: A chopped, unpeeled red apple or 3 to 4 slices crispy fried bacon can be used.

Serves 8

Oriental Pasta Salad

16 ounces vermicelli pasta
1 cup mayonnaise
1 tablespoon Worcestershire sauce
1/4 cup sesame oil
3 tablespoons soy sauce
1 tablespoon hoisin sauce
2 tablespoons cider vinegar
1 tablespoon Dijon mustard
2 cups snow peas, blanched and cut into thirds
1 large red pepper, chopped
4 green onions, chopped (include green tops)
4 ribs celery, chopped
8 ounces marinated baby corn, drained
1 (8-ounce) can sliced water chestnuts, drained
1 cup cooked English peas
1 cup cherry tomatoes, halved and seeded

Cook the pasta in boiling salted water, and drain it thoroughly. Mix mayonnaise with next 6 ingredients until thoroughly blended.

Add vegetables; mix mayonnaise mixture 1/2 cup at a time, stirring after each addition, until the pasta and vegetables are moistened but not overwhelmed. Taste and add salt and cracked pepper if necessary. Refrigerate for several hours, adding more mayonnaise mixture if necessary, before serving.

Note: Add 2 to 3 cups shredded chicken breast for a terrific chicken salad. Great French bread completes the meal.

Serves 6 to 8

Soups, Salads and Sandwiches

Party Relish Tray

1 head cauliflower, cut into florets
1 pound baby carrots (whole with 3 inches of tops left on)
1/2 pound young green snap beans or whole French beans, ends trimmed
1/2 pound celery, cut into 3-inch pieces
1 (16-ounce) jar Kalamata olives packed in vinegar brine or olive oil
1 (11.5-ounce) jar pickled peperoncini
1 (16-ounce) jar pickled hot cherry peppers
1 (10-ounce) jar pickled Spanish Queen olives stuffed with pimentos
1 (8-ounce) jar pickled Holland cocktail onions
15 to 20 fresh basil leaves
6 sprigs fresh thyme
6 sprigs fresh oregano
2 tablespoons chopped fresh parsley leaves
1 teaspoon red pepper flakes
1 cup olive oil

Blanch green beans and carrots separately in a large pot of boiling, salted water for 4 to 5 minutes. Drain, and shock in ice water to stop cooking. Put all ingredients in a large glass bowl and toss to coat evenly. Refrigerate for 8 hours.

Serves 12

Marinated Tomatoes and Cucumbers

Fresh juicy tomatoes and garden cucumbers are a perfect salad for those hot, hot summer days.

3 large tomatoes, unpeeled and sliced
1 large cucumber, thinly sliced
1/2 cup apple cider vinegar
1/2 cup vegetable oil
1 teaspoon sugar
1/2 teaspoon dried dill
1/2 teaspoon salt
1/2 teaspoon black pepper
Lettuce leaves

Place tomato slices and cucumber slices in a large shallow container. Combine vinegar, oil, sugar, dill, salt and pepper. Stir well and pour over vegetables. Cover and refrigerate at least 2 hours. Just before serving, remove tomatoes and cucumbers with a slotted spoon and arrange on lettuce leaves. Spoon some of the remaining marinade over tomatoes and cucumbers if desired.

Serves 6

Summer Tomato Toss

Making use of what you have creates a show-stopper presentation.
Part of summer's pleasure—heirloom tomatoes!

Heirloom tomatoes (all colors and sizes)
Olive oil
Salt and pepper

In bowl, mix tomatoes of all colors and sizes. Quarter large tomatoes but leave salad or grape tomatoes whole. Look for red, yellow and orange ones for color. Toss with small amount of olive oil. Season with salt and pepper.

Soups, Salads and Sandwiches 75

Marinated Vegetable Salad With Dijon Dressing

1 cup cauliflower florets
1 cup broccoli florets
3 ounces green beans, trimmed
1/3 red bell pepper, cut into strips
1 (12-ounce) can hearts of palm, drained, cut into 1/2-inch diagonal slices
5 ounces fresh spinach, thoroughly washed, stems removed and patted dry

Dressing:
1/3 cup extra-virgin olive oil
3 tablespoons red wine vinegar
3/4 tablespoon Dijon mustard
1/4 teaspoon salt
3/4 teaspoon freshly ground black pepper
1/4 teaspoon dried oregano
1/4 teaspoon minced garlic

In a large saucepan, bring 1 1/2 quarts water to a boil. Drop the cauliflower and broccoli into the boiling water. Cook 4 minutes. Remove the florets with a slotted spoon. Drain and rinse under cold water. Drain again.

Return water to a boil and add green beans. Cook 2 minutes. Remove, drain and rinse with cold water. Drain again. Combine the cauliflower, broccoli, green beans, bell pepper and hearts of palm in a bowl.

Put dressing ingredients into a container with a tight-fitting lid and shake well. Pour dressing over the vegetables and toss to mix. Refrigerate for 2 to 3 hours. Prepare a bed of spinach on a serving platter. Spoon vegetables onto spinach.

Serves 6 to 8

Syble Murphy

Roasted New Potato Salad

*Serve this around Roast Chicken with bundles of asparagus
for a simple but elegant meal. Or toss for a tasty potato salad.*

11 tablespoons olive oil
6 cloves garlic, chopped
1 teaspoon salt
1/2 teaspoon pepper
1/2 teaspoon dried thyme
1/2 teaspoon dried rosemary
2 1/2 pounds small new potatoes, white (or red) cut into wedges, unpeeled
2 tablespoons white wine vinegar
1 teaspoon Dijon mustard
Salt and pepper to taste
1/2 cup finely chopped green onions

Preheat oven to 375 degrees. Combine 6 tablespoons olive oil, garlic, salt, pepper, thyme and rosemary in a bowl; mix well. Add the potatoes, tossing to coat. Arrange on a greased baking pan and bake for 55 minutes or until potatoes are brown and tender. Let stand until cool. Transfer potatoes to a bowl. Scrape the pan drippings into a measuring cup. Add enough of the remaining olive oil to measure 6 tablespoons. Whisk the vinegar and mustard in a bowl until smooth. Add olive oil mixture, whisking until blended. Pour over the potatoes, tossing to coat. Season with salt and pepper to taste; sprinkle with green onions. Serve at room temperature.

Serves 6

Summer Potato Salad

Tastes like our mother's potato salad always tasted.

1 1/2 pounds red potatoes, scrubbed but not peeled
6 eggs, hard-cooked, peeled and chopped
3/4 cup diced onion
3/4 cup diced celery
3/4 cup mayonnaise
1/4 cup sweet pickle relish
1 tablespoon yellow mustard
1/2 teaspoon salt
1/2 teaspoon freshly ground black pepper
Mixed greens
1/4 teaspoon paprika
Olives and green bell pepper for garnish

Bring a large saucepan of salted water to a boil. Add the potatoes, reduce heat and simmer for 20 to 25 minutes or until tender. Drain, cool and cut potatoes into 1-inch cubes.

In a large bowl, combine potatoes, eggs, onion and celery. In a small bowl stir together the mayonnaise, relish, mustard, salt and pepper. Pour mixture over potatoes. Toss gently until thoroughly combined.

Serve the salad on a bed of greens and sprinkle with paprika. Garnish with olives and green pepper rings.

Serves 6 to 8

Sweet Potato Salad With Rosemary-Honey Vinaigrette

4 1/2 cups peeled, cubed sweet potatoes
2 tablespoons olive oil, divided
1/4 cup honey
3 tablespoons white wine vinegar
2 tablespoons chopped fresh rosemary
2 garlic cloves, minced
1/2 teaspoon salt
1/2 teaspoon freshly ground pepper

Preheat oven to 450 degrees. Line a 15 x 10-inch jellyroll pan with aluminum foil. Coat foil with vegetable cooking spray. Toss together potatoes and 1 tablespoon oil in pan. Bake for 35 minutes or until potatoes are tender.

Whisk together remaining oil, honey and next 5 ingredients. Add potatoes, toss well, cool and serve.

Serves 6

Syble Murphy

Blue Cheese Coleslaw

1 medium cabbage, shredded (reserve outer leaves)
4 green onions, finely chopped (include green tops)
1 cup mayonnaise
1/4 cup prepared horseradish
1/2 cup (4 ounces) blue cheese, crumbled and divided in half

Reserve outer leaves of cabbage and shred remaining cabbage. Combine shredded cabbage and green onions in a large bowl; mix well. Cover and chill.

Combine mayonnaise, horseradish and 1/4 cup blue cheese. Just before serving, spoon mayonnaise mixture over cabbage and toss gently to blend. Line serving bowl with reserved outer leaves and fill with coleslaw. Sprinkle remaining blue cheese over top.

Serves 6 to 8

Betty Mitchell Sims

Soups, Salads and Sandwiches

Clara's 3-Week Slaw

*This slaw will keep up to 3 weeks in the refrigerator, which
makes it a winner! It's so good you'll never keep it 3 weeks.*

3 pounds cabbage, finely chopped
1 medium onion, finely chopped
1 green bell pepper, finely chopped
1 red bell pepper, finely chopped
1 teaspoon celery seed
1 teaspoon salt
1/2 cup apple cider vinegar
1/2 cup vegetable oil
1/2 cup sugar

Place all chopped ingredients in a large bowl; set aside. Mix celery seed, salt, vinegar, oil and sugar in a
small saucepan and bring to a boil. Pour over chopped vegetables. Cover tightly and refrigerate.

Serves 12 to 14

Carol F. Thompson

Crunchy Cabbage Slaw

*This is an interpretation of Barbara Chenault's slaw. Over the years, she has made a lot of folks happy
sharing this recipe. It's great with hamburgers and chili but it's use is limitless.*

1 medium cabbage, coarsely shredded (8 cups)
1 large unpeeled tomato, coarsely chopped (with most of seeds removed)
1 cucumber, peeled, seeded and chopped (discard seed portion)
2 whole medium dill pickles, chopped
1 small green bell pepper, chopped
1 small onion, chopped (optional)
1/2 to 3/4 cup mayonnaise
Salt and pepper to taste

In large bowl, gently mix all ingredients until mayonnaise is well blended. (This is best done by hand.)
Season with salt and pepper.

Serves 6 to 8

Keb's Slaw

1 medium cabbage, shredded (5 to 6 cups)
1/2 to 1 bunch green onions, chopped (include green tops)
1 (3-ounce) package ramen noodles, crumbled dry (discard seasoning)
1/4 cup almonds, toasted
1/4 cup sesame seeds, toasted

Dressing:
6 tablespoons rice vinegar
1/4 cup sugar
2/3 cup vegetable oil
Salt and pepper to taste

In bowl, mix all slaw ingredients together. Mix all dressing ingredients and set aside. If not serving immediately, refrigerate slaw. Add dressing, toasted nuts and sesame seed just before serving.

Serves 8

Annie Frances Proctor

Best Stuffed Eggs

6 large eggs, hard-boiled and peeled
1/4 cup mayonnaise
1 1/2 tablespoons sweet pickle relish
1 teaspoon prepared mustard
1/8 teaspoon salt
Dash of pepper
Paprika
6 pimento-stuffed olives, halved

Slice eggs in half lengthwise and carefully remove yolks. Mash yolks with mayonnaise. Add relish and next 3 ingredients; stir well. Spoon or pipe yolk mixture into egg whites. Sprinkle with paprika, and top each with an olive half.

Makes 12 eggs

Syble Murphy

Wild Rice Salad

Salad:
1(6.2-ounce) box Uncle Ben's Long Grain Wild Rice
1 cup chopped celery
1 cup pecans, toasted
3 to 4 green onions, chopped (include green tops)

Vinaigrette:
1/4 cup white vinegar
1/2 cup vegetable oil
Juice of 1 lemon

Rice: In pot, cook rice as directed on box omitting the butter. Cool to room temperature. Add the remaining vegetables and set aside to cool.
    Vinaigrette: In bowl, combine vinegar, oil and lemon juice and mix well. When rice is cool, pour vinaigrette over it. Marinate several hours.

Note: Serve cold or at room temperature.

Serves 4 to 6

Egg Salad Sandwiches

4 large eggs, hard-boiled and peeled
1 to 2 green onions, minced (include green tops)
1 rib celery, plus some leaves, chopped
1/3 cup mayonnaise
1 tablespoon Dijon mustard
Salt
Freshly ground black pepper
8 slices whole wheat bread
Mayonnaise
1 head Boston lettuce
2 large tomatoes, thinly sliced

While eggs are still warm, place in a bowl and chop with a pastry cutter. Add onions, celery, mayonnaise and mustard. Season with salt and pepper. Combine well and chill.
    Assemble sandwiches using whole wheat bread, additional mayonnaise, lettuce and tomatoes.

Serves 4

Hot French Cheese Sandwiches

8 ounces sharp Cheddar Cheese, grated
1/2 cup butter, room temperature
2 eggs
1/2 teaspoon garlic salt
1/2 teaspoon onion salt
16 slices white bread
Paprika

Preheat oven to 400 degrees. In mixer bowl, blend cheese and butter. Add eggs and salts and whip until creamy. Spread mixture on slice of bread, place another slice of bread on top and spread it with cheese mixture. Sprinkle with paprika. Cut into halves and bake 10 to 15 minutes. These may be frozen unbaked. Thaw before baking.

Makes 16 sandwich halves

Anne Littrell

Soups, Salads and Sandwiches 83

Betty's Famous Pimento Cheese Sandwiches

Betty Mitchell Sims is well known for her pimento cheese sandwiches. They taste best at tailgate parties, but they'll most assuredly make one who is "under the weather" feel better also.

16 ounces American cheese
3/4 cup Hellmann's mayonnaise
1/4 cup chopped pimento, undrained
1 teaspoon Tabasco
3/4 tablespoon Jane's Crazy Mixed-Up Salt Blend
1 1/2 teaspoons black pepper

Grate cheese into mixing bowl. Add mayonnaise, pimento, Tabasco, salt and pepper. Mix all ingredients together.

Note: Mixture keeps at least 4 days refrigerated. Sandwiches can be made the night before, wrapped well and placed in an air-tight container. Refrigerate. If using as sandwich filling, trim crust from bread, fill and cut in half.

Makes 2 1/2 cups pimento cheese spread

Roasted Pepper and Pork Sandwich

A great sandwich for leftover pork loin! Good enough to start from scratch.

2 teaspoons chopped fresh thyme
1/2 teaspoon salt
1/4 teaspoon pepper
1 clove garlic, finely chopped
1 teaspoon olive oil
1 (3/4-pound) pork tenderloin
1 (12-ounce) jar roasted red peppers, drained
4 slices French bread, toasted (recipe follows)

Heat broiler. Combine thyme, salt, pepper, garlic and oil. Rub over pork. Broil 20 minutes or until internal temperature is 160 degrees. Let stand 10 minutes. Slice thinly.

Arrange pork and peppers on bread. Garnish with thyme sprigs.

Toasted French bread: Combine 1 teaspoon olive oil, 1 chopped garlic clove and 2 teaspoons chopped fresh oregano in small bowl. Spread on bread and toast.

Makes 4 open-face sandwiches

Fresh Salmon BLT Sandwich

1/3 cup mayonnaise
1/2 teaspoon finely minced fresh tarragon
1 shallot, finely minced
3/4 teaspoon lemon juice
Salt and pepper to taste
2 (4-ounce) salmon fillets
1 teaspoon olive oil
4 slices potato-dill bread, toasted (or a substitute)
1 cup shredded lettuce
2 tomatoes, sliced
4 slices fried bacon

Combine mayonnaise, tarragon, shallot and lemon juice in a bowl; mix well. Season with salt and pepper.
Brush the fillets with olive oil; sprinkle with salt and pepper. Grill salmon over medium-high coals or on stove-top grill until salmon is opaque throughout or an instant-read thermometer reaches 137 degrees.
For each serving, spread one slice bread generously with mayonnaise mixture. Add lettuce, tomato, salmon and bacon.
Serve open-face with the second slice of bread cut in half and placed around sandwich on plate.

Note: Good with chips or French fries.

Serves 2

Whitlock Wedges

Cranberry Mayonnaise:
1 cup mayonnaise
1/4 cup whole cranberry sauce

Wedges
1 (16-ounce) loaf wheat or pumpernickel bread, crust removed
16 ounces shaved turkey
Broccoli sprouts or alfalfa sprouts

Cranberry Mayonnaise: Mix the mayonnaise and cranberry sauce in a bowl. Store, covered in the refrigerator until serving time.
Wedges: Spread 1 side of each slice of bread with Cranberry Mayonnaise. Layer half the slices with turkey and broccoli sprouts. Top with the remaining bread slices. Cut each sandwich into wedges.

Makes 20 wedges

Breads, Breakfasts and Brunches

The Dr. Price Irwin House, early 1900's
Moulton, Alabama

Breads, Breakfasts and Brunches

Mexican Cornbread

3 cups self-rising cornmeal
1 1/2 cups vegetable oil
3 eggs
1 teaspoon salt
2 jalapeño peppers, chopped
1/3 cup sugar
1 1/2 cups grated Cheddar cheese
1 1/2 cups milk
1 (8-ounces) can cream style corn
1 large onion, chopped

Preheat oven to 400 degrees. In bowl, mix all ingredients together. Bake in a large greased skillet or a 9 x 13 x 2-inch pan for 35 to 40 minutes.

Serves 12

Lynn Littrell

Skillet Cornbread

A well-seasoned cast-iron skillet is a must for a golden brown crust on cornbread.
Turn hot cornbread onto a plate, bottom side up, to enjoy its crunchy texture.

2 teaspoons bacon drippings
1 large egg
2 cups buttermilk
1 3/4 cups white plain cornmeal
1 teaspoon baking soda
1 teaspoon baking powder
1 teaspoon salt

Preheat oven to 450 degrees. Coat bottom and sides of a 10-inch cast-iron skillet with drippings and heat in oven.

In bowl, stir together egg and buttermilk. Add cornmeal, stirring well. Stir in baking powder, baking soda and salt. Pour batter into hot skillet.

Bake for 20 minutes or until lightly browned.

Serves 6

Corn Muffins

1 cup self-rising corn meal
1 (8-ounce) carton sour cream
1 teaspoon sugar
3 tablespoons vegetable oil
3 eggs, beaten
1 (8-ounce) can white cream-style corn

Preheat oven to 400 degrees. In bowl, mix all ingredients together. Pour into hot, greased muffin tins. Bake 15 to 20 minutes or until golden brown.

Makes 12 muffins

Caryl Ward Littrell

Hush Puppies

Hush puppies are no longer a regional delicacy. There is no better accompaniment to fried fish or seafood of any kind. These are light and delicious. Try serving them piping hot as an hors d'oeuvre with hot pepper jelly or a dash of Tabasco along with little pickles.

2 cups self-rising cornmeal
1 cup self-rising flour
3 small white onions, chopped
1/2 large can evaporated milk (5/8 cup)
1/2 large can water (5/8 cup)
2 eggs, beaten
Vegetable oil for deep frying

Chop onions in food processor. Transfer to large mixing bowl. Add all ingredients and mix together. Let sit in mixing bowl a few minutes (mixture should be medium-thick, as cornbread). In Dutch oven, heat oil to 300 degrees. Drop mix into oil by using two teaspoons. Fry 3 to 4 minutes.

Use a thermometer for correct temperature. The key to golden brown hush puppies is to keep the size small so the cooking time can be shorter.

Makes about 24 hush puppies

Breads, Breakfasts and Brunches

Angel Biscuits

Great to do ahead, freeze and thaw before baking. Be sure to allow time for thawing.

5 cups all-purpose flour
1/4 cup sugar
1 tablespoon baking soda
1 teaspoon salt
1 cup shortening (Crisco)
1 package yeast dissolved in 2 tablespoons warm water (105 to 115 degrees)
2 cups buttermilk, room temperature

Preheat oven to 400 degrees. Sift flour with dry ingredients. Cut in shortening. Add yeast to buttermilk, and stir buttermilk mixture into flour mixture until well moistened and blended. Roll out to 1/2-inch thickness; cut desired size and place on cookie sheet. Bake for 10 to 12 minutes.

If freezing, place biscuits on a cookie sheet and cover. When frozen hard, place biscuits in a plastic bag to store. When ready to bake, remove number needed and thaw for 45 minutes to 1 hour. Preheat oven to 400 degrees. Dip tops in melted butter and bake for 10 to 12 minutes or until lightly brown.

Makes thirty 2-inch biscuits

Hint

Quick-rising yeast may be used interchangeably with regular yeast (with adjustments to rising time). Quick-rising takes about 1/2 as long to leaven bread.

Angel Biscuits II

This dough will keep for 2 weeks refrigerated. Delicious split and filled with thin country ham.

9 cups sifted self-rising flour
1 cup vegetable shortening
1 teaspoon baking soda dissolved in 1/3 cup water
2 cups buttermilk
1/2 cup sugar
2 eggs, well beaten
2 packages yeast, dissolved in 1 cup warm water (105 to 115 degrees)
Melted butter

Sift and measure flour in a large bowl. Cut shortening into flour. Add baking soda, buttermilk, sugar, eggs and dissolved yeast. Mix well and store covered, in refrigerator, until needed. To bake, preheat oven to 400 degrees. Knead dough and roll to 1/2-inch thickness. Cut out and place in a greased pan; brush with melted butter. Bake 10 to 12 minutes.

Makes 8 dozen 1 1/2-inch biscuits or 5 dozen medium biscuits

Mama Berlin's 3-Day Biscuits

*Yum! These are the best! Make the dough, and it will keep refrigerated for 3 days.
The third day's biscuits will be just as good as the first batch.*

3 cups sifted all-purpose White-Lily flour
1 teaspoon baking soda
2 tablespoons baking powder
1 teaspoon salt
1/2 to 3/4 cup shortening
1 1/2 cups buttermilk

Preheat oven to 500 degrees. Mix flour, baking soda, baking powder and salt together in bowl. Cut the shortening into the dry ingredients with a pastry cutter or your fingers until the size of coarse crumbs.

Blend in enough milk with fork until dough leaves sides of bowl. (Too much milk makes dough too sticky to handle; not enough milk makes biscuits dry.)

Knead gently 10 to 12 strokes on a lightly floured surface. Roll dough about 1/2-inch thick. Cut without twisting biscuit cutter. Bake on ungreased baking sheet for 8 to 10 minutes. Serve at once.

Makes about twelve 2 1/2-inch biscuits

Breads, Breakfasts and Brunches

Peppery White Cheddar Biscuit Squares

Mouthwatering right out of the oven! Any Cheddar of choice can be used,
although, white Cheddar is preferred.

4 cups all-purpose White Lily flour
1/2 teaspoon salt
2 tablespoons baking powder
1/2 cup shortening
1/4 cup butter
1 1/2 cups finely crumbled or shredded sharp white Cheddar cheese (6 ounces)
2 to 3 teaspoons coarsely ground black pepper
1 1/2 cups milk
1 egg, beaten
1/2 teaspoon water

Preheat oven to 400 degrees. Lightly grease a large baking sheet; set aside.

In a large mixing bowl, stir together flour, baking powder and salt. Using a pastry cutter, cut in shortening and butter until mixture resembles coarse crumbs. Add cheese and pepper; mix well.

Make a well in the center of the dry mixture. Add milk all at once; stir until just moistened. Turn dough out onto a lightly floured surface. Knead dough 10 to 12 strokes until almost smooth.

Divide dough in half. Roll or pat each half of dough into a 6-inch square, about 1-inch thick. Using a floured knife, cut both squares of dough into 2-inch squares. Combine egg and water. Brush tops of biscuits with egg mixture. Place on prepared baking sheet.

Bake for 13 to 15 minutes or until biscuits are golden on top. Serve warm.

Makes eighteen 2-inch square biscuits

Cream Biscuits

1 1/2 cups self-rising flour
1 cup whipping cream
1/4 teaspoon baking powder

Preheat oven to 450 degrees. Combine all ingredients in a bowl and mix well. Turn dough onto a lightly floured surface and knead briefly. Roll out dough and cut with a floured biscuit cutter. Place on a greased baking sheet. Bake for 10 to 12 minutes or until biscuits are light brown.

Makes 18 biscuits

Betty Mitchell Sims

Genuine Southern Biscuits

The ideal Southern biscuit is feathery light with a light brown crust on top and a moist interior. The quest for the perfect biscuit continues. But we all know real Southern biscuits must be made with lard. Go ahead and sneak it out occasionally!

2 2/3 cups all-purpose Southern flour (White Lily) and more for dusting
1 teaspoon baking soda
1 teaspoon cream of tartar
1 teaspoon salt
1/3 cup plus 4 teaspoons chilled fresh lard, cut into 1-inch chunks
3/4 to 1 cup buttermilk

Place oven rack in center position and preheat oven to 425 degrees. Sift the flour, baking soda, cream of tartar and salt into a large bowl. With a pastry cutter, cut in the lard until it is evenly mixed with the flour and there are no large clumps. Working swiftly, use a rubber spatula to fold in 3/4 cup buttermilk in 3 parts until it's just blended into the dry ingredients; add up to 1/4 cup more buttermilk if needed.

Lightly dust the work surface with flour and scoop the dough onto the counter with the spatula. Dust your fingers with flour. Using your fingertips only, lightly work the dough just until it holds together.

Roll the dough out about 1/2-inch thick and use a biscuit cutter to punch out 12 two-inch biscuits. Quickly, stack up scrap pieces, and roll more biscuits.

Put the biscuits close to each other (but not touching) on an ungreased baking sheet and bake until the tops are light golden brown, 15 to 17 minutes. Serve immediately.

Makes twelve 2-inch biscuits

Breads, Breakfasts and Brunches

Sweet Potato Biscuits

1 1/2 pounds sweet potatoes
4 cups all-purpose flour
1/2 cup sugar
2 tablespoons baking powder
2 teaspoons salt
1 teaspoon baking soda
1 cup (2 sticks) unsalted butter, melted
1 1/3 cups buttermilk

Preheat oven to 400 degrees. Pierce sweet potatoes several times with a small knife. Roast 1 hour or until very soft. Cool; remove skins. Mash until no lumps remain (you should have about 2 cups). Reduce oven temperature to 375 degrees.

In a large bowl, vigorously whisk flour, sugar, baking powder, salt and baking soda until no lumps remain. Make a well in center of dry ingredients. In a 1-quart bowl combine sweet potatoes and melted butter; whisk until combined. Place in well along with buttermilk; combine until soft dough forms.

Turn out onto well-floured surface (dough will be sticky). Flour top of dough. Pat or roll to 1-inch thickness. Using a floured 2 1/2-inch biscuit cutter, cut out biscuits. Transfer with spatula to ungreased baking sheet.

Bake 26 minutes or until lightly golden on bottom.

Note: May cool completely and freeze up to 2 weeks. To serve, preheat oven to 350 degrees. Bake frozen biscuits 16 minutes or until hot.

Makes 24 biscuits

Hint

Try Sweet Potato Biscuits with smoked ham for an appetizer.

Breads, Breakfasts and Brunches

Quick and Easy Biscuits

2 cups all-purpose flour
1 tablespoon baking powder
1 teaspoon salt
1/4 cup shortening
2/3 to 3/4 cup buttermilk

Preheat oven to 500 degrees. Measure flour into bowl; stir in baking powder and salt. Cut in shortening until like coarse crumbs. Blend in milk with a fork until dough leaves sides of bowl. Knead gently 10 or 12 strokes on lightly floured surface. Roll dough about 1/2 inch thick. Cut without twisting cutter. Bake on ungreased baking sheet for 8 to 10 minutes. Serve at once.

Makes twelve 2-inch biscuits

Betty Mitchell Sims

Breads, Breakfasts and Brunches

Advent Bazaar Rolls

Judy Richardson submitted this recipe and was 1 of 3 winners in the "1996 Bread and Justice Cookbook from Tennesseans," compiled by the Tennessee Hunger Coalition in Nashville, Tennessee. The refrigerator roll recipe is Sandy Nix's from "Cotton Country Cooking."

1 cup water
1/2 cup butter (1 stick)
1/2 cup shortening
3/4 cup sugar
1 1/2 teaspoons salt
1 cup warm water (105 to 115 degrees)
2 packages dry yeast
2 eggs, slightly beaten
6 cups all-purpose flour
Melted butter

Bring 1 cup water to boil in saucepan. Remove from heat. Add butter and shortening, stirring until melted. Stir in sugar and salt. Let stand until lukewarm.

Pour 1 cup warm water (105 to 115 degrees) into a large bowl. Sprinkle yeast over the water and stir to dissolve. Add butter, sugar and shortening mixture along with eggs to dissolved yeast and stir to mix. Add flour and mix thoroughly. Cover and chill in refrigerator overnight or 8 to 10 hours.

About 2 1/2 to 3 hours before serving rolls, turn dough out on lightly floured surface and roll 1/3-inch thick. Cut with biscuit cutter and fold in half. Place in greased baking pan; brush with melted butter. Let rise 2 hours. Bake at 400 degrees for 12 to 15 minutes or until browned.

Note: Dough will keep refrigerated several days.

Makes 48 rolls

Destin Trip Rolls

If you will store this dough in a plastic bag in the refrigerator, you can keep it for 2 or 3 weeks. But the rolls are so good, that probably won't ever happen. These are great to do ahead.

1 1/2 packages dry yeast
1/3 cup warm water (110 to 115 degrees)
2 sticks butter, room temperature
1/2 cup sugar
1/2 teaspoon salt
1 cup sour cream
4 cups all-purpose flour
2 eggs, well beaten
Melted butter

Soften yeast in warm water. Let stand for 15 minutes.

Put butter, sugar and salt in a large bowl and put aside until you heat the sour cream.

Sour cream should be carefully heated to a point where yellow begins to show on the edges. Add heated sour cream to butter mixture and stir until butter melts. Cool until bowl feels lukewarm. Blend 1 cup flour into the sour cream mixture and beat until smooth. Mix yeast in and stir until well mixed. Add second cup of flour and beat until smooth. Add beaten eggs. Add the remaining 2 cups of flour, one at a time. Cover and refrigerate at least 6 hours but overnight is better.

Preheat oven to 375 degrees. Roll out dough on floured surface and cut or shape. Brush with melted butter and let rise about 1 hour. Bake for 10 to 15 minutes, or until brown.

Makes twenty 2-inch rolls

Cheddar Dill Scones

Buttered and toasted, this version of scones is good at lunch teamed with tomato soup.
These can be made ahead and refrigerated before baking.

1 1/4 cups sharp Cheddar cheese, grated
1/2 cup fresh dill, chopped
2 cups all-purpose flour
1 tablespoon baking powder
1/2 teaspoon salt
3/4 cup cold unsalted butter, diced
2 eggs, beaten
1/2 cup heavy cream
Egg wash (1 egg yolk mixed with 1 tablespoon heavy cream)

Preheat oven to 425 degrees. Combine the Cheddar and dill and set aside. Place the flour, baking powder and salt in the bowl of a food processor. Add the butter and pulse until the mixture is coarsely crumbled, about 30 seconds. (The mixture should have pieces of butter throughout.) Remove the mixture to a medium bowl; add the eggs and cream and mix. Add the Cheddar-dill mixture and blend until the dough is just soft and sticky. Do not overmix.

Pat or roll out the dough on well-floured board to a thickness of 3/4 inch. Cut with a floured cutter. Place the scones 1 inch apart on a baking sheet. Brush the tops with the egg wash and bake for 15 to 20 minutes, until lightly browned.

Makes 14 scones

Rough-Cut Breadsticks

1 12 x 2-inch loaf of bread
1 tablespoon extra-virgin olive oil
Kosher salt

Preheat oven to 425 degrees. Slice the bread in quarters, lengthwise. Place the 4 breadsticks on a baking sheet and bake until golden brown, about 5 minutes. Drizzle oil over each breadstick and sprinkle lightly with salt.

Makes 4 breadsticks

Parmesan Toast

Use as crackers for appetizers or as croutons topping soup!

1 baguette
1/4 cup extra-virgin olive oil
Kosher salt
Freshly ground black pepper
3/4 cup (3 ounces) freshly shredded Parmesan cheese
Parsley

Preheat oven to 400 degrees. Slice baguette into 1/4-inch-thick slices. Depending on the size of the baguette, you should get about 20 slices. Place one layer of slices on a baking sheet; brush each with olive oil and sprinkle with salt and pepper. Sprinkle with shredded Parmesan and chopped parsley. Bake toast for 15 to 20 minutes until brown and crisp. Serve at room temperature.

Makes 20 to 25 slices

Blackberry Coffee Cake

Shea Patrick was building her wonderful new home overlooking Puget Sound when she served this coffee cake at a fantastic brunch. She's a great gourmet cook and a real foodie! Oh yes, the blackberries, she grew in her yard!

Cake:
1/2 cup (1 stick unsalted butter, softened)
1 cup sugar
2 eggs
1 cup sour cream or plain yogurt or a combination
2 cups unbleached all-purpose flour, sifted
1 teaspoon salt
1 teaspoon baking powder
1 teaspoon baking soda
1 teaspoon vanilla
1 cup blackberries or huckleberries

Topping:
1/4 cup unsalted butter, softened
1/2 cup light brown sugar
1/2 teaspoon cinnamon

Preheat oven to 350 degrees. Grease and flour an 8-inch baking pan.

Cake: In mixer bowl, cream together butter and sugar on high speed until pale and fluffy. Add eggs 1 at a time, mixing thoroughly after each addition. Add sour cream, beating until smooth. Sift together flour, salt, baking powder and baking soda; add to mixture. Fold in blackberries and vanilla.

Topping: Combine ingredients for the topping. Sprinkle on top. Bake approximately 35 minutes or until a toothpick inserted comes out clean.

Serves 6

Hawaiian Banana Nut Bread

3 cups all-purpose flour
2 cups sugar
1 teaspoon baking soda
1 teaspoon salt
1 teaspoon cinnamon
1 cup chopped nuts
1 1/2 cups vegetable oil
3 eggs, beaten
2 cups ripe mashed bananas
1 (8-ounce) can crushed pineapple, drained
2 teaspoons vanilla extract

Preheat oven to 350 degrees. In bowl, combine dry ingredients, stir in nuts and set aside. In mixer bowl, combine remaining ingredients and mix with dry ingredients; stir until blended.

Pour into two 9 x 5-inch loaf pans or three 4 x 8-inch loaf pans. Bake 55 to 65 minutes or until done. Cool 10 minutes in pan before removing.

Serves 8 to 9 per loaf

Jeanette McKelvey

Short and Sweet Caramel Bubble Ring

1/3 cup chopped pecans
3/4 cup sugar
4 teaspoons ground cinnamon
2 (11-ounce) packages refrigerated breadsticks
1/3 cup butter, melted
1/2 cup caramel ice cream topping
2 tablespoons maple-flavored syrup

Preheat oven to 350 degrees. Generously grease a 10-inch fluted tube pan. Sprinkle about half of the pecans in the bottom of the pan. Set aside. Stir together sugar and cinnamon; set aside. Separate each package of breadsticks into 8 spirals. Do not unroll. Cut the spirals in half crosswise. Dip each piece of dough into melted butter, then dip in sugar mixture. Arrange dough pieces, cut sides down, in the prepared pan.

Sprinkle with remaining pecans. Stir together caramel topping and maple-flavored syrup in a measuring cup; drizzle over dough in pan.

Bake about 35 minutes or until dough is light brown. Cover with foil the last 10 minutes to prevent over-browning.

Let stand for 1 minute only. Invert onto a serving plate. Spoon any topping and nuts remaining in the pan onto ring. Serve warm.

Serves 10 to 12

Betty Mitchell Sims

Skillet Coffee Cake

3/4 cup butter or margarine
1 1/2 cups sugar
2 eggs
1 1/2 cups sifted all-purpose flour
Pinch of salt
1 teaspoon almond extract
Slivered almonds
Sugar

Preheat oven to 350 degrees. Melt butter and add to sugar in mixing bowl. Beat in eggs, one at a time. Add flour, salt and almond extract and mix well.

Pour batter into large iron skillet (9 to 11-inch) which has been lined with aluminum foil. (Leave excess foil on either side of pan.) Cover top with slivered almonds and sprinkle with granulated sugar. Bake 30 to 40 minutes.

Remove cake from pan with foil and when cool, wrap tightly to store. Do not try to peel foil off while cake is warm, as it will stick.

Note: Freezes well.

Makes twenty-four 1 1/2-inch squares or 12 wedges

Betty Pickell
Cotton Country Cooking

Pecan Mini-Muffins

2 eggs, slightly beaten
1 cup brown sugar
1/2 cup flour
1/2 teaspoon baking powder
1/2 teaspoon salt
1 cup pecans, chopped

Preheat oven to 350 degrees. In bowl, mix eggs and sugar. Sift flour, baking powder and salt 3 to 4 times. Add to egg mixture. Gently stir in pecans. Blend until batter is just moistened. Spoon into greased miniature muffin tins. Bake for 12 to 15 minutes.

Note: These muffins make delicious hors d'oeuvres filled with turkey slices and cranberry sauce.

Makes 24 miniature muffins

Betty Mitchell Sims

Sweet Potato Muffins

Try these muffins with country ham for an unusual treat!

Muffins:
1 1/4 cups oatmeal
1 cup plain flour
1/3 cup pecans, chopped
1 teaspoon baking powder
1 teaspoon ground cinnamon
1/2 teaspoon baking soda
1/2 teaspoon salt
1/2 teaspoon nutmeg
1 cup canned sweet potatoes, mashed
3/4 cup brown sugar, firmly packed
1/2 cup oil
1/4 cup milk
1 egg
1 teaspoon vanilla

Topping:
1/4 cup oatmeal
1/4 cup flour
1/4 cup brown sugar, firmly packed
1/4 cup pecans, chopped
1 teaspoon ground cinnamon
1/4 cup butter, softened

Muffins: Preheat oven to 400 degrees. In large mixer bowl, combine all ingredients. Stir until moistened. Fill muffin tins 3/4 full.

Topping: Combine all ingredients and sprinkle over muffins. Bake in oven for 20 to 25 minutes.

Makes 18 muffins

Caryl Ward Littrell

Breads, Breakfasts and Brunches

Cinnamon Rolls

1/2 recipe of Advent Bazaar Rolls
1/2 cup butter (1 stick) room temperature
1/2 cup brown sugar
1 tablespoon cinnamon

Glaze:
2 cups confectioners' sugar
5 tablespoons milk

Make recipe of Advent Bazaar Rolls and divide dough in half. Divide this amount of dough in half again. Roll each portion on lightly floured surface into an 8 by 10-inch rectangle.

Stir together softened butter, sugar and cinnamon. Use 1/2 of butter mixture to spread over 1 rectangle of dough recipe. Roll up like a jelly roll. Slice into 16 equal slices. Place rolls into paper-lined muffin pans. Repeat with remaining half of dough. Let rolls rise 2 hours. Bake at 375 degrees for about 15 minutes or until lightly browned.

Glaze: Combine confectioners' sugar and milk. Drizzle over rolls which have cooled slightly.

Makes 32 rolls

Judy Richardson

Orange Rolls

1/2 recipe of Advent Bazaar Rolls
1/2 cup butter (1 stick) room temperature
1/2 cup sugar
1 1/2 teaspoons grated orange zest (1 1/2 teaspoons sweet orange marmalade could be substituted for sugar and orange zest)

Glaze:
2 cups confectioners' sugar
3 to 4 tablespoons orange juice

Make recipe of Advent Bazaar Rolls and divide amount of dough in half. Divide this amount of dough in half again. Roll each portion on lightly floured surface into an 8 by 10-inch rectangle.

Stir together softened butter, sugar and orange zest. Use 1/2 of butter mixture to spread over one rectangle of dough recipe. Roll up like a jelly roll. Slice into 16 equal slices. Place rolls into paper-lined muffin pans. Repeat with remaining half of dough. Let rolls rise 2 hours. Bake at 375 degrees for about 15 minutes or until lightly browned.

Glaze: Combine confectioners' sugar and orange juice. Drizzle over rolls which have cooled slightly.

Makes 32 rolls

Judy Richardson

Simple Orange Rolls

Rolls:
2 (8-ounce) cans crescent rolls
1 stick butter, melted
1/2 cup sugar
1 1/2 tablespoons finely grated orange peel

Icing:
1 cup confectioners' sugar
2 tablespoons fresh squeezed orange juice (juice of 1 orange)

Rolls: Preheat oven to 350 degrees. Divide rolls into rectangles (2 crescent wedges = 1 rectangle.) Mix butter, sugar and orange peel. Spread onto rectangles. Roll up (from short side) and cut each roll in half. (One can crescent rolls makes 8 rolls.) Put in greased muffin pan and slightly press roll down. Bake about 14 minutes.

Icing: In bowl, mix confectioners' sugar and orange juice. Spoon onto rolls while warm.

Note: May use paper muffin liners.

Makes 16 rolls

Carol Buckins

Zucchini Bread

3 eggs
1 cup vegetable oil
2 cups sugar
2 teaspoons vanilla extract
2 cups unpeeled zucchini, grated
3 cups all-purpose flour
2 teaspoons baking soda
1 teaspoon salt
3 teaspoons cinnamon
1 cup pecans, chopped

Preheat oven to 250 degrees. In a large mixer bowl, beat eggs until fluffy. Add oil, sugar, vanilla and zucchini. Mix well and add flour, soda, salt, cinnamon and pecans; mix well and pour into 2 greased and floured 9 x 5-inch loaf pans. Bake 1 1/2 hours.

Each loaf serves 8 to 10

Lynn Littrell

Canadian Egg Casserole

Cheese Sauce:
2 tablespoons margarine
2 1/2 tablespoons flour
2 cups milk
1/2 teaspoon salt
1/8 teaspoon pepper
4 ounces medium Cheddar cheese, shredded

Melt 2 tablespoons margarine in saucepan over low heat. Blend in flour and cook 1 minute. Gradually add milk. Cook over medium heat until thickened, stirring constantly. Add salt, pepper and cheese. Stir until cheese is melted and sauce is smooth.

1/4 cup fresh mushrooms, sliced
1/4 cup green onions, chopped (include green tops)
1 cup cubed Canadian bacon
3 tablespoons margarine
12 eggs, well beaten
1/4 cup margarine, melted
2 1/4 cups soft bread crumbs
1/8 teaspoon paprika

Sauté mushrooms, green onions and Canadian bacon in 3 tablespoons margarine in a large skillet until onion is cooked. Add beaten eggs and stir until softly scrambled. Remove from heat. Pour cheese sauce over egg mixture. Mix carefully. Spoon mixture into a greased 9 x 13 x 2-inch casserole. Combine 1/4 cup margarine and bread crumbs. Spread evenly over egg mixture. Sprinkle with paprika. Cover and chill overnight. Preheat oven to 350 degrees. Uncover and bake for 30 minutes or until heated thoroughly.

Serves 12 to 15

Betty Mitchell Sims

Sausage and Egg Casserole

16 ounces mild sausage
6 eggs
2 cups milk
1 teaspoon salt
1 teaspoon pepper
2 teaspoons prepared mustard
2 slices bread, trimmed and broken up
8 ounces Cheddar cheese, grated

Preheat oven to 350 degrees. Brown sausage; crumble and drain. Mix eggs, milk, salt, pepper and mustard. Stir in bread, sausage and cheese. Pour in greased 9 x 13 x 2-inch baking dish. Bake for 35 to 40 minutes. Note: May be prepared one day ahead, refrigerated overnight and baked the next morning.

Serves 10 to 12

Jeanette McKelvey

"Cook and Hold" Scrambled Eggs

Ever wonder how restaurants manage to serve perfect scrambled eggs for an hour or more on their buffet brunch table? Well, here is one secret. This worked well recently for a pre-golf tournament breakfast and many men and boys enjoyed it!

1/4 cup margarine
12 eggs
1 1/3 cups milk
1 teaspoon salt
Dash of white pepper
2 tablespoons all-purpose flour

Heat large electric skillet to 175 degrees. Melt margarine. Combine eggs, milk, salt, pepper and flour in a large mixing bowl. Beat with electric beater until smooth and well mixed. Pour eggs into skillet. Increase temperature to 250 degrees. Stir eggs from outside edge toward center, allowing uncooked eggs in center to flow to outside. Continue stirring until all the eggs have cooked and are creamy. Lower temperature to 170 degrees. Cover until serving time. They may be held up to 2 hours.

Serves 10 to 12

Breads, Breakfasts and Brunches

Creamy Scrambled Eggs with Chives

2 dozen large eggs
1 cup milk, half-and-half or heavy cream
1 teaspoon salt
1/2 teaspoon pepper
2 tablespoons unsalted butter
2 (3-ounce) packages cream cheese, cut into small chunks
1/4 cup snipped fresh chives

In a large bowl, whisk eggs, milk, salt and pepper. In a deep nonstick skillet, melt butter. Add egg mixture; cook, without stirring, 5 minutes, until eggs start to set on bottom. With heatproof spatula, push across skillet bottom to form large egg curds. Cook another 5 minutes, occasionally pushing eggs with spatula, until set but still creamy (do not overstir eggs as they cook).

Remove from heat; add cheese and chives.

Note: Recipe may be halved.

Serves 12

Asparagus Quiche

4 eggs
1 cup whipping cream
1 cup milk
2 teaspoons sugar
1/2 cup chopped onion
1/2 small bell pepper, chopped
1 (4-ounce) jar sliced mushrooms, drained
1 (16-ounce) can whole-stem asparagus, drained
1 (8-ounce) package Swiss cheese, shredded
2 (9-inch) pie shells, unbaked (not deep dish)

Preheat oven to 475 degrees. In mixer bowl, beat eggs well. Add whipping cream, milk and sugar. Pour into unbaked pie shells and sprinkle onion, pepper, mushrooms and asparagus on top. Add cheese last. Add salt and pepper to taste. Bake for 15 minutes; then lower temperature to 375 degrees for 15 to 25 minutes.

Serves 8

Betty Mitchell Sims

Ambrosia

Ambrosia, in its purest form, consists of sliced oranges and grated coconut. There are many deviations from the basic recipe, depending on the region in which it is prepared. Sometimes ambrosia is served as a salad, but it shows up as a dessert also. If the oranges you use for this recipe are not sweet, sift some confectioners' sugar lightly over each layer of orange sections before sprinkling with coconut. Bananas or pineapple may be used.

8 navel oranges
1 cup flaked coconut
2 tablespoons confectioners' sugar
1/3 cup halved maraschino cherries

Peel oranges. Section the oranges (removing the white membrane) over a small bowl to catch juice; cut orange sections in half. Set juice aside. Place oranges in large bowl; sprinkle with sugar, coconut and cherries and toss gently until combined. Pour 1/4 cup reserved orange juice over mixture. Cover and refrigerate until serving time.

Serves 6 to 8

Breads, Breakfasts and Brunches

Fresh Fruit Salad with Citrus Sauce

Sauce:
2 tablespoons fresh orange juice
2 tablespoons fresh lemon juice
2 tablespoons fresh lime juice
2/3 cup sugar
1/3 cup water

Salad:
2 fresh medium peaches, peeled and sliced
1 cup fresh pineapple, sliced or chunks
1 cup honeydew melon, sliced or chunks
2 medium nectarines, sliced
1 cup blueberries
1 cup strawberries
2 medium bananas

Prepare sauce by thoroughly blending juices, sugar and water in bowl. In bowl, combine peaches, pineapple, honeydew and nectarines. Pour sauce over fruit. Slice and add bananas, strawberries and blueberries just before serving.

Serves 12

Betty Mitchell Sims

Fresh Fruit Tray with Dip

Lettuce (preferably Boston)
Fresh pineapple, cut in chunks
White and red seedless grapes, on the stem
Watermelon, cut in chunks, with seeds removed
Cantaloupe, cut in small wedges
Strawberries, large, with stems

Arrange lettuce to cover a large serving tray. Let leaves slightly extend over sides of tray. Place a small bowl in center for dip and arrange fruit to cover tray.

Cream Cheese Dip
1 (8-ounce) package cream cheese, softened
1 (12-ounce) jar marshmallow cream
2 tablespoons orange juice

In a small bowl, combine all ingredients and mix well.

Betty Mitchell Sims

Instant Fruit Salad

Good enough for brunch and easy enough for a tailgate party. Use the prettiest, freshest fruit of the season, and you'll be making this over and over.

1 (21-ounce) can peach pie filling
Combination of fresh fruit

In large bowl, mix pie filling with strawberries, blackberries, sliced peaches, blueberries, raspberries, bananas or any combination of your choice. Mix gently, cover and refrigerate.

Note: If bananas are used, marinate in pineapple juice; drain before adding to salad.

Hint

Cut a kiwi fruit in half; scoop out the fruit. Mix with fresh sliced strawberries. Return to shell. Garnish with a strawberry.

Hot Sherried Fruit

1 (16-ounce) can peach halves, cut into thirds
1 (16-ounce) can pear halves, cut into thirds
1 (16-ounce) can pineapple chunks
3/4 cup light brown sugar
1/2 cup butter, melted
3/4 cup sherry
2 1/2 cups coconut macaroons (chopped in blender)

One day in advance: Drain fruit well and place in a 2-quart baking dish. Sprinkle with brown sugar. Pour melted butter and sherry over all. Sprinkle coconut macaroons over fruit. Store covered in refrigerator for 24 hours. Bake at 350 degrees for 45 minutes or until hot and bubbly.

Serves 12

Betty Mitchell Sims

Spiced Fruit in Light Syrup

This is delicious as a side dish for so many menus or for an easy dessert,
warm gently and serve over pound cake or vanilla ice cream.

1 cup water
2 cups white grape juice
3/4 cup sugar
2 (3-inch) cinnamon sticks
1 star anise
4 whole cloves
3 medium-sized firm pears, peeled and sliced into 6 or 8 vertical slices
1 cup dried apricots, cut in half
1 cup bite-size prunes
1/2 cup dried cranberries or dried cherries
1 (28-ounce) can sliced peaches, undrained
2 large navel oranges, peeled and sectioned
1 star fruit, sliced for garnish

In a 3-quart saucepan, combine water, grape juice, sugar, cinnamon sticks, star anise and cloves. Bring to a boil over medium heat. Reduce heat to low; add pears, apricots, prunes and cranberries. Simmer uncovered just until fruit softens, about 15 minutes.

Remove pan from heat and let cool 10 minutes. Add peaches and cool 5 more minutes. Remove and discard cinnamon sticks, cloves and star anise.

Pour into serving bowl and garnish with orange segments and star fruit. Can be served at room temperature.

Note: If unable to find star anise, fruit is delicious without it.

Serves 12

Marlynn Rhyne

Summer's Best Fruit Toss

Watermelon, cantaloupe, honeydew, blueberries, strawberries, grapes, pineapple and bananas combine for a real treat during the hottest days of summer.

Cut melons into large bite-size chunks. All other fruits except bananas can be prepared ahead and refrigerated in individual Ziploc bags. At the last minute before serving, slice bananas and dip into pineapple juice.

Gently mix all ingredients and serve from a watermelon half or pretty glass bowl. Garnish with whole strawberries with stems or fresh mint leaves. Pass Poppy Seed Dressing (page 70) to drizzle over fruit.

Warm Berry Compote

An alternative to maple syrup and delicious on pancakes, waffles or French toast.

2 teaspoons unsalted butter
1/2 cup sugar
2 tablespoons fresh orange juice, strained
1 cup fresh blueberries
1 cup fresh blackberries
1 cup fresh raspberries
2 cups fresh strawberries, cut in half

In a medium sauté pan over medium heat, melt butter. Add sugar and orange juice; cook until sugar begins to dissolve, about 2 minutes. Add blueberries and cook until they begin to release juice, about 1 minute. Add blackberries and cook about 2 minutes. Add raspberries and strawberries just before serving. Shake pan gently or stir carefully, being careful not to crush berries. Serve immediately.

Note: Good with Overnight Baked French Toast (page 123).

Serves 8 to 10

Watermelon Quarters

*An easy way to serve watermelon at the pool,
a picnic or a cookout. No utensils required.*

Cut watermelon in half lengthwise; cut each half into 1-to 2-inch slices, then into quarters.

Arrange on large tray and garnish with favorite fruits such as strawberries, grapes, honeydew melon and fresh mint leaves.

Creamy Grits

4 1/2 cups milk
2 tablespoons butter
Salt
Freshly ground white pepper
2 cups quick white grits

In a saucepan over medium heat, add the milk and butter. Season with salt and pepper. Bring the liquid to a boil. Whisk in the grits. Stir constantly for 6 minutes or until tender. Serve immediately.

Serves 4

Hint

For an edible July 4th centerpiece, fill a tall clear compote with large-stemmed strawberries, blueberries and red cherries. Instantly smashing!

Creamy Grits with Mushroom Sauce

Mushroom Sauce:
2 cups fresh mushrooms, sliced
1/4 cup olive oil
1/4 cup finely chopped shallots
3 cups chicken broth
2 tablespoons chopped fresh chervil (parsley may be substituted)
3 tablespoons unsalted butter, softened
1/4 teaspoon salt
1/4 teaspoon pepper
Parmesan cheese, shredded

Creamy Grits:
4 cups milk
1 teaspoon salt
1/4 teaspoon pepper
1 cup regular white grits, uncooked
1 cup whipping cream
3 tablespoons unsalted butter

Mushroom Sauce: Cook mushrooms in olive oil in a large skillet over medium heat, stirring constantly for 2 minutes. Add shallots and cook 1 minute. Gradually add broth; increase heat to high and cook 25 minutes (broth will be reduced and slightly thickened). Stir in chervil or parsley and next 3 ingredients. Serve over creamy grits; top with Parmesan cheese.

Creamy Grits: Combine first 3 ingredients in a large saucepan; bring to a boil over medium heat. Stir in grits; cook 10 minutes or until soft. Add whipping cream and butter, stirring mixture until smooth. Grits may be thinned with a few drops of water if they are too thick.

Makes 4 cups

Betty Mitchell Sims

Creole Grits

A wonderful brunch dish. You'll find many other ways to use it. Good with baked fish.

2 cups quick grits
2 quarts boiling water
2 teaspoons salt
1 stick butter or margarine
1/4 pound thick-sliced bacon, cooked medium and drained (reserve fat)
1 cup green onions, finely chopped (include green tops)
1/2 cup finely chopped celery
1 1/2 cups diced, fresh tomatoes, with juice
Black pepper to taste

Cook grits in boiling, salted water according to package directions. When done, stir in melted butter. Sauté the onions and celery in the reserved bacon drippings. Chop bacon; add the bacon, celery, onions, tomatoes and pepper to grits.

Serves 8

Grits Soufflé

2 1/4 cups milk
1 cup old-fashioned grits
16 ounces Cheddar cheese, coarsely grated
Salt and freshly ground black pepper to taste
5 eggs, room temperature and separated

Heat milk and 2 1/4 cups water in a non-stick saucepan to a boil. Slowly stir in grits. Reduce heat to low and cover pan. Cook grits 12 to 14 minutes or until thickened, stirring occasionally. Remove pan from heat and stir in cheese until thoroughly incorporated. Season with salt and pepper to taste.
    Preheat oven to 350 degrees. Mix egg yolks together in a bowl. Stir into grit mixture. Beat the egg whites in a bowl with an electric mixer until soft peaks form. (Do not overbeat.) Gently fold egg whites into grits mixture. Spoon mixture into a 9 x 14 x 2-inch ovenproof dish. Bake for 1 to 1 1/2 hours or until the top is lightly browned and crisp on the edges. Serve immediately.

Serves 8 to 10

Buttermilk Pancakes

Featherlight pancakes as good as you'll ever taste.

2 cups all-purpose flour
2 tablespoons sugar
2 teaspoons baking powder
3/4 teaspoon baking soda
1/2 teaspoon salt
2 cups buttermilk
1/3 cup milk
2 large eggs
1/4 cup butter or margarine, melted
Butter, vegetable oil or shortening for frying
Pure maple syrup and additional butter, if desired

Preheat oven to 200 degrees. Combine flour, sugar, baking powder, baking soda and salt in a large bowl. Whisk until blended. Combine buttermilk, milk, eggs and melted butter in a medium bowl. Whisk until blended.

Heat a large nonstick griddle or skillet over medium-high heat. When griddle or skillet is hot, add buttermilk mixture to dry ingredients; then stir batter just until blended.

Reduce heat to medium and grease griddle or skillet with butter, oil or shortening. Using a 1/3-cup measure, pour batter onto griddle or skillet. Cook until bubbles form on top, 2 to 3 minutes.

Turn pancakes with spatula. Cook 1 to 2 minutes more, until browned. Serve immediately with maple syrup and butter.

Note: Pancakes can be kept warm in oven until ready to serve.

Makes 14 pancakes

Overnight Baked French Toast

A great dish when guests are expected the next morning for breakfast or brunch.
The overnight soak produces a great French toast.

1 cup heavy cream, half-and-half or whole milk
6 large eggs
1/4 cup pure maple syrup
2 tablespoons light brown sugar, packed
1 teaspoon vanilla
1/4 teaspoon salt
8 slices white bread
Confectioners' sugar

In an 8-inch baking dish, whisk together all above ingredients except bread slices.

Trim the crust from 8 slices of white bread. One slice at a time, turn the bread over in the egg mixture to coat it, then fit the coated bread into the pan in a double layer. Very gently press the bread with the back of a fork to compress the slices slightly. Cover with plastic wrap and press on the plastic to help the bread soak up the egg mixture. Refrigerate overnight.

Preheat oven to 400 degrees. Lightly butter a baking sheet, preferably nonstick.

Using a wide spatula, lift the bread, slice by slice, out of the soaking mixture, allowing the excess to drip back into the pan, and place on the baking sheet. Bake until golden about 12 to 15 minutes, turning the slices over halfway through the baking. Serve immediately with maple syrup or Warm Berry Compote (page 118). Dust with confectioners' sugar.

Note: When doing French toast on the spot, use above recipe and after bread is soaked, melt 2 tablespoons butter in skillet. Place bread slices in skillet, brown on both sides and keep warm in a 200-degree oven while cooking the rest. Dust each slice with confectioners' sugar and serve with syrup and bacon or sausage.

Serves 8

Breads, Breakfasts and Brunches   123

Waffles

Waffles are done when the steaming stops, the lid rises and the visible sides are golden brown.

Never open the waffle iron during the first minute of cooking or the waffle will split apart.

French Toast with Strawberries

Make this French toast part of your Christmas brunch. Prepare the night before and as soon as Santa clears the door, bake and serve.

2 tablespoons light corn syrup
3/4 to 1 cup light brown sugar
5 tablespoons butter
12 slices wheat bread (crusts removed)
5 eggs
1 1/2 cups milk
1 teaspoon vanilla extract
1/2 cup sour cream
1 1/2 cups sliced strawberries
Confectioners' sugar for dusting

Combine corn syrup, brown sugar and butter in a saucepan. Heat until bubbly. Pour into a 13 x 9 x 2-inch baking dish. Place bread slices in dish, making 2 layers. In a separate bowl, combine the eggs, milk and vanilla. Pour over bread. Cover and refrigerate overnight. Preheat oven to 350 degrees and bake for 45 minutes. Spread sour cream over French toast; top with sliced strawberries. Serve hot.

Note: Be sure to sift confectioners' sugar over toast.

Serves 6

Best Breakfast Waffles

Pancakes are nice, but when it comes to holding maple syrup, there's no substitute for the waffle. This batter will keep refrigerated for several days.

4 eggs
1 cup unbleached flour
1 cup whole wheat flour
1 teaspoon salt
1 teaspoon baking soda
1 teaspoon baking powder
1 cup butter, melted
2 cups buttermilk, or 1 cup milk plus 1 cup either yogurt or sour cream

Preheat waffle iron. Beat eggs until light. Mix together dry ingredients and add dry mixture and milk alternately to beaten eggs, beating well after each addition. Begin and end with dry mixture. Add melted butter. Blend thoroughly. Pour onto waffle iron. Most waffle irons will need 1/2 to 3/4 cup batter. Serve hot.

Serves 4

Wonderful Waffles

The Painted Table restaurant at the historic Alexis Hotel in downtown Seattle serves great Belgian waffles with a blueberry in each square. This is not their recipe but it brings back pleasant memories! Don't forget a dollop of whipped cream and a sprig of mint!

2 cups biscuit mix
1/2 cup vegetable oil
1 egg
1 1/3 cups club soda (10-ounce bottle)
3/4 cup fresh blueberries (optional)

In bowl, combine biscuit mix, oil and egg. Stir well. Add club soda, and mix well. Pour batter onto a greased waffle iron. Most waffle irons will need 1/2 to 3/4 cup batter. Cook 4 to 5 minutes or until done. Add blueberries.

Note: Makes 3 to 4 Belgian waffles or 10 to 12 regular waffles

Peppered Ranch Bacon

Sprinkle 1 pound of thick-sliced bacon with coarsely ground black peppercorns, pressing the peppercorns into the bacon with the back of a spoon. Fry bacon in a cast-iron skillet over medium heat until crisp. Drain. (Begin with a cold skillet to prevent curling.)

Do-Ahead Broiled Bacon for a Crowd

2 pounds bacon

Preheat broiler. Place bacon in batches on rack in broiler pan. Broil for 1 to 2 minutes per side or until desired crispness. Drain well. Pack in freezer bags and freeze. Remove desired number of slices and heat slowly in a conventional oven or microwave.

Serves 8 to 10

Sugared Bacon Twist

The aroma of bacon, brown sugar and cinnamon is irresistible. Serve these for brunch or as an hors d'oeuvre.

1 pound bacon, room temperature (regular bacon, not thick sliced)
1 1/4 cups brown sugar
1 tablespoon cinnamon, optional

Preheat oven to 350 degrees. Cut each slice of bacon in half, crosswise. Mix sugar and cinnamon together and thoroughly coat each slice of bacon. Twist slices (or leave flat) and place on rack in a broiler pan or jellyroll pan in oven. Bake until bacon is crisp and sugar is bubbly, 15 to 20 minutes. Watch closely as the sugar burns quickly. Cool on foil. Serve at room temperature. These may be made hours ahead and left at room temperature.

Serves 16

Country Ham with Red-Eye Gravy

This is the traditional way of serving country ham in most parts of the South. It's usually served with grits and hot biscuits for a hearty breakfast!

1/4 inch-thick center cut of country ham
4 tablespoons brewed black coffee

Trim off skin from ham slices. Fry the ham quickly in an ungreased hot skillet for 2 to 3 minutes on each side. Remove the ham from the pan and set ham aside.
    To the hot fat remaining, add the black coffee. Cover, and simmer for 2 to 3 minutes. Pour the gravy over the ham slices and serve.

Serves 1 or 2

Entrées

Close-up of the Main House porch balusters, 1870's
Pond Spring (Wheeler Plantation)
Hillsboro, Alabama

Entrées

Chutney Beef Tenderloin

Beef Tenderloin:
1 (4-pound) beef tenderloin
4 slices bacon
2 teaspoons freshly ground pepper
1/3 cup Major Grey Chutney

Tangy Pineapple Marinade:
3/4 cup unsweetened pineapple juice
1/4 cup steak sauce
1/3 cup Worcestershire sauce
1/3 cup port wine
1/4 cup fresh lemon juice
1 teaspoon pepper
1 teaspoon lemon pepper seasoning
1 teaspoon dry mustard

In medium bowl, stir together all marinade ingredients.

Beef Tenderloin: Place tenderloin in plastic storage bag, pour in Tangy Pineapple Marinade, and seal securely. Refrigerate several hours or overnight, turning occasionally.

When ready to cook, preheat oven to 425 degrees. Drain tenderloin, reserving marinade. Rub beef with pepper. Place on rack in shallow pan. Top with bacon and roast uncovered until meat thermometer registers 135 degrees, in thickest part, 45 to 55 minutes. Baste twice with marinade during cooking.

Remove bacon, spoon chutney over roast and bake 10 minutes longer or until thermometer reaches 140 degrees in thickest part. Remove to serving platter and allow to sit 15 minutes before slicing. This recipe works equally well on the grill.

Serves 6 to 8

Walt and Betty Sue Smith

Filet with Red Onion Confit

Filets with mustard port sauce:
2 tablespoons olive oil
4 5-to-6-ounce filets mignons (each 1 1/2-inch thick)
3 tablespoons minced shallot
1/3 cup tawny port wine
2/3 cup dry red wine
1 cup beef broth

1 1/2 teaspoons Dijon-style mustard
A beurre manié made by kneading together 1 tablespoon softened, unsalted butter and
    1 tablespoon all-purpose flour
Flat-leafed parsley sprigs for garnish
Red Onion Confit as accompaniment

Red Onion Confit:
1 tablespoon minced garlic
1/4 cup minced shallot
1/2 teaspoon dried thyme, crumbled
1 tablespoon olive oil
2 1/2 cups thinly-sliced red onion
1/4 cup tawny port wine
1/2 cup dry red wine
1 teaspoon sugar, or to taste
1 tablespoon balsamic vinegar, or to taste
3 tablespoons minced fresh parsley leaves

In a heavy skillet, heat oil over moderately high heat until hot, but not smoking, and in it brown the filets, patted dry and seasoned with salt and pepper for 2 minutes on each side. Sauté the filets, turning them on both sides and edges, for 4 to 6 minutes, more for medium-rare meat. Transfer them to a cutting board; let stand covered loosely with foil while making the sauce.

Using fat remaining in the skillet, cook shallots over moderately low heat, stirring until softened. Add port and red wine, and boil mixture until it is reduced by 2/3. Add broth, boil the mixture until it is reduced by half and strain mixture through a fine sieve into a small saucepan. Whisk in mustard, bring the mixture to a boil; and add the beurre manié, a little at a time, whisking until sauce is smooth. Simmer sauce, whisking occasionally, for 2 minutes. Whisk in any juices that have accumulated on the cutting board, and season sauce with salt and pepper.

Cut the filets mignons into 1/4-inch-thick slices, divide slices among 4 plates and spoon sauce over them. Garnish the filets with the parsley and serve with Red Onion Confit.

Confit: In a heavy skillet, cook garlic and shallot with thyme, salt and pepper in oil over moderately-low heat, stirring until the shallot is softened. Add red onion and cook the mixture, stirring for 5 to 10 minutes, or until onion is very soft. Add the port, red wine, sugar and vinegar and simmer mixture, uncovered, for 5 to 10 minutes, or until almost all the liquid has evaporated. Stir in parsley, salt and pepper to taste, and cook mixture, stirring for 1 minute.

Note: The confit may be made 1 day in advance, kept covered and refrigerated. Reheat to serve. Divide among 4 plates.

Serves 4

Philip Reich

Shallots

More subtle than onions and less pungent than garlic, shallots are indispensable for many French sauces. They are particularly delicious used in wine cooking.

Marinated Eye of Round Roast

1 (3-to 4-pound) eye of round roast
1/2 cup cracked black peppercorns (or coarsely ground black pepper)

Marinade:
1 tablespoon tomato paste
1 teaspoon paprika
1/2 teaspoon garlic powder
1 cup soy sauce
3/4 cup white vinegar

Press pepper onto outside of roast, using hands. Using a heavy Ziploc bag as a container, carefully pour marinade over roast and refrigerate overnight. Turn at least 1 time, trying not to disturb pepper.
    Allow roast to come to room temperature (about 1 hour). Preheat oven to 500 degrees. Bake, uncovered, for 5 minutes per pound for medium cooked roast. Turn oven off and leave roast in oven for 2 hours. DO NOT OPEN OVEN DOOR! Cool and slice to serve. You will have a beautiful pink roast with au jus gravy.

Note: Excellent thinly sliced as an entrée or served with bite-size rolls for hors d'oeuvres. Be sure to slice very thin.

Makes 8 to 10 dinner servings

Celebration Roast with Horseradish-Peppercorn Cream

A tender rib eye roast suitable for holiday magic or any special occasion.

2 tablespoons cream-style prepared horseradish
4 cloves garlic, minced
5 teaspoons pink and black peppercorns, coarsely cracked; or cracked black pepper
1/2 teaspoon salt
1 (4-to 6-pound) boneless beef rib eye roast
6 medium onions
1 tablespoon olive oil
1 recipe Horseradish-Peppercorn Cream (optional – recipe follows)

Entrées

Preheat oven to 350 degrees. Combine cream-style horseradish, garlic, 3 teaspoons of the cracked peppercorns and salt; rub mixture onto meat. Place beef roast, fat side up, on a rack in a shallow roasting pan. Do not add liquid. Do not cover. Roast, uncovered, 1 1/2 to 2 hours or until thermometer in thickest section reaches 135 degrees for medium rare; 2 to 2 1/2 hours or until thermometer in thickest section reaches 150 degrees for medium. (The meat's temperature will rise about 10 degrees while standing.)

Meanwhile, slice root ends from onions. Brush onions with olive oil. Sprinkle with remaining cracked peppercorns. During the last 1 1/4 hours of roasting time, arrange onions around the roast, pepper side up. If desired, serve with Horseradish-Peppercorn Cream or pan gravy.

Serves 12

Horseradish-Peppercorn Cream:
1/2 cup whipping cream
2 tablespoons cream-style prepared horseradish
1 teaspoon Dijon-style mustard
1 to 2 tablespoons pink and black peppercorns, cracked

In a chilled mixing bowl, beat whipping cream just until soft peaks form. Fold in horseradish and Dijon-style mustard. If not using immediately, cover and store in refrigerator for up to 6 hours. Serve with Celebration Roast or other beef roasts. Sprinkle each serving of cream with cracked peppercorns.

Makes 1 cup

You'll Never Believe It Rib Roast

A wonderful roast for guests since it is cooked in 2 steps and can be easily timed for serving.

Any size beef rib roast (rib eye or standing rib)
Salt and pepper (rub into roast)

Step 1:
Preheat oven to 375 degrees. Place beef in roasting pan uncovered, (rack optional) and place in oven for 1 hour. Turn off oven, and don't open oven door for a maximum of 2 hours before final cooking.

Step 2:
Preheat oven to 300 degrees. For rare beef roast-1 hour before serving: Bake for 45 minutes; let roast stand 15 minutes before slicing.

For medium beef roast-1 hour and 5 minutes before serving: Bake for 50 minutes; let roast stand 15 minutes before slicing.

For medium to well done beef roast-1 hour and 10 minutes before serving: Bake for 55 minutes; let roast stand 15 minutes before slicing.

Marlynn Rhyne

Beef and Vegetable Stir-Fry

1 pound boneless round steak
1 pound small fresh mushrooms
1 small bunch fresh broccoli
2 tablespoons peanut oil or vegetable oil
4 to 5 carrots, diagonally sliced
1 (6-ounce) can sliced water chestnuts, drained
1/4 cup soy sauce
2 tablespoons cornstarch
1/2 teaspoon sugar
1 1/2 cups beef broth
Hot cooked rice (6 servings)

Partially freeze steak; slice steak across grain into 3 x 1/4-inch strips. Set aside. Clean mushrooms and remove stems. Set aside. Wash broccoli and remove florets. Set aside.

Heat oil in preheated wok, coating sides. Allow to heat at 325 degrees for 1 minute. Add steak; stir-fry until browned. Add mushrooms, carrots, water chestnuts and soy sauce, stirring well. Cover, reduce heat to 225 degrees and cook 10 minutes. Add broccoli, cover and cook 5 minutes or until crisp-tender.

Combine cornstarch, sugar and beef broth, mixing well. Add to meat mixture and cook, stirring constantly, until thickened. Serve over rice.

Serves 6

Syble Murphy

Cheesy Beef Enchiladas

1 (10-ounce) can cream of mushroom soup
1 (10-ounce) can tomato soup
1 (10-ounce) can enchilada sauce, hot or mild
1 pound ground beef, cooked and drained
1 pound hot sausage, cooked and drained
1/2 cup chopped and cooked onion (optional)
(15-ounce) package flour tortilla shells, 8 to 10 count
1 (12-ounce) package grated Cheddar cheese

Preheat oven to 350 degrees. Mix soup and enchilada sauce together and heat in a saucepan until warm and bubbly, stirring often. Brown the ground beef and sausage and drain well. May add chopped onion to meat mixture, if desired. Warm flour tortillas according to package directions until soft and easy to handle. Add 1 cup of soup mixture to meat mixture. Heat and stir well.

Take 1 to 2 tablespoons of meat mixture and fill tortilla shell in middle. Add 1 to 2 tablespoons of cheese and layer on meat. Fold and place seamside down in a large baking dish. Continue process until all meat mixture is used.

Cover enchiladas with remaining soup mixture. Spread evenly over enchiladas. Cover with grated cheddar cheese. Bake until bubbly brown, about 30 minutes.

Note: Serve with salsa and sour cream, Mexican rice or refried beans for a real Mexican dinner!

Makes 8 to 10 enchiladas

Cathy Sanderson

Entrées   133

Eggplant Parmesan

1 medium eggplant
1 teaspoon salt
1 tablespoon butter or margarine
1 medium onion, chopped
1/3 cup chopped green pepper
1 pound ground beef
1 (28-ounce) can whole tomatoes, undrained and coarsely chopped
1 (6-ounce) can tomato paste
1/2 teaspoon dried oregano
1/2 teaspoon dried whole basil
1/2 teaspoon dried marjoram
1 teaspoon salt
1/2 teaspoon pepper
2 eggs, beaten
3/4 cup dry bread crumbs
1/2 cup butter or margarine, divided
2 cups shredded mozzarella cheese
3/4 cup grated Parmesan cheese
Green pepper rings for garnish
Parsley sprigs for garnish

Cut eggplant into 1/4-inch slices. Sprinkle with salt and let stand one hour. Melt 1 tablespoon butter in heavy saucepan. Add onion, green pepper and ground beef. Cook over medium heat, stirring to crumble beef, until beef is brown. Drain. Add next seven ingredients. Stir well. Bring to a boil. Reduce heat and simmer uncovered 30 minutes.

Preheat oven to 350 degrees. Dip eggplant slices in egg. Coat with breadcrumbs. Melt 1/4 cup butter in heavy skillet. Arrange a single layer of eggplant slices in skillet and brown on both sides. Drain on paper. Repeat eggplant slices, adding more butter as needed.

Layer 1/3 of meat sauce, 1/2 of eggplant, 1/2 of mozzarella cheese and 1/4 cup of Parmesan cheese in lightly greased 13 x 9 x 2-inch baking dish. Repeat layers. Add remaining meat sauce and top with Parmesan cheese. Bake 30 to 35 minutes. Garnish with green pepper rings and parsley.

Serves 6

Pie Weatherwax

Mustard-Topped Steak With Caramelized Onions

1 tablespoon Zatarain's Creole Mustard
1 tablespoon prepared horseradish, drained
1 garlic clove, minced
1 boneless beef sirloin steak, 1 1/2 inches thick (about 2 pounds)

Preheat broiler. In cup, mix mustard, horseradish and garlic. Place steak on rack in broiling pan. Place pan in broiler at closest position to source of heat; broil steak 10 to 12 minutes for medium-rare or until desired doneness; with tongs, turn steak once. Spread mustard mixture evenly over steak and broil 1 to 2 minutes until golden. Cut steak into thin slices to serve.

Serves 4

Caramelized Onions:
2 large onions (1 pound)
1 tablespoon salad oil
1 tablespoon red wine vinegar
1 tablespoon light brown sugar

Cut onions into thick slices. In 10-inch skillet, over medium heat in hot oil, cook onions until tender. Stir in vinegar and brown sugar; cook until golden.

Marlynn Rhyne

Entrées 135

Sunday Pot Roast With Vegetables

How can so many mothers juggle Sunday church and a family meal? Probably pot roast with vegetables!

1 (3-to 4-pound) sirloin tip, rump or boneless chuck pot roast
1/2 cup self-rising flour
1 teaspoon salt
1 teaspoon pepper
2 tablespoons vegetable oil
1 (10-ounce) can cream of mushroom or cream of celery soup
1 cup water
1 or 2 onions, quartered
2 or 3 carrots
4 or 5 potatoes

Preheat oven to 350 degrees. Pat roast dry and rub with flour. Sprinkle with salt and pepper.

In a Dutch oven, heat oil over moderately high heat. Add roast and brown on all sides, about 15 minutes total. Combine soup and water and pour over roast. Bring to a simmer on top of stove and add vegetables. Cover tightly and place in lower third of oven.

The liquid needs to maintain a gentle simmer; so after first hour, lower heat if needed and continue to simmer 3 or 4 hours or until roast is fork-tender.

Serves 6

Jane McCullough

Onion-Stuffed Burgers

1 onion (Vidalia or other sweet onion)
2 pounds ground sirloin
3 tablespoons Worcestershire sauce
Salt and freshly ground black pepper
6 ounces sliced Monterey Jack cheese

Preheat grill to medium high. Thinly slice onion and grill until translucent. Remove onion from heat and separate into rings while still warm. Set aside to cool.

In a large bowl, combine sirloin with Worcestershire; season with salt and pepper. Form hamburger patties using about 1/3 pound sirloin for each. Slice uncooked patties in half horizontally. Place 1 or 2 onion rings and a few slices of cheese between the 2 sirloin halves and press down.

Pinch the edges of the patties to keep the "sandwich" together. Grill about 7 minutes per side.

Makes 6 burgers

Entrées   137

July 4th Hamburgers

A 4th of July event usually leads to the all-American hamburger and an outdoor buffet!
These hamburgers have a hidden surprise for extra moistness.

1 pound unsalted butter, at room temperature
1 tablespoon chopped fresh thyme
1 tablespoon chopped fresh sage
2 tablespoons chopped flat-leaf parsley
1 tablespoon chopped chives
1 teaspoon chopped fresh rosemary
2 pounds freshly ground sirloin or round

Coarse salt and freshly ground pepper
Vegetable oil for grill
4 onion rolls, split
Lettuce
Sliced tomatoes

In a medium bowl, make herb butter by combining softened butter, thyme, sage, parsley, chives and rosemary; this can also be done in a food processor. Turn out onto parchment or plastic wrap and roll in a log, 1 1/2 to 2 inches in diameter. Chill until firm, or freeze for up to one month.

Heat grill or grill pan to medium high. Form four 8-ounce, 1-inch thick burgers. Cut four 1/8-inch thick slices of butter from the log. Make an indentation in the center of each burger, and place a slice of compound butter inside. Reshape meat to cover butter, making sure it is not visible from either side; season both sides with salt and pepper. Oil grill with a small amount of vegetable oil to prevent sticking. Grill burgers 5 to 7 minutes per side for medium doneness. Remove from grill and place each burger on a bun and serve garnished with lettuce and tomato.

Variation: Substitute herb butter with 1 tablespoon blue cheese or Boursin cheese (preferably peppered).

Serves 4

Barbecue Chicken

2 whole chickens, (3 pounds each) cut in half
1/2 stick butter, room temperature
Salt and pepper to taste
White Barbecue Sauce (page 170)

Preheat oven to 375 degrees. Wash chickens well and pat dry. Line baking pan with aluminum foil. Place chickens in pan. Spread butter over chickens and salt and pepper to taste. Place in oven and bake for 2 to 2 1/2 hours or until browned nicely. Baste 2 or 3 times during the last 45 minutes with White Barbecue Sauce (page 170). Serve sauce with meal.

Serves 4

Whole red chili peppers punctuate a platter of hamburgers.

Southern Corn Bread Dressing with Giblet Gravy

Thanksgiving and other family holidays are not times for culinary experimentation. Everyone is looking forward to a taste of tradition. So don't even try to sneak in anything different, for the aroma will give you away!

6 cups crumbled corn bread (recipe follows, or your favorite recipe)
4 cups crumbled day old breads (biscuit or sandwich bread)
1 cup margarine
1 cup chopped celery
1 cup chopped onion
4 eggs, slightly beaten
1/4 cup sage, or to taste
2 1/2 teaspoons poultry seasoning, or to taste
2 1/2 teaspoon salt, or to taste
2 1/2 teaspoons pepper, or to taste
3 to 4 cups Rich Chicken Broth (recipe follows) or Turkey Stock (page 320)
Giblet Gravy (recipe follows)

Corn Bread for Dressing:
5 eggs, beaten
2 cups buttermilk
2 cups self-rising cornmeal
1/2 teaspoon baking soda
2 teaspoons baking powder
1/2 teaspoon salt
1 teaspoon sugar
2 sticks margarine, melted

Rich Chicken Broth:
3-pound fryer
1 cup butter or margarine
Salt and pepper to taste

Rich Chicken Broth: Place fryer in large saucepan. Cover with water. Add butter, salt and pepper. Cook on medium heat until chicken is tender, about 45 minutes. Remove chicken from broth and set broth aside. Should have 4 cups.

Corn Bread for Dressing: Preheat oven to 350 degrees. Beat eggs and add buttermilk. Mix all dry ingredients together and add to egg mixture. Add melted margarine. Pour into a 10-to 11-inch greased skillet and bake for 1 hour or until slightly brown.

Dressing: Preheat oven to 375 degrees. Sauté celery and onions in margarine until tender and translucent, about 15 to 20 minutes.

In a large bowl, combine crumbled breads, celery and onion mixture, eggs, seasonings and enough broth for mixture to be pourable for a moist dressing, about 4 cups. Reduce amount of broth for a dryer dressing if desired.

Pour mixture into a greased 10 x 14 x 3-inch (or 4 1/2 quart) baking dish. Bake for 35 to 45 minutes or until dressing has a firm center and is light brown in color.

Note: If highly-seasoned dressing is not your favorite, adjust as follows: 3 teaspoons sage, 1/2 teaspoon each of poultry seasoning, salt and pepper. Add more to taste.

Serves 10

Caryl Ward Littrell

Giblet Gravy

Giblets and neck reserved from turkey
1/2 teaspoon salt
1 egg, hard-boiled and chopped

In pan, cover giblets and neck with water; add 1/2 teaspoon salt and bring to a boil. Simmer until tender and chop into small cubes. Add 1 chopped boiled egg and giblets to Basic Turkey Gravy.

Basic Turkey Gravy

1 tablespoon shortening
2 tablespoons flour
1/2 teaspoon salt
1/4 teaspoon pepper
2 cups turkey stock (or chicken stock)

In skillet, heat shortening; add flour and cook until brown. Add salt, pepper and stock. Stir constantly until thickened.

Caryl Ward Littrell

Hoisin Chicken with Grilled Peppers and Onions

Sauce:
1 tablespoon vegetable oil
2 tablespoons minced ginger
1 tablespoon minced garlic
1/3 cup hoisin sauce
1/4 cup fresh lime juice (about 2 limes)
1/2 cup roughly chopped fresh basil
1 teaspoon red pepper flakes
Salt and freshly cracked white (or black) pepper to taste

4 boneless chicken breast halves, with skin
Salt and freshly cracked black pepper to taste
2 red bell peppers, halved and seeded
1 large red onion, peeled and sliced into rings about 1-inch thick
1 tablespoon olive oil

Sauce: In a small saucepan, heat oil over medium heat until hot but not smoking. Add the ginger and garlic and sauté, stirring occasionally, for 2 minutes. Add the hoisin sauce and lime juice and simmer for 5 minutes. Remove from the heat, stir in the basil, red pepper flakes, and salt and pepper to taste, and set aside (do not refrigerate).

Sprinkle the chicken breasts with salt and pepper to taste and place on the grill, skin side down, over a medium-hot fire. Cook for 8 to 10 minutes, at which point the skin should be crispy. Turn the breasts over and cook for another 5 to 6 minutes. To check for doneness: Cut into the thickest part of one of the breasts and check to be sure that there is no pink color and the flesh is consistently opaque.

Meanwhile, rub the bell pepper halves and onion rings with the olive oil, sprinkle with salt and pepper to taste, and place on the grill. Cook for 2 to 3 minutes per side; you want them to have color and to be fairly firm. Remove from the grill when done.

Place the chicken breasts on a platter, arrange the peppers and onions around the breasts, drizzle the sauce over everything, and serve.

Note: Thighs, legs and wings can also be used.

Serves 4

Garlic and Oregano Marinated Chicken

2 tablespoons sherry vinegar
2 tablespoons fresh lemon juice
2 tablespoons fresh lime juice
2 tablespoons honey
1 tablespoon ancho chile powder
8 garlic cloves, coarsely chopped
1/4 cup fresh oregano leaves
2 cups olive oil
Salt and pepper
4 chickens, 2 pounds each, quartered
Olive oil to sauté chicken
Roasted Pepper and Black Olive Relish (page 306)

Combine vinegar, lemon juice, lime juice, honey, ancho chile powder, garlic and oregano in a blender and blend for 30 seconds. With motor running, slowly add olive oil until emulsified. Season to taste with salt and pepper. Place marinade in a large shallow baking dish, add chicken pieces and turn to coat. Cover and let marinate for 2 hours in refrigerator. Preheat oven to 375 degrees. Heat a large sauté pan until almost smoking. Remove chicken from marinade and season with salt and pepper to taste. Sauté chicken until golden brown on both sides. Place chicken on a large baking sheet and place in oven, bake for 45 to 60 minutes or until tender and brown. Remove from oven and let rest, 5 minutes. Serve with Roasted Pepper and Black Olive Relish.

Serves 8

Entrées 143

Grilled Chicken with Balsamic Peaches

In the summer when peaches are ripe and juicy, their flavor is strong enough to stand up to a few minutes on the grill. If the peaches are underripe or very firm, leave them on the grill a little longer.

1 cup balsamic vinegar
1/4 cup molasses
2 to 3 tablespoons freshly cracked black pepper
1/2 cup roughly chopped fresh basil
3 tablespoons minced garlic
1/4 cup olive oil
4 boneless chicken breast halves, with skin
Salt and freshly ground black pepper to taste
4 peaches, halved and pitted

In a small saucepan over medium-high heat, bring the vinegar to a boil and cook until it is reduced by half, 20 to 25 minutes. Stir in the molasses and black pepper, remove from the heat and set aside.

Meanwhile, in a small bowl, combine the basil, garlic and olive oil and mix well. Rub the chicken breasts with this mixture, sprinkle lightly with salt and pepper and grill over a medium fire, skin side down, until the skin is crispy, 8 to 10 minutes. Turn the breasts over and grill for another 6 minutes.

As the chicken breasts are finishing up, place the peaches on the fire, cut side down, and grill until they are nicely browned, about 2 minutes. Flip them over, brush the cut side with the balsamic glaze and continue to cook for another 2 minutes. Remove the peaches from the grill, give them another coat of glaze and serve whole or sliced with the chicken breasts.

Note: The balsamic glaze keeps forever so double or triple the batch and keep in the refrigerator. It's good brushed on any grilled meat at the last minute or two of cooking.

Serves 4

Grilled Lemon Chicken

This can be served whole for dinner, or sliced in 1/2-inch thick slices for an appetizer or atop a green salad.

3/4 cup freshly squeezed lemon juice (4 or more lemons)
3/4 cup extra virgin olive oil
2 teaspoons kosher salt
1 teaspoon freshly ground black pepper
1 tablespoon minced fresh thyme leaves or (1/2 teaspoon dried)
2 pounds boneless chicken breasts, halved and skin removed

Whisk together the lemon juice, olive oil, salt, pepper and thyme. Pour over the chicken breasts in a nonreactive bowl. Cover and marinate in the refrigerator for 6 hours or overnight.

Heat a charcoal grill and cook the chicken breasts for 10 minutes on each side, until just cooked through. Cool slightly and serve or cut diagonally in 1/2-inch thick slices for appetizers.

Note: If using as an appetizer, skewer on wooden sticks and serve with Peanuty Dip (page 22).

Serves 4

Chicken with Lime Butter

6 chicken breast halves, boneless and skinless
1/2 teaspoon salt
1/2 teaspoon pepper
1/3 cup vegetable oil
1 lime, juiced
8 tablespoons butter
1/2 teaspoon minced chives
1/2 teaspoon minced dill

Sprinkle chicken on both sides with salt and pepper. In a large frypan, place oil and heat to medium temperature. Add chicken and sauté about 4 minutes or until light brown on each side. Turn chicken, cover and reduce heat to low. Cook 10 minutes or until fork can be inserted into chicken with ease.

Remove chicken and keep warm; drain off oil and discard. In same frypan, add lime juice and cook over low heat until juice begins to bubble. Add butter, stirring until butter becomes opaque and forms a thickened sauce. Stir in chives and dill. Spoon sauce over chicken.

Serves 6

Entrées 145

Luncheon Chicken

4 chicken breast halves
1/4 cup butter
1 (10-ounce) can cream of chicken soup
3/4 cup white sauterne
1 (5-ounce) can water chestnuts, drained
1 (3-ounce) can sliced mushrooms, drained
2 tablespoons chopped green pepper
1/4 teaspoon thyme

Preheat oven to 350 degrees. In large skillet, brown chicken in butter and place in casserole. In same skillet, mix all the other ingredients, bring to a boil and pour over chicken. Bake covered for 30 minutes and uncovered for 30 minutes.

Serves 4

Dianne Norwood

Roast Chicken

Saluting the "whole bird," roasted in a pan with vegetables.
There's not a better, simpler, one-dish American meal!

1 3-to 4-pound chicken
1 lemon, halved
Fresh rosemary sprigs
Fresh thyme sprigs
2 cloves garlic, peeled and crushed
4 tablespoon butter, room temperature
Salt and freshly ground black pepper
4 small red onions, halved
8 small potatoes, halved
4 medium carrots, peeled
4 medium parsnips, peeled
Extra-virgin olive oil

Preheat oven to 450 degrees. Rinse chicken; then pat dry with paper towels. Put chicken in a large cast-iron skillet or roasting pan; squeeze lemon over chicken to cover all surfaces, inside and out, with juice. Use squeezed lemon halves, several sprigs each of rosemary and thyme, and garlic in cavity of the bird. Tie legs together with kitchen string; then rub butter all over chicken. Season liberally with salt and pepper.

Arrange onions, potatoes, carrots and parsnips around chicken. Brush vegetables with a little olive oil and season to taste with salt and pepper.

Roast in the oven for 15 minutes; then baste chicken and vegetables with pan juices. Reduce temperature to 375 degrees and continue to roast, basting occasionally, until skin is crisp and golden, about 45 minutes more.

Turn off heat and allow chicken to rest in the oven, with the oven door ajar, for about 15 minutes before carving. Garnish with additional fresh rosemary and thyme sprigs, if you like.

Serves 4

Entrées 147

Southern Fried Chicken

Fried chicken is just that, chicken that is fried and there's no getting around it. Oh yes, there's one more thing; the truly correct way to cook Southern Fried Chicken is in a cast-iron skillet most likely handed down from your mother. If you must ever buy a new one, be sure to season it before using (page 329).

1 3-pound chicken, cut up
1 cup buttermilk
2 cups all-purpose flour
2 teaspoons black peppercorns, cracked
1 teaspoon cayenne pepper
2 teaspoons salt
2 cups vegetable shortening
1 stick (1/2 cup) unsalted butter

Wash chicken thoroughly and pat dry. Place in a large shallow dish and pour buttermilk over chicken. Cover and chill for at least 1 hour or up to 1 day.

In a large shallow bowl, mix together flour, peppercorns, cayenne and salt. Dredge chicken pieces in flour mixture and shake off excess. (Flour may be placed in brown paper bag and chicken pieces can be floured by shaking in bag.)

Place floured pieces of chicken on a piece of wax paper to stand 15 minutes. Generously sprinkle more flour mixture over chicken, patting it to adhere to chicken, and let stand 15 minutes more.

In two 10-inch skillets, melt 1 cup vegetable shortening and 4 tablespoons butter in each skillet over high heat just until butter begins to turn golden. Fill each skillet with chicken pieces and turn heat to medium high. Cook chicken pieces 8 to 10 minutes per side or until deep golden color. Drain on paper towels.

Note: If only 1 skillet is needed for amount of chicken used, use 1 cup shortening and 4 tablespoons butter. Successive batches of chicken cannot be fried in shortening-butter mixture as it becomes too dark.

Serves 4

Chicken Milk Gravy

2 tablespoons flour
2 cups milk
Salt and pepper to taste

After all the chicken is fried, turn the heat off and pour out all but 2 tablespoons of the fat, leaving the un-burned residue. Add an equal amount of flour to the skillet (2 tablespoons), and stir with a whisk until the fat and the flour are incorporated. With the heat off, add 2 cups milk to the flour and fat mixture and whisk thoroughly to remove all lumps. Turn the heat back to medium, and heat to the boiling point, whisking constantly. Cook 1 or 2 minutes.

Note: Serve over rice, fried chicken, biscuits or corn bread.

Make 2 cups gravy

Chicken and Artichoke Casserole

3-pound fryer plus 4 extra breast halves
1 cup butter
1/2 cup flour
3 1/2 cups milk
3 ounces Cheddar cheese or Gruyère cheese, grated or cut in small pieces
1 tablespoon Accent
2 cloves garlic, minced
1/2 tablespoon red pepper (according to taste)
2 (13-ounce) cans mushrooms, drained
2 (14-ounce) cans whole artichoke hearts, drained and chopped
1/2 cup tomato sauce

In pot, cook chicken in seasoned water. Remove skin and bones and cut meat into bite-size pieces. Set aside. Preheat oven to 350 degrees. In pan, melt butter; stir in flour. Slowly add milk and stir until sauce is smooth. Add cheese and seasonings. Stir until cheese melts and sauce bubbles. Add chicken to sauce. Add mushrooms, chopped artichoke hearts and tomato sauce. Pour into a 3-quart casserole dish. Top may be sprinkled with toasted breadcrumbs. Bake for about 30 minutes.

Note: Can be prepared several days in advance and either refrigerate or freeze until time for use.

Serves 10 to 12
Marlynn Rhyne

Entrées

Best Chicken Divan

6 small chicken breast halves
1 cup water
1 teaspoon salt
1/2 teaspoon pepper
3 celery tops
1 ounce sherry
4 (10-ounce) packages frozen broccoli

Sauce:
1 stick margarine
1/2 cup flour
1 cup milk
1 cup chicken stock
1/2 teaspoon salt
1/4 teaspoon pepper
1 1/2 tablespoons grated Parmesan cheese
1/2 teaspoon Worcestershire sauce
1 ounce sherry
1/2 cup hollandaise sauce
1 cup heavy cream, whipped
1 cup grated Parmesan cheese
Buttered bread crumbs, optional

In pot, cook chicken with next 5 ingredients until done. Cool and slice or pull chicken from bone in medium-large chunks. Set aside. Cook broccoli in salted water and drain when done.

Sauce: Cook first 6 ingredients over medium heat until thickened. Add cheese, Worcestershire and sherry. Remove from heat, fold in hollandaise and whipped cream.

Line a shallow 9 x 13 x 2-inch baking dish with well-drained broccoli. Add chicken, sauce and sprinkle with more cheese. Brown under broiler. Add buttered bread crumbs and brown slightly if desired.

Serves 10 to 12

Cheesy Chicken Crescents

1 3/4 cups diced cooked chicken
1/2 cup shredded Cheddar cheese
1 (10-ounce) can cream of chicken soup
1 cup milk
1 (8-ounce) can crescent rolls
Paprika

Preheat oven to 375 degrees. In a bowl, combine chicken and half of cheese; set aside. Combine soup, milk and remaining cheese in saucepan. Heat just enough to melt cheese. Pour into a 9 x 9-inch square baking dish. Separate crescent rolls into 8 triangles. Place chicken and cheese mix on wide end and roll up. Arrange crescents in soup mixture. Sprinkle with paprika. Bake for 20 to 25 minutes.

Serves 4

Cindy Tidwell

Cornish Game Hens

4 Cornish game hens
Salt
Black peppercorns, cracked

Stuffing:
2 1/2 cups boiling water
1/2 cup long grain rice
1/4 cup wild rice
4 tablespoons melted butter
1 1/2 cups blackberries
1 apple, chopped
1/4 cup light brown sugar
4 green onions, chopped
1/2 cup chopped pecans
1/2 teaspoon thyme
1/2 teaspoon marjoram
1/2 teaspoon white pepper
1 1/2 cups dry white wine (to pour over hens)

Sauce:
1 cup melted butter
1/2 cup ground pecans

Preheat oven to 350 degrees. In pan, boil both rices for 15 minutes on high (cook longer if you do not want crunchy wild rice). Combine the rice with the other stuffing ingredients.

Remove giblets and rinse hens. Sprinkle salt and peppercorns in cavity of each hen and stuff each hen with rice mixture. Close cavities. Truss and secure with wooden toothpicks. Place hen breast side up in an uncovered roaster. Pour wine over each hen. Make melted butter and pecan sauce and spread on each hen, coating completely. Bake for 1 hour, basting frequently with drippings.

Serves 4

Caryl Ward Littrell

Fried Catfish with Sunflower Seed Crust

A recipe that truly glamorizes catfish! You must try this. Serve with Cilantro Tartar Sauce.

8 whole small catfish (or fillets), skin removed
1 cup flour (seasoned with 1 teaspoon salt and 1/2 teaspoon ground black pepper)
Vegetable oil for frying

Batter:
2 large eggs
2/3 cup flour
1 teaspoon salt
1/3 cup cornmeal
1 cup flat beer
2 jalapéno peppers, seeded and finely diced
1/3 cup red bell peppers, seeded and finely diced
1 cup sunflower seeds (or pumpkin seeds)
1 teaspoon chili flakes

Beat eggs in medium bowl. Add flour and salt to blend; add cornmeal and beer, a little of each at a time, whisking lightly to blend.

Batter should be a little lumpy. Let stand at room temperature for 1 hour. Lightly fold in remaining ingredients.

Pour oil to depth of 2 inches in an electric skillet or Dutch oven; heat to 375 degrees. Dust fish with seasoned flour and then place in batter to coat. Fry for 3 or 4 minutes or until medium brown. Serve with Cilantro Tartar Sauce (page 307).

Serves 4

Caryl Ward Littrell

Entrées

Keep Parsley Fresh

To keep your parsley fresh and green, cut about 1/2 inch off the stems. Remove the rubber band or string and place the stems in an inch of water in a glass. Cover with a plastic bag and store in the refrigerator. Every couple of days recut the stems, change the water and pick off any yellowing leaves. You can also simply rinse off the parsley, shake dry and store in a plastic bag.

Deep-Fried Catfish

The favorite way to prepare catfish in the South is to fry it until tender inside and crispy golden brown outside. This calls for a shade tree and an "ole-time" fish fry. If you don't do it outside, go out to eat it!

10 pounds catfish fillets
1 1/2 cups salt
3/4 cup black pepper
2 1/2 pounds self-rising flour
5 pounds self-rising cornmeal
2 gallons peanut oil

Thoroughly wash and drain catfish fillets. Liberally sprinkle with salt and pepper (more rather than less is good.)
    Mix flour and cornmeal together. Roll catfish fillets in cornmeal-flour mixture and place in skillet of hot peanut oil (360 to 375 degrees).
    Cook until fillets float in oil and are golden brown all over (3 to 5 minutes per side). Remove from oil and drain on paper towels. Serve hot with lemon wedges and parsley as a garnish!

Makes 33 fillets

Bobby Murphy

Saucy Catfish Bake

1 cup chopped onion
1 cup chopped celery
1/2 cup chopped parsley
2 pounds catfish fillets
1 teaspoon salt
1/2 teaspoon pepper
1/4 cup vegetable oil
1/2 to 3/4 teaspoon paprika or cayenne pepper
2 (8-ounce) cans tomato sauce
2 tablespoons Worcestershire sauce
1/4 cup lemon juice

Preheat oven to 375 degrees. In bowl, combine onion, celery and parsley; mix well. Spoon into a greased 13 x 9 x 2-inch baking pan.
   Sprinkle each fillet with salt and pepper; arrange over vegetables. Pour oil over fish and sprinkle with paprika or cayenne. Bake for 10 minutes.
   In bowl, combine tomato sauce, Worcestershire and lemon juice. Pour over fish and bake 30 minutes longer or until fish flakes easily when tested with a fork.

Serves 4 to 5

Syble Murphy

Is It Done?

To test fish for doneness, prod it with a fork at its thickest point. A properly cooked fish is opaque, has milky white juices, and just begins to flake easily. Undercooked fish is translucent and has clear and watery juices.

Entrées

Chili-Crusted Salmon And Roasted Scalloped Potatoes

Salmon fillets are coated with a simple chili rub and roasted over a bed of sliced potatoes for a tasty, no-fuss meal.

1 tablespoon chili powder
1 tablespoon light brown sugar
1 teaspoon salt
1 1/2 pounds russet potatoes, peeled and cut into thin slices
3 green onions, chopped (with green tops)
1 tablespoon olive oil
1/4 teaspoon coarsely ground black pepper
4 (6-ounce) salmon fillets
Green onions for garnish

Preheat oven to 450 degrees. In small bowl, combine chili powder, brown sugar and salt until blended.
    In a 9 x 13 x 2-inch baking dish, toss potatoes with onions, olive oil, pepper and 1 tablespoon chili mixture until evenly coated. Cover with foil and roast 20 minutes.
    Meanwhile, with hand, rub remaining chili mixture on top of salmon fillets. Place fillets over potatoes and roast, uncovered, 10 to 12 minutes longer or until fish flakes easily when tested with a fork and potatoes are tender. Garnish with green onions.

Serves 4

Scallions can be thought of as teenage onions. They add color and flavor to soups and salads and are great garnishes.

Coconut Shrimp with Mustard Sauce

1 1/2 pounds unpeeled, jumbo fresh shrimp
2 cups biscuit mix, divided
1 cup beer
1/2 teaspoon salt
1/8 to 1/4 teaspoon ground red pepper or cayenne
3 cups flaked coconut
Vegetable oil

Peel shrimp, leaving tails intact; devein. Set aside. Stir together 1 cup biscuit mix and beer until smooth. Stir together remaining biscuit mix, salt and ground red pepper. Coat shrimp with dry mixture, dip into beer mixture, allowing excess coating to drip, and gently roll in coconut. Pour vegetable oil to a depth of 3 inches in a large saucepan, and heat to 350 degrees. Cook shrimp, a few at a time, 1 to 2 minutes or until golden; remove and drain on a rack, not paper towels. Serve immediately with Mustard Sauce.

Serves 4

Mustard Sauce:
1/2 cup Dijon mustard
2 tablespoons light brown sugar
2 tablespoons pineapple juice
1/8 to 1/4 teaspoon ground red pepper or cayenne
Stir together all ingredients.

Makes 2/3 cup sauce

Christy Wright

Entrées   157

Shrimp-Chicken Étouffé

1 cup vegetable oil
1 cup all-purpose flour
1 cup chopped green onions (include green tops)
1 cup chopped onions
2 garlic cloves, minced
1/2 cup chopped green pepper
1/2 cup chopped celery
1 bay leaf
1/4 teaspoon thyme
1 teaspoon basil
1 (8-ounce) can tomato sauce
1/2 teaspoon white pepper
2 teaspoons salt
1 tablespoon Worcestershire
Tabasco to taste
2 cups liquid (see below)
1 pound boneless chicken breast, cooked and chopped
2 pounds raw shrimp, peeled
1 tablespoon lemon juice
Zest of 1 lemon
1/4 cup minced parsley
1/2 cup chopped green onion tops, (optional)
Liquid should be one of the following:
1 cup dry white wine plus 1/2 cup water or 2 cups chicken broth

Combine oil and flour in a large Dutch oven; cook over medium-low heat stirring constantly until roux is caramel-colored (30 to 45 minutes). Stir in both onions, garlic, green pepper, celery, bay leaf, thyme and basil. Sauté uncovered over medium heat for 30 minutes. Add tomato sauce, white pepper, salt, Worcestershire, Tabasco and liquid. Bring to boil, reduce heat and simmer slowly uncovered for 1 hour, stirring occasionally. Add shrimp and chicken; cook 15 minutes. Turn off heat. Add lemon juice, lemon zest and parsley.

Note: This is better made the day before or early in the morning. Cover and refrigerate. Remove from refrigerator 1 hour before serving. Heat quickly without boiling and serve immediately over steamed rice or in ramekins with French bread. If desired, garnish with raw green onion tops. It is recommended that if you use wine, omit the onion garnish.

Serves 6 to 8

Judy Richardson

Shrimp and Crab Supreme

If fresh lump crab is not available, double the amount of shrimp.

1 1/2 tablespoons butter
1/2 cup chopped green pepper
1/4 cup minced green onion
1 1/2 cups finely chopped celery
1 cup mayonnaise
1 tablespoon Worcestershire sauce
2 ounces diced pimentos
2 tablespoons fresh lemon juice
1/2 teaspoon salt
1 pound cooked shrimp, chopped coarsely
1 pound crab meat (lump)
2 cups crushed potato chips

Preheat oven to 400 degrees. Melt butter in saucepan with tight-fitting lid. Add the pepper, onion and celery and cover. Cook over medium heat for 5 minutes, stirring occasionally. Set aside and allow to cool.

Combine mayonnaise, Worcestershire sauce, pimentos, lemon juice and salt until well blended. Fold in the cooked vegetables.

Fold the shrimp and crab into the mayonnaise-vegetable mixture. Do not overmix. Use a light hand so as not to break up crab meat.

Pour into 2-quart buttered casserole dish. Top with 2 cups crushed potato chips. Bake for 25 to 30 minutes.

Note: Can be served in individual pastry shells, baked for 20 minutes.

Serves 6

Marlynn Rhyne

Entrées 159

Barbecued Shrimp

Spread the dining table with newspapers and serve shrimp in the baking pan. Peel and eat the shrimp, sopping up the sauce with lots of French bread. Serve with vegetable crudités with Ranch-style dip. Great for river or beach party.

2 to 3 pounds large shrimp, heads removed

Sauce:
16 ounces butter or margarine
4 lemons, sliced
1 tablespoon rosemary
1 teaspoon Tabasco
2 to 4 cloves garlic, minced
2 teaspoons salt
1 tablespoon black pepper
3/4 cup Worcestershire sauce

Preheat oven to 400 degrees. In a saucepan melt butter or margarine. Add lemon slices, rosemary, Tabasco, garlic, salt and pepper. Mix thoroughly. Add Worcestershire sauce and stir over medium-low heat until heated thoroughly. Arrange shrimp in large shallow baking pan and pour heated sauce over them. Bake about 15-20 minutes, turning once. Shrimp are ready when their shells are pink and the meat is white, not translucent.

Serves 4

Basic Shrimp Boil

1 gallon water (no salt added)
1 (3-ounce) bag Zatarain's Crab Boil
1 lemon, cut in half, not squeezed
6 to 10 bay leaves
3 tablespoons white vinegar
1 tablespoon unsalted butter
1 1/2 pounds fresh medium shrimp, heads off, not peeled, never frozen

Place water, crab boil, lemon, bay leaves, vinegar and butter in a large Dutch oven or soup pot. Stir the crab boil bag around to release flavoring. Cover loosely. When water has boiled 1 to 2 minutes, add 1/2 to 3/4 pound shrimp. Continue to heat, even allowing a rolling boil to develop. When shrimp float to the top and have turned pink, they are ready to remove (about 5 minutes). Remove shrimp with a slotted spoon to a serving platter. Add additional batches of shrimp into same broth, repeating until all the shrimp are cooked. Peel and eat. Serve with Hot Cocktail Sauce (page 310)

No-No's:
Don't overcook the shrimp (remove promptly)
Don't add salt to water (harder to peel)

Serves 4

Horseradish Sauce

*1 cup ketchup
2 tablespoons horseradish
2 teaspoons fresh lemon juice.*

Thoroughly blend all ingredients and chill.

Makes 1 cup sauce

Entrées

Baked Plantation Country Ham

You will not believe how tender and delicious this ham is!

1 (14-to 16-pound) hickory-smoked country ham
1/2 gallon apple juice
Whole cloves
1 1/2 cups firmly packed light brown sugar
1 tablespoon white vinegar
2 teaspoons prepared mustard
1 teaspoon ground cloves

Place ham in a very large container; cover with water and soak 8 to 24 hours. Pour off water. Scrub ham with warm water using stiff brush and rinse well.

Preheat oven to 325 degrees. Place ham in a large roasting pan; pour apple juice over ham. Cover and bake for 3 hours. Carefully remove ham from pan, reserving 1 tablespoon pan juices. Discard remaining juices. Let ham cool 10 minutes.

Remove skin and score fat in a diamond design using a sharp knife; return ham to pan, fat side up. Stud with whole cloves. Combine reserved pan juices, brown sugar and remaining 3 ingredients. Coat exposed portion of ham evenly with brown sugar mixture.

Bake ham, uncovered, 30 to 40 minutes or until a meat thermometer inserted into thickest part of meat registers 142 degrees and brown sugar coating is crusty. To serve, slice ham across grain into very thin slices.

Serves 26

Betty Mitchell Sims

Baked Easter Ham

As tradition has it, certain holidays are linked to certain foods. At Thanksgiving, there's turkey; at Christmas, roast beef or turkey again. At Easter it's lamb or if you're eating at my house—ham! Someone once defined eternity as a ham and 2 people! So bake this ham to feed a large group of people!

1 (17-to 18-pound) smoked, fully cooked, bone-in ham

Glaze:
1 1/2 cups orange marmalade
1 cup Dijon mustard
1 1/2 cups firmly packed light brown sugar
1 rounded tablespoon whole cloves

For ham, preheat oven to 300 degrees. Trim outer skin and excess fat from ham. Put ham in a large roasting pan and score, making crosshatch incisions all over ham with a sharp knife. Roast for about 5 hours.

For glaze, combine orange marmalade, mustard and brown sugar in a medium bowl. Stud ham with cloves and brush the entire surface with glaze at least 3 times. Cook ham 1 hour more. Transfer to cutting board and allow to sit for 30 minutes. Carve and serve warm or at room temperature.

Note: Don't forget to line roasting pan with heavy-duty foil for an easy clean-up!

Serves 20 to 30

Baked Ham with Mustard-Apricot Glaze

1 (6-to 8-pound) smoked, fully-cooked, bone-in ham half

Glaze:
1/2 cup Dijon mustard
1 cup apricot jam
1/2 cup light brown sugar, plus extra for crusty glaze
1/4 cup light corn syrup
Whole cloves

Preheat oven to 300 degrees. Remove hard outer skin from ham, leaving a thin layer of fat. Place ham, fat side up, on rack in shallow roasting pan. With sharp knife, score fat in a diamond pattern.
Bake ham for 3 1/2 hours. Remove ham from oven and leave oven on. Make glaze and spread on ham. Pat more sugar on top of glaze, add cloves and return to oven for 30 to 45 minutes for sugar to melt.

Note: Ham is done when an instant-read thermometer inserted in the thickest part of ham not touching bone reads 140 degrees.

Serves 12

Leg of Lamb Roast With Lemon Or Saffron Sauce

Leg of lamb
Flour
Garlic powder to taste
Salt to taste
Lemon pepper to taste

Lemon Sauce:
2 tablespoons flour
Fresh lemon juice, to taste
Pan drippings

Saffron Sauce:
1/2 pint sour cream
3/4 teaspoon saffron
1 teaspoon cornstarch
3 tablespoons water.
1 (3 1/2-ounce jar) capers, drained

Leg of Lamb: Rub leg of lamb with flour. Sprinkle garlic powder, salt and lemon pepper over flour and rub into roast. In roasting pan, brown in a 500-degree oven for about 20 minutes. Reduce heat to 350 degrees and cook 15 minutes per pound for medium rare or use meat thermometer to read internal temperature. Rare is 130 to 140 degrees, medium 150 to 160 degrees and well done is 160 to 170 degrees in thickest part. Use a small amount of water if necessary.

When roast is done, place lamb on platter and serve with Lemon Sauce or Saffron Sauce.

Lemon Sauce: Skim fat from pan drippings and add 2 tablespoons flour per cup of pan drippings. Heat and stir, add fresh lemon juice to taste and serve with roast.

Saffron Sauce: Skim fat from pan drippings and add sour cream and saffron. Bring to a boil, stirring constantly. Mix cornstarch and water. Add to sour cream mixture and boil gently for about 4 minutes. Add drained capers and cook for 1 minute more. Cover until ready to serve.

Serves 8

Caryl Ward Littrell

Entrées

Grilled Pork Tenderloin

1(2 1/2-to 3-pound) pork tenderloin

Marinade: (make twice)
1/2 cup soy sauce
1/4 cup chopped green onion
2 cloves minced garlic
1 teaspoon ginger
1/2 teaspoon pepper
1/4 cup sesame seeds

Sauce:
1/2 cup sour cream
1/2 cup mayonnaise
1 teaspoon dry mustard
1 teaspoon white wine vinegar
1/2 cup chopped green onion

Sauce: In bowl, combine all ingredients for sauce. Refrigerate several hours.
   Tenderloin: Make marinade and marinate tenderloin 2 hours to overnight.
   Grill over medium-hot coals 30 minutes or until done, basting with marinade.
   To serve, dilute a new recipe of marinade with 5 parts water. Simmer 10 or 15 minutes. Slice pork very thin and place with some of the marinade in a chafing dish. Serve with sauce on dinner rolls.

Serves 4 to 6 or makes 20 cocktail servings

Bobbi Shelton

Marinated Pork Tenderloin with Mustard Sauce

3 pork tenderloins, 3/4 pound each
1/2 cup soy sauce
1/2 cup bourbon
1/4 cup packed light brown sugar

Mustard Sauce:
1/4 cup sour cream
1/2 cup mayonnaise
1 tablespoon dry mustard
1 tablespoon chopped scallions or onions
1 1/2 tablespoons white wine vinegar

Tenderloins: In a shallow dish, blend soy sauce, bourbon and brown sugar. Add the tenderloins, turning to coat with the sauce, and marinate in the refrigerator several hours.

While tenderloins are marinating, prepare sauce by mixing all ingredients together. Let stand at room temperature at least 4 hours.

Preheat oven to 325 degrees. Bake tenderloins in the marinade for 45 minutes, basting frequently. Slice and serve with Mustard Sauce on yeast rolls.

Serves 6 to 8

Syble Murphy

Pork Roast With Peppers

1 tablespoon vegetable oil
3 tablespoons unsalted butter
1 small onion, finely chopped
1/2 green bell pepper, finely chopped
1/2 stalk celery, finely chopped
1 tablespoon minced garlic
1 1/2 teaspoons salt
2 teaspoons black pepper
1 teaspoon cayenne pepper
1 teaspoon paprika
1 teaspoon dried thyme
1/2 teaspoon dry mustard
1 (4-pound) boneless pork loin roast
1 each red, yellow, orange and green bell peppers, cut in 1-inch pieces
1/4 cup extra virgin olive oil, or more
2 tablespoons balsamic vinegar, or to taste
Salt and pepper to taste

Preheat oven to 275 degrees. In skillet, sauté onion, green pepper, celery and garlic in butter and oil. Add salt, black and cayenne peppers, paprika, thyme and mustard. With pork roast fat side up, make several slits and stuff with vegetable mixture. Rub surface of roast with remaining vegetable mixture. In roasting pan, bake uncovered for 3 hours or until internal temperature reaches 160 degrees, then raise heat to 425 degrees and continue baking until brown on top, 15 minutes more. Sauté bell pepper pieces in olive oil and balsamic vinegar. Salt and pepper to taste and serve roast on large platter surrounded with sautéed peppers.

Serves 8

Roasted Pork Boston Butt

If you're interested in starting an all-out war, just declare exactly who has the best barbecue and sauce. Battles rage all around the country and even in the same state. There's yellow mustard sauce from South Carolina, white mayonnaise sauce from Alabama, bacon and pecan sauce from Louisiana and the list goes on and on. You can grill, smoke or roast pork and enjoy the results. But that's just the tip of the iceberg; so have a simple pork roast or a pile of sandwiches if you're tired already!

1 (4-to 5-pound) pork Boston butt, untrimmed
Salt
Freshly ground black pepper

Preheat oven to 400 degrees. Season pork with salt and pepper. Place roast, fat side up, in shallow roasting pan lined with heavy foil. Place 1 cup water in pan. Cook pork for 1 hour. Reduce heat to 300 degrees and continue to cook for 6 hours. Remove from oven and cool completely. Remove meat from bone with fingers and shred. Serve with White Barbecue Sauce (page 170) and Vinegar Hot Sauce (recipe follows).

Serves 6

Vinegar Hot Sauce

*Serve this hot sauce as an accompaniment to cooked barbecue pork.
It is a must for each and every barbecue sandwich!*

1 cup white wine vinegar
2 tablespoons ketchup
2 tablespoons honey
3/4 teaspoon cayenne pepper
1/4 teaspoon salt
1/2 teaspoon black pepper

In a medium saucepan, mix together all ingredients. Simmer 10 minutes over low heat. Serve at room temperature.

Makes 1 1/2 cups sauce

Entrées 169

Hotter Hot Sauce

If you enjoy eyes that water, sprinkle this sauce on cooked barbecue pork! It can be mixed into chopped pork.

1 1/2 cups cider vinegar
2 teaspoons hot red pepper flakes
2 teaspoons Tabasco
1 tablespoon Worcestershire sauce
Salt and pepper to taste

Mix all ingredients in small saucepan and heat on medium. Remove from heat and serve warm or at room temperature.

Makes 1 3/4 cups sauce

White Barbecue Sauce

North Alabama's version of the best sauce! This is delicious with barbecue pork or chicken. It is an old, old recipe but grown children still call home for it. So this is for our children, again!

1 1/2 cups mayonnaise
3/4 to 1 cup white vinegar
4 tablespoons sugar
1/4 cup black pepper, or to taste
Juice of 1 lemon (1 1/2 tablespoons)

Mix all ingredients in a jar with lid. Shake vigorously to mix. Serve with Barbecue Chicken (page 139) or Roasted Pork Boston Butt (page 169).

Makes 1 1/2 pints sauce

Barbecue Sandwiches

Soft buns and slaw—indispensable accompaniments for barbecue! Mound buns generously with pork and slaw and sprinkle with Vinegar Hot Sauce. Most will add White Barbecue Sauce also!

Roasted Pork Boston Butt (page 169)
12 hamburger buns
Coleslaw (recipe follows)
Vinegar Hot Sauce (page 169)
White Barbecue Sauce (page 170)

Make sandwiches and just pile them into a napkin-lined bowl. Good for a crowd! Potato chips are a must here; so are dill pickles.

Serves 6

Coleslaw

Coleslaw is a must with barbecue pork or chicken.
This is the correct coleslaw to use on barbecue sandwiches.

1 large head cabbage or 2 small cabbages with nice green outer leaves (about 7 cups cabbage when grated and drained)
1 cup white vinegar
1 cup water
1 3/4 cup sugar
1/2 teaspoon salt

Using food processor, fill container about 1/2 full of water. Add chopped cabbage and pulse cautiously until cabbage is correct grated size. Drain and repeat if necessary.

In saucepan, mix vinegar, water, sugar and salt. Boil until sugar and salt dissolve. Cool completely before adding to drained cabbage. Refrigerate overnight.

Serves 6

Entrées 171

Slow-Simmered Pork Roast

3 scallions, cut into 1-inch pieces (with green tops)
1 teaspoon julienned fresh ginger
2 star anise, whole
2 tablespoons Black Bean Garlic Sauce
2 tablespoons soy sauce
2 teaspoons light brown sugar
1/2 cup dry sherry or Chinese rice wine
2 cloves garlic,thinly sliced
1/2 teaspoon ground white pepper
2 cups water (more if needed)
1 (3-to 4-pound) Boston butt pork roast

Mix all ingredients together except the roast. Place roast into a 3-to 4-quart ovenproof dish. Pour sauce over the top, cover the dish and bake at 275 degrees from 5 to 8 hours, depending upon desired tenderness.

Marlynn Rhyne

Roast Turkey

1 (10-to 12-pound) turkey
Salt
Pepper
1 cup water
1 to 1 1/2 sticks butter, room temperature

Preheat oven to 325 degrees. Remove giblets and neck; save to use in giblet gravy. Wash turkey thoroughly; pat dry. Sprinkle generously inside and out with salt and pepper.

Place bird, breast side up, on a rack in roasting pan. Add 1 cup water to bottom of pan. Rub the outside skin all over with 1 to 1 1/2 sticks butter. Place an aluminum tent over the bird, making tent large enough to cover loosely. Do not let foil touch heating unit.

During cooking, lift foil tent and baste several times with juice in bottom of pan. Baste every 30 minutes.

Roast in oven until tender. The drumstick will move easily when turkey is done, about 4 to 4 1/2 hours.

Serves 15 or more

Good Chicken Salad

1 (4-to 6-pound) hen or 4 cups cooked chicken breasts, torn or chopped
1/2 cup slivered almonds, toasted
1 cup finely chopped celery
1 cup white seedless grapes, cut into halves
1 cup Cooked Salad Dressing (recipe follows)
Salt and pepper to taste
Lettuce leaves

Cooked Salad Dressing:
2 eggs
3 tablespoons vinegar
1/3 cup milk
1 tablespoon margarine
1/2 teaspoon salt
1/2 teaspoon sugar
1/2 teaspoon powdered mustard
Dash paprika
Dash black pepper

In pan, beat eggs and vinegar until smooth. Add other ingredients and cook over low heat until as thick as heavy cream. Cool. If you feel more dressing is needed, add mayonnaise.
    Combine chicken, almonds, celery, grapes, Cooked Salad Dressing, salt and pepper in large bowl. Stir gently to blend. Chill until serving time. Serve over lettuce leaves.

Serves 6

Cutting Into Julienne

To cut vegetable slices into small strips, stack slices, a few at the time and cut into very thin strips (less than 1/8-inch thick) to make a julienne.

Chicken Salad with Currants

1 recipe Good Chicken Salad (leave out grapes and almonds)
3/4 cup currants
1/2 to 3/4 cup chopped green onions (with green tops)
1 cup chopped red apples with peel
1/2 cup chopped pecans

Note: Makes great sandwiches! Use on multi-grain bread.

Entrées

Chicken Salad and Artichokes

Make this with homemade Herbed Mayonnaise for the best chicken salad ever.

6 chicken breast halves, boneless and skinless
2 large celery ribs, cut in half
1 onion, peeled and sliced
4 ribs celery, chopped
1 (14-ounce) can artichoke hearts, drained and coarsely chopped
1 cup Herbed Mayonnaise (recipe follows)
Salt and pepper to taste
1 cup slivered almonds, toasted

Cook chicken breast in large pot with the celery ribs, onion and water to cover for about 45 minutes over medium heat. Let cool in broth while preparing the rest of the salad.

When chicken is cool, chop or pull chicken into fairly large pieces. Mix with the chopped celery, the drained and chopped artichoke hearts, and about 1 cup of the mayonnaise. Add salt and pepper to taste. Chill at least 2 hours. Serve topped with toasted slivered almonds.

Note: Serve on Boston lettuce.

Serves 6 to 8

Herbed Mayonnaise:
3 whole eggs
2 teaspoons dry mustard
2 teaspoons each: chives, tarragon and salt
1 1/2 cups light vegetable oil
3 tablespoons cider or sherry vinegar

Put the whole eggs, dry mustard, chives, tarragon and salt in a processor and process until light yellow.

With the machine still running, add the oil 1 teaspoon at a time until 1/2 cup has been incorporated into the eggs. Then add the rest of the oil, with the machine still running, in a steady stream until all the oil is used up and the mayonnaise is thick. Turn the machine off, and add the vinegar. Process until the vinegar is just mixed in. Taste and add more salt if necessary.

Makes about 1 1/2 cups mayonnaise

Vegetables and Side Dishes

1887 Smokehouse
Robert M. Byars, Sr. Property
Moulton, Alabama

Vegetables and Side Dishes

Marinated Asparagus

3/4 cup extra-virgin olive oil
1/3 cup red wine vinegar
1 tablespoon salt
1 teaspoon sugar
1/4 cup chopped green pepper
1 tablespoon chopped fresh parsley
2 tablespoons chopped green onion
2 tablespoons chopped pimento
1 pound thin, fresh asparagus
    (trimmed, blanched 1 or 2 minutes and plunged into ice water a second before draining)

Combine oil, vinegar, salt, sugar, pepper, parsley, onion and pimento in a shallow, nonmetallic bowl. Add asparagus, tossing to coat. Cover and marinate several hours in refrigerator. Serve chilled or at room temperature.

Serves 4

Steamed Asparagus with Lemon Butter

1/2 pound fresh asparagus
Salt
2 tablespoons unsalted butter
1 tablespoon lemon juice
1 teaspoon lemon zest

Wash asparagus and trim bottom of stems if needed. In a large skillet, bring about 1/2 inch of water to a rapid boil. Season water with salt and add the asparagus. Cook for 2 to 3 minutes, uncovered, or until asparagus is bright green and just tender. Remove asparagus from skillet and plunge into a bowl of ice water. Drain immediately. Add the butter, lemon juice and lemon zest to the skillet. Return the drained asparagus to the skillet and toss to coat. Serve immediately.

Note: Asparagus may also be served cold.

Serves 4

Best Baked Beans

4 slices bacon
1 green pepper, finely chopped
1 small onion, finely chopped
1/2 cup brown sugar
1/2 cup ketchup
1 teaspoon mustard
1 teaspoon Worcestershire sauce
1 (53-ounce) can pork and beans

Preheat oven to 325 degrees. Combine all ingredients except bacon. Pour into a 9 x 13 x 2-inch baking dish and top with bacon. Bake uncovered 1 1/2 hours.

Note: Add 1 (14-ounce) can diced tomatoes for a slightly different twist.

Serves 8

Green Beans with Bacon Dressing

3 pounds fresh whole green beans, trimmed
4 slices bacon
1/2 cup chopped shallots
3 tablespoons coarsely chopped pecans
1/3 cup white wine vinegar
2 tablespoons sugar
3/4 teaspoon salt
1/2 teaspoon freshly ground black pepper

In a 4-quart saucepan, bring 2 1/2 quarts water to a boil. Add green beans and cook 2 to 4 minutes. Drain, cool in ice water, drain again and set aside.
    In a large skillet, cook bacon until crisp, about 7 minutes. Drain bacon on paper towels. Add shallots to bacon drippings and sauté 2 minutes. Add pecans and cook 1 minute more. Remove skillet from heat and add vinegar and sugar, stirring until sugar has dissolved.
    Add green beans to skillet and cook over low heat until vegetables are heated through; sprinkle with salt and pepper. Transfer to serving platter; crumble reserved bacon over green beans and serve immediately.

Serves 10 to 12

Fresh Asparagus

If asparagus isn't thin and tender, gently bend each stalk and the woody end will snap off at just the right spot. Any tough spots can be removed with a vegetable peeler.

Vegetables and Side Dishes

Blanching Tips

Blanch vegetables by placing them in boiling water 1 to 2 minutes. Plunge into ice water, drain and chill.

Never cover green vegetables while blanching.

Never try to keep vegetables warm after blanching. They will turn soft and lose their color. It is best to reheat them in their seasoning sauce or butter.

Green Beans with Honey Cashew Sauce

3 tablespoons unsalted butter
1/2 cup coarsely chopped salted cashews
2 tablespoons honey
1 pound fresh young, whole green beans, blanched and drained

In pan, sauté cashews in butter over low heat for 5 minutes. Add honey and cook 1 minute longer, stirring constantly. Pour sauce over beans and toss until coated.

Serves 4

Green Beans and Red Bell Pepper

2 tablespoons extra-virgin olive oil
1 red bell pepper, cut in 1/4-inch strips
2 cloves garlic, finely minced
1 1/2 pounds fresh young whole green beans, blanched
1/4 cup balsamic vinegar
Salt and freshly ground black pepper to taste
Freshly grated Parmesan cheese, optional

In skillet, sauté bell pepper in oil until tender. Add garlic, green beans, vinegar, salt and pepper. Heat until beans are warmed.

Serves 4

Green Beans, Southern Style

1 pound fresh green beans
2 1/2 cups hot water
One 2 x 2-inch piece salt pork
Salt to taste
Pepper to taste
1/2 teaspoon sugar
1 tablespoon vinegar, or to taste
1 onion, quartered

Wash beans, string, break into pieces and set aside. Score salt pork in several places. Place all ingredients in large saucepan and cook on simmer 1 1/2 to 2 hours, or until very tender. Add more water as necessary.

Serves 4

Caryl Ward Littrell

Broccoli Cheese Soufflé

Served with a fresh tomato salad and good bread, this makes a nice lunch.

1 bunch broccoli
1 medium onion, chopped
2 tablespoons butter
2 tablespoons oil
2 cups grated cheese (Swiss or Cheddar)
4 ounces cream cheese
1 1/2 cups breadcrumbs (trim crust from bread)
8 eggs, beaten
4 cups heavy cream or milk
Dash of Tabasco
Salt and pepper to taste

Preheat oven to 375 degrees. Trim the broccoli stems. Separate the broccoli into florets. In Dutch oven sweat the broccoli and onion in the butter and oil over low heat for 10 minutes, until the vegetables are slightly cooked. Stir in grated cheese, cream cheese, breadcrumbs, eggs and cream. Season the mixture to taste with Tabasco, salt and pepper.

Pour mixture into a lightly oiled 9 x 13 x 2-inch baking dish and bake for 45 minutes or until the top is lightly browned and the soufflé has set. Serve hot or at room temperature.

Note: This dish may be prepared and baked 1 or 2 days in advance and reheated. It also freezes very well after baking.

Serves 10

Charred Brussels Sprouts, Carrots, Onions and Garlic

1 pound brussels sprouts, "X" cut in bottoms and outer layers removed
4 to 6 garlic cloves, peeled
2 medium onions, cut in wedges
2 carrots, peeled and julienned
3 to 6 tablespoons olive oil
Salt
Freshly ground black pepper
2 lemons for juicing (2 tablespoons)
3 tablespoons chopped fresh parsley

Preheat oven to 425 degrees. In bowl, toss the brussels sprouts (you may parboil these 3 to 4 minutes before adding to mixture), garlic, onions and carrots with the olive oil and arrange in an oiled pan in a single layer. Bake 30 to 45 minutes, stirring occasionally, or until the vegetables are crisp, tender and charred to your taste. Season with salt and pepper. Squeeze lemon juice over vegetables and sprinkle with parsley.

Serves 4 to 6

Pecan-Glazed Brussels Sprouts

1 1/2 pounds fresh brussels sprouts
1/2 cup water
1/4 cup unsalted butter or margarine
1/3 cup firmly packed light brown sugar
3 tablespoons soy sauce
1/4 teaspoon salt
1/2 cup finely chopped pecans, toasted

Wash brussels sprouts thoroughly, and remove discolored leaves. Cut off stem ends and slash bottom of each sprout with a shallow "X." Bring 1/2 cup water to a boil in a large saucepan; add brussels sprouts. Cover, reduce heat and simmer 8 to 10 minutes, or until sprouts are crisp-tender; drain and set aside.

Melt butter in a medium skillet; stir in brown sugar, soy sauce and salt. Bring butter mixture to a boil, stirring constantly. Add pecans; reduce heat and simmer, uncovered, 5 minutes, stirring occasionally. Add brussels sprouts; cook over medium heat 5 minutes. Stir well before serving.

Note: Use tiny brussels sprouts, which are more tender.

Serves 4 to 6

Butterbeans and Peas

2 (10-ounce) packages frozen baby lima beans
2 (10-ounce) packages frozen green peas
2 cups water
1 teaspoon salt
1/4 teaspoon garlic salt
1 teaspoon seasoned salt
2 tablespoons butter
1/2 cup finely chopped onions
1 1/2 tablespoons all-purpose flour
3 tablespoons milk
1 cup light cream
1/4 teaspoon salt
Cayenne pepper
Paprika

Preheat oven to 325 degrees. In a large saucepan, bring water to a boil. Add salt, garlic salt, 1/2 teaspoon seasoned salt, beans and peas. Cook until tender. Drain, and place into a 2-quart casserole.

Heat butter in skillet and sauté onions until tender. Remove onions to casserole, leaving butter in skillet. Add flour and stir gradually, adding milk and cream until slightly thickened. Add 1/4 teaspoon salt, 1/2 teaspoon seasoned salt, cayenne and paprika.

Pour over beans and peas. Stir gently; cover and bake until warm.

Serves 8 to 10

Caryl Ward Littrell

Carrot-Pecan Casserole

3 pounds carrots, sliced
2/3 cup sugar
1/2 cup butter or margarine, room temperature
1/2 cup chopped pecans, toasted
1/4 cup milk
2 large eggs, lightly beaten
3 tablespoons all-purpose flour
1 tablespoon vanilla extract
1 teaspoon grated orange zest
1/4 teaspoon ground nutmeg
Carrot curls and fresh parsley for garnish

Preheat oven to 350 degrees. Cook carrots in a small amount of boiling water in a medium saucepan 12 to 15 minutes or until tender.

Drain carrots, and mash. Stir in sugar and next 8 ingredients. Spoon into a lightly greased 2-quart casserole.

Bake for 40 minutes. Garnish if desired.

Serves 10 to 12

Ginger and Honey-Glazed Carrots

No more ho-hum carrots! Who said carrots needed to be stubs? The visual appeal of these carrots is such that you'll want to have them often. They taste great lightly coated with a buttery glaze.

6 cups water
3/4 teaspoon salt
2 pounds young, peeled, small carrots with tops trimmed (not removed) to 2 inches
2 tablespoons butter
2 tablespoons honey
4 teaspoons minced fresh ginger

In a large heavy skillet, combine water and salt. Bring to a boil. Add carrots and return to boil; reduce heat. Cover and simmer 10 to 12 minutes or until carrots are just tender, then drain.

To glaze carrots, in the same heavy skillet, combine butter, honey and ginger. Stir constantly over medium heat until butter is melted. Carefully add carrots as the green tops are fragile. Toss gently for 2 to 3 minutes or until carrots are thoroughly coated with glaze and heated completely.

To serve, arrange carrots in a shallow bowl or on a platter; drizzle with remaining glaze.

Note: To make ahead, carrots may be cooked, cooled, covered and refrigerated up to one day. Bring to room temperature (takes about an hour) when ready to glaze. Heat carrots in glaze for 4 to 5 minutes.

Serves 6 to 8

Macaroni and Cheese

4 cups (16 ounces) elbow macaroni
1/2 cup chopped onion
1/4 cup margarine
2 cups sour cream
1 cup cottage cheese
1/4 cup chopped parsley
1 teaspoon salt
8 ounces sharp shredded Cheddar cheese

Preheat oven to 350 degrees. Cook macaroni according to package directions. Sauté onion in margarine until tender. Combine macaroni, sour cream, cottage cheese, sautéed onion, parsley and salt. Mix well. Pour into greased 2-quart casserole and sprinkle top with shredded cheese. Bake for 30 minutes.

Serves 8 to 10

Caryl Ward Littrell

The Ultimate Macaroni and Cheese

Is it macaroni and cheese or cheese and macaroni? Whichever, this may become a family favorite.

1 3/4 cups large elbow macaroni, uncooked
Salt
1 1/4 cups of 1/2-inch cubes of Velveeta cheese (about 5 ounces)
2 tablespoons plus 2 teaspoons all-purpose flour
1 1/2 teaspoons salt
1 1/2 teaspoons dry mustard powder
1/4 teaspoon freshly ground black pepper
1/8 teaspoon cayenne pepper
1 1/3 cups half-and-half
1 1/3 cups whipping cream
2/3 cup sour cream
2 large eggs, slightly beaten
3/4 teaspoon Worcestershire sauce
1 1/4 cups sharp Cheddar cheese, grated for topping (may also use shredded Velveeta or a shredded 4-cheese mixture)

Preheat oven to 350 degrees. Lightly butter a 13 x 9 x 2-inch glass baking dish. Cook macaroni in a large saucepan of boiling, salted water until just tender but still firm to bite. Drain pasta. Transfer to prepared dish. Mix in cubed cheese.

Whisk flour, salt, mustard, black pepper and cayenne pepper in medium bowl until smooth. Gradually whisk in half-and-half, then whipping cream and sour cream. Add eggs and Worcestershire sauce; whisk to blend. Add to macaroni. Sprinkle grated cheese over top.

Bake macaroni and cheese until just set around the edges but sauce is still liquid in center, about 25 minutes. Remove from oven; let stand 10 minutes to thicken slightly. (Sauce will be creamy.)

Note: Also very good topped with buttered breadcrumbs.

Serves 8 to 10

Vegetables and Side Dishes   185

Everyday Macaroni and Cheese

All children seem to like macaroni and cheese, even picky eaters.
This version is quick and doesn't require a trip to the store.

2 tablespoons butter
1/2 teaspoon salt
2 tablespoons all-purpose flour
1 3/4 cups milk
8 ounces Velveeta cheese, coarsely chopped
8 ounces large elbow macaroni, cooked and drained

Melt butter in medium saucepan. Whisk in salt and flour. Stir milk into flour mixture and whisk until blended. Cook on low heat 2 minutes or until slightly thickened. Add Velveeta cheese and stir until melted. Pour over drained macaroni in a deep 2-quart dish to serve.

Serves 4 to 6

Corn on the Cob

When serving this corn, a bowl of melted butter flavored with lime juice and cayenne pepper, needs to be within reach of everyone at the table.

12 ears fresh corn, husked
2 tablespoons sugar
2 sticks butter, melted
Juice of 3 limes
1/2 teaspoon cayenne pepper
4 tablespoons chopped fresh parsley
Salt

Bring large stockpot of water to a rapid boil over high heat. Add sugar and corn and cook for 8 to 10 minutes.
        In bowl, mix melted butter, lime juice, cayenne pepper and parsley. Remove corn from water with tongs and brush with butter. Sprinkle with salt and serve immediately.

Serves 6

Grilled Corn in Husks with Basil Butter

12 fresh ears of corn
1/2 cup (1 stick) butter, room temperature
1/4 cup snipped fresh basil
2 tablespoons snipped fresh parsley
Salt
Freshly ground black pepper

Basil Butter: In a small bowl combine the butter, basil and parsley. Set aside.

Corn: Peel back the cornhusks, but do not remove. Using a stiff brush or your fingers, remove the silks from the corn; discard. Rinse the ears. Lower the ears into a large container, with the stem ends on the bottom. (Select a container that's deep enough to allow the husks to be covered with water.) Fill with water just covering the folded-back husks and stem ends. Do not cover corn kernels with water. Soak for 30 to 60 minutes.

Remove the corn from the soaking water, shaking the ears to remove the excess water from the husks. Place each ear of corn on a piece of heavy foil. Spread each ear with basil butter; sprinkle lightly with salt and pepper. Pull the husks back up around the corn. Wrap each ear securely with foil.

Grill the corn on the rack of an uncovered grill directly over medium coals for 20 to 25 minutes or until the corn kernels are tender, turning frequently so the corn gets evenly cooked.

Serves 12

Grilled corn is done when the husk begins to pull away from the tip of the ear.

Vegetables and Side Dishes

Shoe Peg Corn Casserole

1 (12-ounce) can white shoe peg corn
1 (16-ounce) can French-cut green beans
1/2 cup chopped bell pepper
1/2 cup chopped celery
1/2 cup chopped onion
1/2 cup sharp grated, shredded Cheddar cheese
1/2 cup sour cream
1 (10-ounce) can cream of celery soup
Salt and pepper to taste

Topping:
1 1/2 cups Ritz cracker crumbs
1 stick margarine

Preheat oven to 350 degrees. Drain corn and green beans. Mix corn, beans, celery, bell pepper, onion, cheese, sour cream and celery soup. Salt and pepper to taste. Place in a 9 x 13 x 2-inch baking dish. Melt butter and stir crumbs into butter. Top casserole with crumbs and bake for 45 minutes.

Serves 6 to 8

Soaking Dried Beans

Pick over beans, removing any blemished ones. Place beans into a large bowl; add water to cover by 2 inches. Cover with plastic wrap and soak overnight at room temperature. The next day, drain and rinse beans, cover with new water and cook.

Vegetables and Side Dishes

Jalapeño Black-Eyed Peas

Forged in hardship, the early settlers made them staples. Today, most of us still revere these simple heritage foods. Black-eyed peas with cornbread are true soulmates! They are required eating for all Southerners on New Years' Day to bring good luck in the coming year.

1 (16-ounce) package dried black-eyed peas, soaked overnight, drained and rinsed
5 cups water
2 medium onions, quartered
2 garlic cloves, minced
3 large jalapeño chilies, seeded
2 bay leaves
1 ham hock
1 (4-ounce) jar diced pimento, drained
Salt and pepper

Place black-eyed peas in large saucepan. Add water, onions, garlic, jalapeño chilies, bay leaves and ham hock; bring to a boil. Reduce heat and simmer until peas are tender, stirring occasionally, about 2 or 3 hours.
Mix pimento into peas. Season with salt and pepper.

Serves 6

To Quick-Soak Dried Beans

In a large saucepan, combine picked-over dried beans with triple their volume of cold water. Bring water to a boil and cook beans, uncovered, over moderate heat 2 minutes. Remove pan from heat and soak beans 1 hour.

Vegetables and Side Dishes

English Pea and Asparagus Casserole

1 (15-ounce) can Le Seur peas, drained, but reserve the liquid
1 (15-ounce) can whole asparagus, drained, but reserve the liquid
2 eggs, boiled and chopped
1 recipe White Sauce
1 cup saltine cracker crumbs (page 312)
3/4 cup grated Cheddar cheese

White Sauce:
2 tablespoons butter
2 tablespoons flour
1 teaspoon salt
Reserved asparagus and pea liquid
1 (10-ounce) can cream of mushroom soup, undiluted

Casserole: Preheat oven to 350 degrees. Assemble all ingredients for layering. Layer in a greased 1 1/2 quart baking dish as follows: 1/2 of the peas, 1/2 of the asparagus, 1/2 of the chopped eggs and 1/2 of the white sauce. Repeat for second layer. Top with cracker crumbs and sprinkle with cheese. Bake for 30 minutes.

White Sauce: Melt 2 tablespoons butter in a medium saucepan. Stir in 2 tablespoons flour and 1 teaspoon salt. Whisk until smooth. Add enough water to the pea and asparagus reserved liquid to make 1 cup. Stir this into the flour mixture and cook slowly until it comes to a boil. Add mushroom soup.

Note: Recipe may be doubled. Use a 9 x 13 x 2-inch baking dish.

Serves 6 to 8

Betty Mitchell Sims

Do you Know How To Boil An Egg?

Begin boiling eggs in already boiling water, not cold water. Boil 20 minutes. Drain hot water, crack shells and cover with cold water for 10 minutes and peel. Easy and no dark yolks!

Vegetables and Side Dishes

Roasted Sweet Onions

Great with roasted meats!

4 medium sweet onions (Vidalia, Maui or Walla Walla) peeled and cut in half
3 tablespoons olive oil
Salt
White pepper
1 to 2 tablespoons water
1/3 cup balsamic vinegar
2 tablespoons light brown sugar
2 tablespoons butter

Preheat oven to 350 degrees. Brush onion halves with olive oil. Sprinkle with salt and pepper. Place onions, cut-side down, in large ovenproof skillet. Bake about 1 hour and place in a serving dish. Stir together water, vinegar and brown sugar. Deglaze skillet using the water, vinegar and brown sugar mixture. Add butter. Heat to a boil reducing liquid somewhat. Spoon over onions. Add salt if needed. Serve hot or at room temperature.

Serves 8

Deglazing

Deglazing is a technique for creating a simple sauce or gravy by dissolving the tasty browned bits left in a roasting pan or skillet in which meat, poultry or fish has been cooked. Pour off most of fat left in pan before deglazing. Make sure pan is hot. Add 1/4 cup or more liquid to pan and cook for a few minutes, stirring and scraping up bits from bottom and sides of pan.

Vegetables and Side Dishes

How To Save Vidalia Onions

Vidalias can be wrapped separately in foil and preserved for as long as a year refrigerated. Vidalias can also be frozen. Chop and place in a single layer on a baking sheet in the freezer. When frozen, remove and place in freezer containers or bags, and seal. This allows you to remove the amount you want when you want it. Or, freeze whole. Jumbos can be peeled, washed, cored and dropped into a plastic bag. Once frozen, they can be removed like ice cubes. Freezing changes the texture of onions, so frozen onions should be used forcooking only. Whole frozen Vidalias can be baked.

Sweet Pepper Gratin

This vegetable dish pairs best with roasted or grilled meats and chicken. Roast the peppers ahead for quicker preparation.

6 fresh red or yellow sweet peppers, roasted and cut into 3/4-inch-wide strips or two 7-ounce jars roasted sweet peppers
2 tablespoons olive oil
3 anchovy fillets, drained and finely chopped
1/2 cup Greek black olives, pitted and coarsely chopped
1/8 teaspoon cracked black pepper
1 1/4 cups fresh bread crumbs, crust removed
2 cloves garlic, minced
1/3 cup chopped fresh parsley
1 or 2 ounces goat cheese, crumbled

Preheat oven to 350 degrees. In a large bowl toss pepper strips with olive oil, anchovy fillets, olives and pepper. Transfer mixture to a 9-inch pie plate. Place bread crumbs, garlic and parsley in food processor. Process until combined. Add cheese; process just until combined. Crumble cheese mixture over pepper mixture. Bake, uncovered 30 minutes or until top is browned. Serve warm.

Serves 4 to 6

192 Vegetables and Side Dishes

Boursin Mashed Potatoes

Boursin cheese makes these potatoes wonderfully creamy. A white cheese with a buttery texture, it is often flavored with herbs, garlic or pepper.

3 1/2 pounds potatoes, peeled and cut into 2-inch chunks (about 10 medium potatoes)
3 to 5 ounces boursin cheese, with garlic and herbs or pepper (or to taste)
1/2 cup whole milk, half-and-half, or cream
Salt and black pepper

Preheat oven to 350 degrees. In saucepan, cook potatoes, covered, in enough boiling water to cover, 20 to 25 minutes or until tender. Drain. Return to saucepan. Mash with potato masher or beat with mixer on low speed until smooth. Add cheese; beat until combined. Beat in milk until combined. Season with salt and black pepper. Transfer to a 2-quart casserole. Cover; bake 25 minutes or until heated through.

Note: Potatoes can be refrigerated for up to 24 hours. To reheat, bake, covered, in a 350-degree oven for 1 1/2 hours or until heated through.

Serves 6 to 8

Vidalia Onions

If Vidalias or other sweet onions are not available, use yellow or red onions and soak in milk for 1 hour to sweeten and soften their bite.

Vegetables and Side Dishes

To Roast Peppers

Preheat oven to 425 degrees. To roast peppers, cut peppers in half; remove stems, membranes and seeds. Place peppers, cut side down, on foil-lined baking sheet. Bake 20 to 25 minutes or until skin is bubbly and browned. Place in a new brown paper bag. Seal; let stand 30 minutes. Remove skin.

Company Potatoes

6 medium potatoes
1 teaspoon salt
1/4 cup butter
1/8 teaspoon paprika
1/2 cup milk
3/4 cup heavy cream, whipped
1/2 cup shredded American cheese
1/3 teaspoon onion salt
Freshly ground black pepper to taste
Paprika

Preheat oven to 350 degrees. Wash and peel potatoes. Cut into thirds, crosswise. Cover potatoes in saucepan with cold water. Add salt and cook until tender, about 30 minutes. Drain thoroughly. Place potatoes and butter in electric mixer bowl. Add paprika and milk and beat until light and fluffy. Spread mashed potatoes in a buttered 2-quart baking dish (or larger to deter topping from spillage.) Fold grated cheese, onion salt and pepper into whipped cream. Spread this mixture over potatoes and sprinkle lightly with paprika. Bake for 6-8 minutes for topping to turn a delicate brown.

Serves 6 to 8

French Fries

*For the best French fries, fry them twice.
It gets the fries to the table hot and delicious.*

4 medium Idaho or russet potatoes
Olive oil
Coarse salt, to taste

Peel potatoes, slice lengthwise into 1/4-inch slices and cut again into 1/4-inch strips. Place in a nonreactive bowl and cover with water.

Drain potatoes and dry with paper towels. Heat about 3 to 4 inches of oil in a heavy-bottomed pot over medium heat (325 degrees). Add potatoes in small batches so as not to lower oil temperature. Cook for 5 to 6 minutes, turning occasionally. Transfer to paper towels to drain and cool.

To fry the second time, raise oil temperature to 375 degrees and fry 1 to 2 minutes until crisp and golden. Remove from oil; drain and sprinkle with salt before serving.

Serves 4

How many potato dishes should a cookbook have? We stopped at 14, not because we ran out of ideas, but because we ran out of room!

Vegetables and Side Dishes

Do-Ahead Stuffed Potatoes

What a great thing— a do-ahead dish that everyone loves. These potatoes can be done several hours before the final baking or they will freeze beautifully. Why not make extra to keep in the freezer?

10 medium Idaho potatoes
1/2 cup chopped onions
1/2 to 3/4 cup butter
1/2 to 1 cup milk, warmed
1 tablespoon salt
1/4 teaspoon red pepper
1 cup sour cream
2 cups Cheddar cheese, grated and divided
1 1/2 teaspoons dried chives

Preheat oven to 450 degrees. Place washed, ungreased potatoes in a shallow pan and loosely cover. Bake 1 hour. While potatoes are baking, sauté onions in butter and heat milk.

After baking, slice off the top of each potato and set aside. Reduce oven temperature to 375 degrees. Scoop potato pulp into the largest electric mixer bowl (work fast for best results). Add the sautéed onions, salt, red pepper, sour cream, 1 cup grated cheese, chives and hot milk. Mix together. Stuff potato shells and top with remaining 1 cup of cheese. Bake 15 minutes at 375 degrees.

Serves 10

Garlic Mashed Potatoes

Garlic Sauce:
1 head garlic (about 8 to 9 cloves, or to taste)
1/4 cup butter
2 tablespoons flour
1 cup hot milk
Salt and pepper to taste

Mashed Potatoes:
2 1/2 pounds Idaho potatoes, peeled and cubed
1/4 cup butter
3 to 4 tablespoons heavy cream
Salt and pepper to taste

Garlic Sauce: Separate the cloves from the head and drop them into pan of boiling water; boil 2 minutes, drain and peel. (This blanches and mellows the garlic.)

In a separate saucepan, simmer the peeled garlic cloves and butter for about 20 minutes. Blend in the flour, and cook for 2 minutes more. Whisk in the hot milk and continue whisking until the Garlic Sauce is thick and creamy. Set aside to keep warm.

Mashed Potatoes: In pot, cook potatoes in salted water over medium-high heat until tender, about 15 to 20 minutes. Drain water and mash the potatoes, adding the butter, cream and seasoning. Add the Garlic Sauce and serve. (Garlic cloves can be removed at this point or they can be mashed into the potatoes.)

Serves 4

Vegetables and Side Dishes

Glorified Potatoes

2 medium white onions, diced
3 bell peppers, diced large
2 sticks margarine
1/4 cup all-purpose flour
1 1/2 cups milk
5 medium Idaho potatoes, cooked with skins on and diced into 3/4-inch cubes
1 (4.5-ounce) can button mushrooms
1/2 cup (2 to 3 ounces) sharp Cheddar cheese, cut into 1-inch cubes
1 (4-ounce) jar pimento

Preheat oven to 350 degrees. Sauté onions and peppers in margarine until tender. Add flour and make a paste. Add milk and stir to make a gravy. Stir in diced potatoes, mushrooms, cheese, pimento, salt and pepper. Gently distribute. Bake in a 9 x 13 x 2-inch baking dish until bubbly, about 30 minutes.

Serves 6 to 8

Mashed Potatoes With Butter

Even the humble mashed potato can't just be simple anymore. So, as the saying goes, there's more than one way to mash a potato. The old-fashioned potato masher will leave a few lumps, which some foodies consider not just acceptable but downright essential. Use an electric mixer if you have lots of potatoes to mash, but never the food processor.

3 pounds russet or Idaho potatoes, peeled and cut into pieces (about 1 1/2-inch slices)
Salt
1/2 to 1 cup milk
6 tablespoons butter
Freshly ground black pepper

Place potatoes in a medium saucepan and cover with cold water. Add a generous pinch of salt and bring to a boil over medium-high heat. Lower heat to medium and simmer until potatoes are easily pierced with a knife, about 20 minutes.

While potatoes cook, warm the milk and 4 tablespoons butter in a small saucepan and bring to a simmer over low heat.

When potatoes are done, drain and transfer to large electric mixer bowl. Mix on medium-low speed until lumps have disappeared, about 1 minute. On low speed, add warm milk and melted butter and taste again for salt seasoning. Add pepper. Serve immediately with remaining 2 tablespoons butter on top of potatoes.

Variation: For smashed potatoes, remove pot from heat. Drain water and mash the potatoes slightly with potato masher. Add butter, a little milk and seasoning at this point.

Variation: After potatoes are mashed, stir in 1 diced red pepper and 1 or 2 diced green onions. Garnish top with a spoonful of the peppers and onions.

Serves 4 to 6

Oven-Fried Potatoes

6 to 8 medium baking potatoes, unpeeled
1/2 cup olive oil
2 tablespoons grated Parmesan cheese
1 teaspoon salt
1/4 teaspoon black pepper
1/2 teaspoon garlic powder (or more to taste)
Paprika

Preheat oven to 375 degrees. Cut each potato in half lengthwise. Repeat lengthwise cuts to form long thick strips. Arrange potato strips, peel side down, in pan. Combine remaining ingredients except paprika and brush over potatoes. Sprinkle with paprika. Bake, uncovered, for 45 minutes, basting several times.

Serves 12

Potatoes Romanoff

2 teaspoons salt
2 cups cottage cheese
1 cup sour cream
1/4 cup minced green onions
1 small clove garlic, minced
5 cups peeled, cubed, cooked potatoes
1/2 cup grated sharp Cheddar cheese
Paprika

Preheat oven to 350 degrees. Mix first 6 ingredients and put in greased 3-quart casserole dish. Top with cheese and paprika and bake 40 minutes.

Serves 8

Caryl Ward Littrell

Roasted New Potatoes with Rosemary

These may become your all-time favorite! Make a few or make dozens;
they are always delicious with very little effort!

1/4 cup extra-virgin olive oil
4 cloves garlic, crushed
20 new potatoes, halved and unpeeled
1 tablespoon chopped fresh rosemary
Salt and pepper to taste
Fresh rosemary for garnish

In bowl, combine olive oil and garlic and allow flavors to blend at least 1 hour. Preheat oven to 400 degrees. Place potatoes in baking dish and sprinkle with rosemary, salt and pepper. Pour oil and garlic over potatoes and toss well. Roast until potatoes are tender and crusty, stirring occasionally, about 45 minutes. Serve hot and garnish with fresh rosemary sprigs.

Variation: Substitute russet or sweet potatoes (or a combination).

Serves 6

Stove-top Potatoes

These crispy fried potatoes are Louisiana's version of French fries.

4 medium baking potatoes, peeled and cut into 1/2-inch cubes
2 tablespoons vegetable oil
3/4 teaspoon salt
1/4 teaspoon freshly ground black pepper
1/4 cup chopped scallions
2 tablespoons fresh chopped parsley
1 tablespoon Worcestershire sauce
1 tablespoon minced garlic
1 tablespoon butter

In large pot, cook potatoes in boiling water to cover, 5 to 10 minutes or until almost tender. Drain and cool slightly. Heat oil in a large nonstick skillet over medium high heat. Add potatoes, salt and pepper. Cook, shaking pan back and forth and turning potatoes often with a spatula, 12 to 15 minutes until golden brown and crisp. Add the scallions, parsley, Worcestershire and garlic. Shake pan 1 minute. Add butter and continue shaking pan and turning potatoes until butter melts.

Serves 4

Vegetables and Side Dishes 201

Candied Sweet Potatoes

*My mother, "Miss Rubye" as she is known, always prepared sweet potatoes this way,
never mashed, casserole-style. When I want sweet potatoes, this is what I like to have.*

3 medium sweet potatoes
1 1/2 cups sugar
1 stick margarine, cut into chunks
1 cup marshmallows, optional

Preheat oven to 350 degrees. Peel and quarter 3 sweet potatoes. In a saucepan, cover with water and cook until almost done, about 20 minutes. Drain off part of water and spoon potatoes and remaining water into a heavy skillet. Sprinkle sugar and margarine over potatoes and cook slowly on top of stove until sugar and margarine make a thick syrup, about 40 minutes or longer. Do not boil.

When done, remove to an 8 x 8-inch ovenproof serving dish. Place marshmallows on top and bake for 5 to 10 minutes.

Serves 4

Sweet Potato-Praline Casserole with Marshmallows

5 cups cooked, mashed sweet potatoes (about 3 1/2 pounds)
2 beaten eggs
1/2 cup milk
1/3 cup granulated sugar
3 tablespoons melted butter or margarine
2 tablespoons frozen orange juice concentrate, thawed
1/2 teaspoon salt
2/3 cup chopped pecans
1/3 cup packed light brown sugar
2 tablespoons all-purpose flour
2 tablespoons melted butter or margarine
1 1/2 cups miniature marshmallows

Preheat oven to 350 degrees. In a large mixing bowl stir together the mashed sweet potatoes, eggs, milk, sugar, 3 tablespoons melted butter, orange juice concentrate and salt until smooth. Spread the mixture into a greased 2-quart rectangular baking dish.

In a small bowl stir together the pecans, brown sugar, flour and 2 tablespoons melted butter. Sprinkle evenly over the sweet potato mixture.

Bake about 30 minutes or until nearly heated through in the center. Remove the casserole from the oven; sprinkle with marshmallows. Return the casserole to the oven; bake 5 to 10 minutes more or until the marshmallows are lightly browned. Let stand about 5 minutes before serving.

Serves 12

Caryl Ward Littrell

Vegetables and Side Dishes 203

Spinach and Artichoke Casserole

2 (10-ounce) packages frozen chopped spinach
1/2 cup chopped onion
1 stick margarine
1/2 cup shredded Parmesan cheese
1 (14-ounce) can artichokes, drained and chopped
1 pint sour cream
Parmesan cheese for topping

Preheat oven to 350 degrees. Cook spinach as directed. Drain. In large skillet, sauté onions in margarine and add spinach, cheese, artichokes and sour cream. Place in 9 x 13 x 2-inch baking dish. Add extra cheese to top and bake 20 to 30 minutes.

Serves 8

Dianne Norwood

Greek Spinach Casserole

16 ounces feta cheese
7 eggs, beaten
7 tablespoons flour
1/2 cup butter, room temperature
32 ounces cottage cheese
12 ounces Cheddar cheese, grated
3 (10-ounce) packages frozen spinach, thawed and drained
1 large onion, minced
1 teaspoon minced garlic
1 1/2 teaspoons oregano

Preheat oven to 350 degrees. Butter a 9 x 13 x 2-inch casserole. Rinse feta cheese to remove salty liquid and crumble. In bowl beat eggs with flour and combine with feta cheese. Add butter, cottage cheese, Cheddar cheese, spinach, onion, garlic and oregano. Pour into casserole and bake for 1 hour.

Note: This casserole freezes very well after baking.

Serves 12 to 14

Betty Mitchell Sims

Wilted Spinach with Cranberries

1/4 cup pine nuts, toasted (page 329)
1/2 cup dried cranberries or dried cherries, soaked in hot water 30 minutes
2 tablespoons extra-virgin olive oil
2 1/2 pounds fresh, cleaned spinach leaves
Fresh lemon juice (1 lemon)
Salt to taste
Freshly ground black pepper to taste

Toast pine nuts in large Dutch oven to be used for spinach. Drain cranberries or cherries and set them aside along with the pine nuts.

Just before serving, place the Dutch oven over high heat and add oil. Dump 1/2 the spinach into pan and stir-fry for 2 minutes. Add the remaining spinach and stir. When wilted, remove from heat, season to taste with lemon juice, salt and pepper. Add pine nuts and cranberries or cherries.

Serve immediately.

Serves 6

Squash Dressing

2 cups cooked yellow squash, drained, cut into 1-inch pieces
2 cups crumbled cornbread
2 eggs, beaten
1 (10-ounce) can cream of mushroom soup or cream of chicken soup, undiluted
1/2 teaspoon sage
1 medium onion, chopped
1 cup chopped celery
2 tablespoons margarine

Preheat oven to 375 degrees. In pan, cook squash until tender. Drain and add cornbread, eggs, soup and sage, Sauté onion and celery in margarine until tender. Add to first mixture and stir until blended. Pour into buttered 9 x 13 x 2-inch baking dish and bake for 30 minutes or until lightly browned.

Serves 8 to 10

Carol Buckins

Baked Tomatoes

Serve as a side dish for brunch or anytime tomatoes are needed.
Especially good when tomatoes are out of season as the heat enhances the flavor.

6 small whole tomatoes
1 1/2 teaspoons salt
1/2 teaspoon freshly ground black pepper
2 to 3 tablespoons olive oil

Preheat oven to 375 degrees. Lightly oil a 9 x 13 x 2-inch baking dish. Remove tops from tomatoes and season with salt and pepper. Drizzle tomatoes with olive oil. Bake 15 minutes or until flesh is warmed throughout.

Note: Add more tomatoes and seasoning to serve an additional number. Tomatoes can also be topped with bread crumbs.

Serves 6

Fried Green Tomatoes

3 green tomatoes, each cut into 4 slices
1 cup cornmeal
1/3 cup flour
Salt and freshly ground black pepper
Pinch of cayenne
3 eggs, beaten
Vegetable oil for frying

Mix the cornmeal, flour, salt, pepper and cayenne in a bowl. Dip the sliced tomatoes in the eggs and coat with cornmeal mixture.

Heat oil in large skillet to 375 degrees. Add tomatoes, a few at a time. Fry for 2 to 3 minutes per side or until golden brown; drain and serve.

Note: Mix green tomatoes with okra and fry the same way. Very, very good!

Serves 6

Sautéed Cherry Tomatoes

This is a quick, easy and colorful vegetable side dish or a great garnish. The few minutes of heat enhances the natural sweetness of tomatoes. Sprinkle them with basil, tarragon or rosemary if desired.

5 tablespoons unsalted butter
2 pints cherry tomatoes, stemmed, rinsed and dried
Salt and freshly ground pepper to taste

Melt butter in heavy skillet. Add tomatoes and raise heat to medium high. Shake and roll the tomatoes around in the butter until they are shiny and heated through, no more than 5 minutes. Season with salt and pepper and serve immediately.

Serves 4 to 6

Summer Squash and Green Tomatoes

1/4 cup olive oil
2 tablespoons balsamic vinegar
1 teaspoon salt
1/2 teaspoon pepper
4 garlic cloves, minced
4 medium green tomatoes cut into 1/4-inch-thick slices
1 pound yellow squash, cut diagonally into 1/2-inch slices

Combine the first 5 ingredients in a shallow dish or a Ziploc bag; add tomato and squash. Cover or seal; chill 30 minutes. Remove vegetables and reserve marinade. Grill on stove-top grill skillet over medium-high heat or on the gas grill. Turn occasionally. Toss with the reserved marinade.

Serves 6

Vegetables and Side Dishes

Fresh Turnip Greens

8 pounds fresh turnip greens or collard greens
3/4 cup olive oil
1/3 cup butter
1/4 cup minced fresh garlic
1/2 cup water
1 teaspoon sugar
1 teaspoon salt, or to taste
1/2 teaspoon pepper, or to taste

Remove and discard stems from greens. Wash thoroughly and drain. Tear into bite-size pieces. Set aside.

Combine olive oil and butter in a large stockpot; add garlic and cook over medium heat, stirring constantly, until tender. Add water and greens and simmer covered for 40 minutes or until tender. Stir occasionally. Add sugar, salt and pepper to taste.

Serves 12

Caryl Ward Littrell

Vegetable Sauté

This dish gets a visual A+! It's especially good served with baked ham.

4 bunches fresh baby carrots (3/4 pound)
1 bunch fresh asparagus trimmed and cut into 2-inch pieces
2 cups sugar-snap peas, strings removed
2 tablespoons unsalted butter
3 scallions, thinly sliced
1 tablespoon chopped fresh dill
1 teaspoon grated orange zest
1/2 teaspoon salt

In large saucepan, bring 2 inches lightly salted water to a boil. Add carrots; cook 6 minutes, until crisp-tender. With slotted spoon, remove carrots to bowl. When water returns to a boil, add asparagus; cook 3 to 6 minutes, until crisp-tender. Remove to carrot bowl. When water returns to a boil, add sugar-snap peas; cook 4 to 6 minutes, until crisp-tender; drain and add to bowl of vegetables.

Heat butter in large nonstick skillet over medium-high heat. Add scallions, chopped fresh dill, orange zest and salt; sauté 1 minute longer or until heated through and evenly coated. Toss with vegetables.

Note: I like to make twice as much butter sauce to use liberally when served.

Serves 8

Vegetables and Side Dishes 209

Roasted Autumn Vegetables

These vegetables have been mistreated for generations. They've mostly been boiled into submission!
But the fall vegetables benefit greatly from roasting. Pile your platter high for a great presentation.

8 to 10 pounds vegetables such as butternut squash, shallots, yellow onions, carrots, beets,
    pumpkin, whole garlic or parsnips
Extra-virgin olive oil
Fresh herbs, such as thyme, sage or oregano
Salt and freshly ground black pepper

Preheat oven to 350 degrees. Peel and seed vegetables as necessary, or if small and tender enough, trim and scrub well.

Leave carrots and garlic whole, cut onions and butternut squash in half and cut any other vegetable you use as chunky as possible, but of approximate size.

Arrange vegetables in large baking pan and brush with oil. Scatter sprigs of herbs on top of vegetables. Season to taste with salt and pepper. Roast in oven, turning occasionally, until golden on edges and tender, about 1 hour. Pile on a large platter and garnish with sprigs of herbs.

Serves 6 to 8

Roasted Vegetable Assortment

3 tablespoons olive oil
3 garlic cloves, peeled and sliced
8 carrots, peeled and cut into 1-inch pieces
16 small brussels sprouts
8 new potatoes, halved
2 large onions, peeled and coarsely chopped
1 green pepper, stemmed, seeded and cut into 1/2-inch cubes
2 leeks, cleaned and cut into 1/4-inch rings
2 medium-size eggplants, halved, seeded and cut into 1/2-inch cubes
Fresh basil for garnish

Place olive oil and garlic in a large roasting pan and bake in a preheated 350-degree oven for 10 minutes. Add carrots, brussels sprouts and potatoes to pan. Bake, turning occasionally, until vegetables can be pierced with a fork. Add remaining cut vegetables to pan. Bake, turning every 10 minutes, until vegetables are lightly browned and crisp on the edges, about 40-50 minutes or longer. Remove pan from oven and transfer vegetables to a serving platter. Garnish with basil.

Serves 8

Apple and Cheese Bake

2 (20-ounce) cans sliced apples, drained
2 sticks margarine, room temperature
2 cups sugar
16 ounces Velveeta cheese, cubed
1 1/2 cups all-purpose flour

Preheat oven to 350 degrees. Place drained apples into a buttered 9 x 13 x 2-inch baking dish. Cream margarine and sugar. Add Velveeta and blend well. Beat in flour gradually. Smooth on top of apples and bake for 20 minutes.

Serves 6 to 8

Annie Frances Proctor

Stove Top Apples

8 apples, (Rome, McIntosh or Granny Smith) cored and peeled around top
1 1/2 cups sugar
1 cup water
1/4 cup cinnamon candy (for color)
1 teaspoon lemon juice
10 teaspoons sugar
3 to 4 tablespoons dried cherries or raisins
1/2 cup walnut pieces
4 tablespoons unsalted butter, room temperature
8 large pieces lemon peel (optional)

Peel the skin from the top 1/4 of each apple. Boil sugar, water and cinnamon candy in large enough skillet to hold 8 apples. Add lemon juice. Cook apples on low heat until fork tender (about 45 minutes). Turn apples at least one time. Spoon syrup over apples several times.

Fill the center of each apple with sugar. Add cherries, a walnut or two, and top with butter. Add a lemon peel to each apple. Spoon more syrup over apples. Scatter any stray cherries or walnuts around apples on serving dish. Top with more syrup. Garnish with lemon peel.

Note: Apples can be peeled if desired.

Serves 8

Rubye Little

Fettucini Alfredo

1 (16-ounce) package fettucini pasta
1/2 cup butter
1 cup heavy whipping cream
1 cup sour cream
1 cup grated Parmesan cheese
1/2 cup fresh or dried chives, minced
Salt and pepper to taste

Cook fettucini according to package directions until tender but still firm. While noodles are cooking, melt butter in a saucepan. Add cream and cook over medium heat. Reduce heat to low; add sour cream and stir constantly, but do not let boil. Add cheese, chives, salt and pepper.
    Drain noodles; toss with sauce until well-blended. Serve immediately.

Serves 6

Betty Mitchell Sims

Pineapple Casserole

1/2 cup sugar
5 tablespoons flour
1 (20-ounce) can pineapple chunks, undrained
1 cup shredded Cheddar cheese
1/2 cup butter, melted
1 sleeve Town House crackers, crushed

Preheat oven to 350 degrees. Combine sugar and flour set aside. Combine pineapple and cheese and spoon into a buttered 1 1/2-quart casserole dish. Sprinkle flour and sugar mixture over pineapple-cheese mixture. Top with combined butter and crackers. Bake uncovered for 20 minutes or until lightly browned.

Note: Recipe can be doubled.

Serves 4

Annie Frances Proctor

Wild Rice with Mushrooms

1 cup wild rice (about 6 ounces)
1 cup regular long-grain rice
1 teaspoon salt
3 tablespoons margarine or butter
1 small onion, diced
1 medium celery rib, diced
10 ounces white mushrooms, sliced
8 ounces shiitake mushrooms, stems discarded, caps sliced
1/4 teaspoon coarsely ground black pepper
1/8 teaspoon dried thyme
1 cup chicken broth
1/2 cup loosely packed fresh parsley leaves, chopped

Prepare wild rice and white rice, separately, as labels direct, adding 1/4 teaspoon salt to each rice, but omitting margarine or butter.

Meanwhile, preheat oven to 350 degrees. In 12-inch skillet, melt margarine or butter over medium heat. Add onion and celery, and cook until tender, about 10 minutes, stirring occasionally. Increase heat to medium-high; add mushrooms, pepper, thyme and remaining 1/2 teaspoon salt, and cook 15 minutes longer, stirring occasionally, until mushrooms are tender and golden and liquid evaporates. Stir in chicken broth. Remove skillet from heat. Add rice and mix. Pour into a 9 x 13 x 2-inch dish and bake 15 to 20 minutes. Sprinkle parsley on top.

Serves 8

Vegetables and Side Dishes 213

Wild Rice with Dried Cranberries and Apricots

8 ounces (1 1/3 cups) wild rice
4 cups reduced-sodium chicken broth
3/4 cup dried cranberries
3/4 cup dried apricots, diced
4 green onions sliced (include green tops)
Zest of 1/2 orange
3/4 cup orange juice
1/4 cup olive oil
2 tablespoons minced fresh rosemary
1 teaspoon salt
1/2 teaspoon ground black pepper

In a medium saucepan over high heat, bring wild rice and chicken broth to a boil. Reduce heat to low; cover and simmer 50 minutes or until tender. Drain rice; discard broth. Add cranberries, apricots, green onions, orange zest, orange juice, olive oil, rosemary, salt and pepper and mix well.

Serve warm or chilled. For food safety reasons, do not let salad sit at room temperature for more than two hours.

Makes 6 cups

Desserts

The Ice House, 1947
Moulton, Alabama

Desserts

Carrot Cake

This carrot cake has been a favorite for many, many years.

Cake:
3 cups unbleached all-purpose flour
3 cups sugar
1 teaspoon salt
1 tablespoon baking soda
1 tablespoon ground cinnamon
1 1/2 cups corn oil
4 large eggs, lightly beaten
1 tablespoon vanilla extract
1 1/2 cups chopped walnuts
1 1/2 cups shredded coconut
1 1/3 cups puréed cooked carrots
3/4 cup crushed pineapple, drained

Cream Cheese Frosting:
1 (8-ounce) package cream cheese, room temperature
6 tablespoons unsalted butter, room temperature
3 cups confectioners' sugar
1 teaspoon vanilla extract
Juice of 1/2 lemon

Cake: Preheat oven to 350 degrees. Grease two 9-inch layer cake pans and line bottom with waxed paper.

Sift dry ingredients into bowl. Add oil, eggs and vanilla. Beat well. Fold in walnuts, coconut, carrots and pineapple.

Pour batter into prepared pans. Place on middle rack of oven and bake for 30 to 35 minutes, until edges have pulled away from sides and a cake tester inserted in center comes out clean.

Cool on a cake rack for 3 hours. Frost cake.

Frosting: Cream together cream cheese and butter in mixing bowl. Slowly sift in confectioners' sugar and continue beating until fully incorporated. Mixture should be free of lumps.

Stir in vanilla and lemon juice.

Note: This cake serves nicely if you completely frost each layer individually. Eat one now and freeze one for later. Great with coffee!

Serves 10 to 12

Perfect Chocolate Cake

These chocolate cake layers are dark and not too sweet when compared to other chocolate cakes. The layers are unbelievably moist! This is truly the Perfect Chocolate Cake with Whipped Cream Filling and Creamy Chocolate Frosting.

Layers:
4 ounces unsweetened chocolate
2 cups sugar
1 1/2 cups sifted all-purpose flour
3/4 teaspoon baking soda
1/2 teaspoon salt
1 cup hot strong brewed coffee or 5 teaspoons instant coffee dissolved in 1 cup hot water
1/2 cup sour cream, room temperature
1/2 cup vegetable oil
2 large eggs, room temperature, lightly beaten with a fork

Whipped Cream Filling:
1 cup whipping cream
1/4 cup confectioners' sugar
1 teaspoon vanilla extract

Creamy Chocolate Frosting:
1 cup (6 ounces) semisweet chocolate morsels
1/2 cup half-and-half
1 cup butter
2 1/2 cups confectioners' sugar

Layers: Preheat oven to 345 degrees. Lightly grease two 8-inch layer cake pans with vegetable oil or butter.

Melt chocolate in top of double boiler placed over simmering water; then turn off heat. Sift sugar, flour, baking soda and salt together into a large mixer bowl.

In a separate bowl, blend the hot coffee, sour cream and vegetable oil with a whisk.

With an electric mixer on low speed, add the coffee mixture in a stream to the dry ingredients and mix until blended, about 35 seconds. Stop mixer to scrape bowl several times with a rubber spatula.

Add eggs 1 at a time and mix on medium-low speed after each addition until smooth, about 15 seconds. Scrape bowl each time. Add chocolate and mix until batter is uniform in color, about 10 seconds more.

Divide batter evenly between the prepared pans and place them on the center oven rack. Bake until cake springs back to the touch, 35 to 38 minutes.

Allow cake to cool in pans before frosting.

Desserts

Unsweetened Chocolate

Unsweetened chocolate is also known as baker's chocolate and is cocoa solids with no additional flavorings or sugar. In a pinch, 3 tablespoons unsweetened cocoa powder plus 1 tablespoon unsalted butter can be substituted for 1 ounce unsweetened chocolate.

Whipped Cream Filling: Beat all ingredients at medium speed with an electric mixer until stiff peaks form. Spread between layers and refrigerate until ready to frost.

Creamy Chocolate Frosting: Cook first 3 ingredients in a heavy saucepan over medium heat, stirring until chocolate melts. Remove from heat; cool 15 minutes. Stir in confectioners' sugar.

Place pan in ice and beat with wooden spoon about 8 to 10 minutes or until of spreading consistency. Must work fast! With spatula, frost sides first, covering all whipped cream; use remaining frosting on top of cake. Refrigerate at least 1 hour before serving. Makes 3 cups

Note: To cut, use a thin-edged sharp knife; slice with sawing motion.

Serves 10 to 12

Chocolate Grand Marnier Torte

Torte:
8 ounces semisweet chocolate squares, coarsely chopped
3/4 cup butter, room temperature
1 cup sugar
1/2 cup cake flour, sifted
6 large eggs, separated
1/4 teaspoon salt

Whipped Cream Filling:
1 envelope unflavored gelatin
1/4 cup cold water
2 cups whipping cream
1/2 cup sugar
1/4 cup orange liqueur
1 teaspoon vanilla

Chocolate Glaze:
8 ounces semisweet chocolate squares, coarsely chopped
1/3 cup whipping cream
1/4 cup butter, room temperature

Torte: Coat three 8-inch cake pans with vegetable cooking spray; line bottoms with wax paper, and coat with cooking spray. Set aside. Preheat oven to 350 degrees.

Melt chocolate in a large, heavy saucepan over low heat, stirring often. Remove from heat. Add butter, 2 to 3 tablespoons at a time, and whisk until melted. Gradually whisk in sugar, then flour. Add yolks, 1 at a time, whisking until blended after each addition.

In large mixer bowl, beat egg whites and salt until stiff but not dry; fold 1/4 of egg whites into chocolate mixture. Gradually fold in remaining egg whites. Spoon evenly into prepared pans.

Bake for 18 to 20 minutes or until a tester inserted in center comes out clean. Cool completely in pans on wire racks.

Loosen edges of cake layers by running a thin metal spatula around edges. Insert spatula under each layer to loosen. Gently lift first layer and invert onto a serving plate. Layers will be very tender. Peel wax paper from all layers.

Whipped Cream Filling: Sprinkle gelatin over cold water in a small saucepan; let stand 1 minute. Cook over low heat, stirring constantly until gelatin dissolves.

Beat whipping cream at low speed with an electric mixer, gradually adding gelatin mixture. Beat at medium speed until mixture begins to thicken. Gradually add sugar, beating well. Add liqueur and vanilla; beat until stiff peaks form.

Spread whipping cream between cake layers. Cover and chill at least 2 hours.

Makes 4 cups

Chocolate Glaze: Combine chocolate and whipping cream in a heavy saucepan. Cook over low heat, stirring often, until chocolate melts. Remove from heat; stir in butter. Let stand 30 minutes or until slightly thickened. Pour the glaze over torte, spreading a thin layer on sides. Chill.

Serves 10 to 12

Tortes

A torte is similar to a cake, except in place of flour, dry bread crumbs, ground nuts or a combination of the two are used. Tortes can be conveniently baked in a springform pan with a removable bottom as they are very delicate in texture and cannot withstand much handling.

Desserts

Chocolate Torte With Strawberry Filling

This torte is sinfully delicious and well worth the effort. You might want to make it in stages.

Torte:
3/4 cup butter or margarine, room temperature
2 cups sugar
8 eggs
2 tablespoons vanilla extract
1/4 teaspoon salt
12 ounces bittersweet or semisweet chocolate, melted
3 1/2 cups finely ground pecans

Buttercream:
1 1/4 cups butter, sliced and at room temperature
2 cups confectioners' sugar, sifted
4 egg yolks
1/2 cup puréed fresh strawberries
3 tablespoons strawberry preserves

Glaze:
3 ounces semisweet chocolate, coarsely chopped
6 tablespoons butter or margarine
1/2 cup water
3 tablespoons safflower oil
3/4 cup cocoa
1/2 cup plus 2 tablespoons sugar
15 whole strawberries

Torte: Line 4 greased 9-inch cake pans with parchment paper. Preheat oven to 375 degrees.
Cream butter in mixer bowl until light. Add sugar; beat until fluffy. Beat in eggs 1 at a time. Add vanilla and salt; mix well. Fold in chocolate and then pecans. Spoon into prepared pans. Bake for 22 minutes or until a cake tester inserted in center comes out fudgy but not wet; tops may crack. Cool in the pans on a wire rack for 5 minutes. Loosen from the sides of the pans with a knife. Invert onto rack; remove parchment. Cool completely.
Buttercream: Cream butter and confectioners' sugar in a mixing bowl until light and fluffy. Beat in egg yolks. Add strawberries and preserves; mix well.

Glaze: Combine chocolate, butter, water and safflower oil in a double boiler. Heat over simmering water until chocolate and butter melt, stirring to mix well; remove from heat.

Add cocoa and sugar; mix until sugar dissolves and glaze is smooth. Chill until slightly thickened. Dip strawberries in glaze; let stand until set.

Assemble: Place 1 torte layer bottom side up on a cake plate. Spread with 3/4 cup of the buttercream. Repeat with the remaining layers, ending with the top layer bottom side up; press lightly.

Chill, covered, for 6 hours or longer. Trim the edges of the torte with a serrated knife if necessary.

Pour the glaze over top and side of torte; arrange glazed strawberries around the edge. Let stand at room temperature for 1 hour before serving.

Note: The torte and buttercream may be made up to 2 days in advance and stored in refrigerator. Wrap the layers individually in plastic wrap to store; allow buttercream to return to room temperature before spreading.

Serves 15

Swiss Chocolate Cake

This cake is very delicious served with Raspberry Sauce (page 296)
between the layers in addition to the frosting the recipe calls for!

Cake:
1(18.25-ounce) box Duncan Hines Swiss Chocolate cake mix
1 (3-ounce) package instant vanilla pudding mix
3 eggs
1 1/2 cups milk
3/4 cup oil

Frosting:
1 (8-ounce) package cream cheese, room temperature
1 cup confectioners' sugar
1 cup sugar
1 (12-ounce) container whipped topping
1/2 cup chopped pecans
2 (1.55-ounce) Hershey bars, chopped

Cake: Preheat oven to 325 degrees. In large mixer bowl, mix all ingredients well. Bake for 20 to 25 minutes in 3 greased and floured 9-inch cake pans.

Frosting: In mixer bowl, cream together the cream cheese, confectioners' sugar and sugar. Add whipped topping, nuts and Hershey bars. Frost when layers are completely cooled and store cake in refrigerator.

Serves 10 to 12

Jane McCullough

Desserts 221

Mattie B's Fabulous Fresh Coconut Cake

Along with being a family tradition, some recipes, such as this one, are certainly a family treasure. What better way to honor a Mother's memory than to share her delicious, fabulous coconut cake recipe for many to enjoy. Just get tough—this one is definitely worth the effort!

Cake Layers:
1 cup butter, room temperature
2 cups sugar
5 eggs
1 teaspoon baking soda
Dash salt
2 3/4 cups cake flour
1 teaspoon baking powder
1 cup buttermilk
2 teaspoons vanilla

Cake Frosting/Filling:
6 to 8 cups (3 to 4 coconuts) fresh grated coconut (reserve coconut milk and 2 cups coconut to sprinkle)
1/2 cup all-purpose flour
2 1/2 cups sugar
4 cups milk
1 cup coconut milk
1/4 cup butter
2 teaspoons vanilla

Cake Layers: Preheat oven to 350 degrees. In mixer bowl, cream butter and sugar until smooth (about 15 minutes). This is a very important step, so do not under beat. Add eggs one at a time, beating after each addition. Sift dry ingredients and add in small amounts to the creamed mixture alternately with buttermilk. Stir in vanilla.

Bake in 3 greased and floured 9-inch cake pans for 20 minutes. Be careful not to overbake as oven temperatures vary. Allow to cool completely before frosting.

Frosting/Filling: Reserve 2 cups grated coconut to sprinkle over filling between layers and on top and sides of cake. Mix remaining coconut, flour and sugar in heavy saucepan. Add milk and coconut milk. Heat at a low temperature and cook until thick enough to spread. Stir in butter and vanilla. Continue to cook until butter is melted. Remove from heat and cool completely. Chill in refrigerator for 30 to 40 minutes. Spread between layers and on top and sides of cake. Sprinkle reserved grated coconut between layers and on top and sides of cake.

Note: This makes a large cake which should be stored in the refrigerator. It is at its best if served at room temperature. Cake also freezes well.

Serves 15

Syble Murphy

European Cake with Ambrosia Icing

This cake stands tall and proud at the Christmas buffet at Ott's parents' home. Mama Berlin has made it every Christmas for 50 years. That means she's made this cake just 50 times!

Cake:
1/2 cup butter, room temperature
2 cups sugar
5 eggs, separated
1 teaspoon baking soda
2 teaspoons ground cinnamon
1/2 teaspoon ground cloves
2 tablespoons cocoa
4 cups all-purpose flour (reserve 1/2 cup to dredge fruit in)
1 cup buttermilk
1 1/2 cups blackberry jam
1 cup seedless raisins
1 1/2 cups chopped pecans
1 cup candied cherries, cut in half

Icing:
2 fresh coconuts, grated (may use 4 cups frozen)
Grated rind and juice from 4 oranges
1 (15-ounce) can crushed pineapple, undrained
2 cups sugar
2 tablespoons flour

Desserts 223

Cake: Preheat oven to 325 degrees. In mixer bowl, cream butter and sugar well. Add beaten egg yolks and mix well. Sift all dry ingredients and add flour alternately with buttermilk, beginning and ending with flour.

Add jam, raisins, nuts and cherries. (Dredge raisins, nuts and cherries in reserved flour before adding.)

Beat egg whites until stiff. Add to cake mixture and fold evenly into mix. Grease and flour three 9-inch cake pans and fill with batter. Bake for 1 hour or until cake tester inserted in center comes out clean. Do not overbrown. Watch carefully and check after 45 minutes.

Icing: Mix all ingredients except coconut together in a small saucepan and cook until thick. Spread between layers and sprinkle coconut on top of icing. Spread icing on sides and top of cake. Add coconut over icing, using spatula or hands to press into icing. Keep refrigerated.

Serves 12 to 14

Italian Cream Cake

Cake:
1/2 cup butter or margarine, room temperature
1/2 cup shortening
2 cups sugar
5 large eggs, separated
1 tablespoon vanilla extract
2 cups all-purpose flour
1 teaspoon baking soda
1 cup buttermilk
1 cup flaked coconut
Toasted pecan halves and chopped pecans for garnish

Nutty Cream Cheese Frosting:
1 cup chopped pecans or black walnuts
1 (8-ounce) package cream cheese, room temperature
1/2 cup butter or margarine, room temperature
1 tablespoon vanilla extract
16 ounces confectioners' sugar, sifted

Cake: Preheat oven to 350 degrees. Beat butter and shortening at medium speed with electric mixer until fluffy; gradually add sugar, beating well. Add egg yolks, one at a time, beating until blended after each addition. Add vanilla; beat until blended. Combine flour and soda; add to butter mixture alternately with buttermilk, beginning and ending with flour mixture. Beat at low speed until blended after each addition. Stir in coconut.

In large mixer bowl, beat egg whites until stiff peaks form; fold into batter. Pour batter into 3

224   *Desserts*

greased and floured 9-inch cake pans. Bake for 25 minutes or until a cake tester inserted in center comes out clean. Leave oven on for toasting pecans.

Cool layers in pans on wire racks 10 minutes; remove from pans and cool on wire racks.

Nutty Cream Cheese Frosting: Place pecans in a shallow pan; bake for 5 to 6 minutes, stirring occasionally. Cool. Beat cream cheese, butter and vanilla at medium speed with electric mixer until creamy. Add sugar, beating at low speed until blended. Beat at high speed until smooth; stir in pecans.

Serves 10 to 12

Fresh Peach Meringue Cake

Serve this when peaches are at their ripest and best.

1 (18.25-ounce) box White cake mix
4 egg whites
1 1/4 cups sugar
3/4 cup chopped pecans, walnuts or almonds
Vanilla ice cream
1 quart fresh peaches, peeled, sliced and macerated
1/2 cup sugar (or to taste)
2 tablespoons Grand Marnier

Toss peaches with 1/2 cup sugar and Grand Marnier in a heavy-duty Ziploc bag. Refrigerate 45 minutes to 1 hour, turning once or twice. Preheat oven to 325 degrees. Prepare cake according to package instructions. Spread in 2 greased and floured 8-inch cake pans. In mioxer bowl, beat egg whites until stiff. Gradually add sugar, beating thoroughly. Spread meringue over cake batter. Sprinkle with chopped nuts. Bake for 30 minutes, or until cake tester inserted in center comes out clean. Cool and cut into pie-shaped wedges. With each wedge, serve a scoop of vanilla ice cream and peaches.

Variation: If fresh peaches are not available, other fresh fruit or berries may be substituted.

Serves 12

Macerated Fruit

Macerated fruit is fruit which is allowed to sit in sugar for about 45 minutes, creating extra juices.

Plain Sponge Cake

Not extremely exciting on its own, this wonderfully light layer benefits from the addition of a simple syrup, other filling or frosting.

4 eggs
Pinch salt
2/3 cup sugar
1/2 cup cake flour
3 tablespoons cornstarch

Butter a 2 1/2 to 3-inch deep springform pan and line with wax paper. Preheat oven to 350 degrees.

Break eggs into a mixer bowl and whisk until liquid. Beat in salt, then the sugar, in a stream. Place bowl over, not in, a pan of simmering water and stir constantly with whisk to keep eggs from scrambling. Heat the egg mixture to about 100 to 110 degrees. The egg mixture should feel lukewarm.

Immediately remove bowl from pan of water and whip egg mixture on maximum speed until cool and increased in volume, 4 or 5 minutes. The egg foam should increase to 5 times its original volume and become very pale yellow.

While egg foam is beating, mix cake flour and cornstarch together on wax paper. Sift onto another piece of wax paper; sift 3 times.

When egg foam is beaten, sift 1/3 of the dry ingredients onto the egg foam. Fold in with rubber spatula and continue in 2 more batches.

Pour batter into pan immediately. Drop pan onto a solid surface from a height of about 3 inches to settle contents. Bake for 30 minutes. Immediately remove from oven and invert cake onto work surface, then using a wide spatula turn right side up on a rack to cool.

Note: Can be frozen or refrigerated for up to 5 days. To freeze, wrap and slide back into pan for protection.

Variation: Cover with whipping cream. Add strawberries, peaches, etc. or slice the layer in half horizontally and fill with pastry cream (page 267).

Serves 6

Peter Paul Mounds Cake

Cake:
2 cups sugar
1 cup shortening
5 eggs
1 cup all-purpose flour
1 cup self-rising flour
1 cup milk
2 teaspoons vanilla extract

Preheat oven to 350 degrees. In large mixer bowl, cream sugar and shortening. Add eggs one at a time. Sift all-purpose and self-rising flour together. Add flour, alternately with milk, to sugar mixture. Add vanilla. Bake in three 9-inch greased and floured pans for 25 to 30 minutes until center springs back when touched.

Filling:
1 cup milk
1 cup sugar
1 (16-ounce) package frozen coconut
12 large marshmallows
1 teaspoon vanilla

In pan, boil milk and sugar 5 minutes. Add other ingredients and mix. Put mixture between layers while hot.

Frosting:
2 cups sugar
1 (5-ounce) can evaporated milk
2 to 3 tablespoons cocoa
1 stick margarine

In pan, cook ingredients over medium heat until near the soft ball stage (232 degrees). Beat until frosting cools and is thickened to spreadable consistency. Frost cake.

Serves 14 to 16

Jane McCullough

Dividing a Cake Layer

When slicing the layer in half horizontally, use a long serrated knife. To remove the top section easily without breaking it, slide the bottom of a springform pan between the two sections as you cut the layer.

Fresh Pineapple Upside-Down Cake

This fresh version of the classic takes pineapple upside-down cake to new heights!

Topping:
1/4 cup (1/2 stick) unsalted butter
1/2 cup firmly packed dark brown sugar
1 ripe pineapple, peeled, cored and cut into at least 8 rings
8 to 12 pecan halves
Maraschino cherries

Layer:
2 cups cake flour, sifted
2 teaspoons baking powder
1/4 teaspoon salt
1/2 cup (1 stick) unsalted butter, room temperature
1 cup sugar
2 large eggs
2 teaspoons vanilla extract
1 cup pineapple juice (fresh or canned)

Topping: Preheat oven to 350 degrees. Place butter and brown sugar in an 11-inch cast-iron skillet and put in the oven until butter melts, about 7 minutes. Mix well.
    Over sugar and butter mixture place 1 pineapple ring in center and arrange others around it. In the center of each ring, place a maraschino cherry. Fill in the spaces with pecans, face side down. Set aside.
    Layer: Mix cake flour, baking powder and salt. In large mixer bowl, cream butter and sugar until fluffy, about 3 minutes. Add the dry mixture a little at a time, beating well after each addition. Add the eggs, 1 at a time, beating well after each addition. Add vanilla and pineapple juice and beat well.
    Pour the batter over the pineapple layer and smooth the top.
    Bake 40 to 45 minutes or until deep golden brown and a cake tester inserted in center comes out clean. Cool cake on rack for 2 to 3 minutes.
    Invert a plate (make sure the size is ample) on top of skillet. Turn the cake onto the plate. Remove skillet.

Note: Serve warm with whipped cream or at room temperature.

Serves 8 to 10

Strawberry Cake

Cake:
1(18.25-ounce) box White cake mix
1 (3-ounce) package strawberry Jell-O
3/4 cup vegetable oil
3/4 cup milk
4 eggs, separated
1 cup shredded coconut
1 cup chopped pecans
2 cups frozen and sliced strawberries

Frosting:
1/2 stick margarine, room temperature
1 (16-ounce) box confectioners' sugar
1/2 of strawberry mixture

Cake: Preheat oven to 350 degrees. In bowl, combine cake mix and Jell-O and mix together by hand. Add oil, milk and egg yolks; beat just enough to mix. In a separate bowl, mix coconut, nuts and strawberries. Put half of this mixture in the batter, reserving the remaining half for frosting. In a mixer bowl, beat egg whites until stiff, but not dry. Fold into batter. Pour into three 8-or 9-inch greased and floured cake pans and bake 25 to 30 minutes.

 Frosting: In mixer bowl, cream margarine. Stir in confectioners' sugar. Add remaining half of strawberry mixture and beat well. Allow cake to completely cool before frosting.

Serves 10 to 12

Desserts

Apple Cake

3 cups sifted all-purpose flour
1 teaspoon baking soda
1 teaspoon ground cinnamon
2 cups sugar
3 eggs
1 1/4 cups vegetable oil
1 teaspoon vanilla
1/4 cup orange juice
2 cups grated fresh apples (with peel)
1 cup chopped walnuts
1 cup flaked coconut

Buttermilk Sauce:
1 cup sugar
1/2 cup butter
1/2 teaspoon baking soda
1/2 cup buttermilk

Preheat oven to 325 degrees. Sift flour, baking soda and cinnamon. Combine sugar, eggs, oil, vanilla and orange juice in a large bowl. Beat with electric mixer until well blended. Stir in flour mixture until well mixed. Fold in apples, walnuts and coconut. Spoon into well-greased and floured 10 x 4-inch tube pan. Bake for 1 hour and 15 minutes to 1 1/2 hours or until top springs back to the touch. Cool in pan on wire rack 15 minutes. Remove cake from pan to serving plate (with a raised edge).
    Buttermilk Sauce: Cook all ingredients until thick. Puncture top of cake all over with fork tines. Spoon hot Buttermilk Sauce over warm cake until cake absorbs most of it. Let stand 1 hour before serving.

Serves 12

Marlynn Rhyne

Deep Chocolate Cake

8 plain (1.5-ounce) Hershey bars
2 (16-ounce) cans chocolate syrup
2 teaspoons vanilla extract
2 sticks margarine
2 cups sugar
4 eggs
1/2 teaspoon baking soda
2 1/2 cups flour
1 cup buttermilk
1 cup pecans

Preheat oven to 350 degrees. Melt candy and syrup in double boiler. Add vanilla and set aside to cool. In large mixer bowl, cream margarine and sugar. Add eggs, one at the time, beating after each addition. Add chocolate mixture and mix well. Sift together baking soda and flour. Add to the chocolate mixture alternately with buttermilk. Add nuts. Bake in a 10-inch tube pan 1 1/4 to 1 1/2 hours. Cool and remove from pan and let sit for 24 hours before cutting.

Serves 10

Caryl Ward Littrell

Desserts 231

Chocolate Pound Cake

Cake:
3 cups sugar
1/2 cup vegetable shortening
2 sticks margarine or butter
5 large eggs
3 cups all-purpose flour
2/3 cup cocoa
1/2 teaspoon baking powder
1/2 teaspoon salt
1 cup milk
1 tablespoon vanilla extract

Icing:
1 stick butter or margarine
2 cups sugar
3 tablespoons cocoa
1/2 cup milk
1/4 cup light corn syrup

Cake: Preheat oven to 325 degrees. In large mixer bowl, cream sugar, shortening and margarine. Beat in eggs, one at a time. Add flour, cocoa, baking powder and salt that have been sifted together, alternately with milk. Mix well. Add vanilla extract. Bake for 1 1/2 hours.

Icing: In pan, melt butter; add sugar and cocoa (which have been mixed together). Add milk and corn syrup and boil for 1 minute. Remove from heat and beat until cool. Spread on cooled cake.

Serves 10 to 12

Jane McCullough

Lemon-Almond Buttermilk Loaf with Balsamic Strawberries

Loaf:
2 1/4 cups all-purpose flour
1/2 teaspoon salt
1/2 teaspoon baking soda
2 cups sugar
3/4 cups (1 1/2 sticks) unsalted butter, room temperature
3 large eggs
1/4 teaspoon almond extract
3/4 cup buttermilk
3/4 cup ground almonds—about 3 1/2 ounces (do not grind fine.)
1 tablespoon grated lemon peel
5 tablespoons fresh lemon juice

Balsamic Strawberries:
3 1/2 cups fresh strawberries, hulled and sliced
1/4 cup sugar
1 1/2 tablespoons balsamic vinegar

Loaf: Preheat oven to 350 degrees. Butter and flour 9 x 5 x 2 1/2-inch metal loaf pan.

Sift flour, salt and baking soda into medium bowl. Using electric mixer, beat 1 1/2 cups sugar and butter in large bowl until well-blended.

Add eggs, 1 at a time, beating well after each addition. Mix in almond extract. Add dry ingredients to egg mixture alternately with buttermilk in 3 additions, beating until well-blended after each addition. Add ground almonds and lemon peel and beat 1 minute. Transfer batter to prepared pan.

Bake cake until deep golden brown, cracked on top, and tester comes out clean (about 1 hour and 25 minutes). Cool cake in pan on rack 15 minutes.

Meanwhile, stir remaining 1/2 cup sugar and 5 tablespoons lemon juice in a small bowl until sugar dissolves.

Place rack on baking sheet. Turn cake out onto rack, top side up. Punch holes 1 to 2 inches apart all over cake. Brush top and sides of cake with all of lemon glaze, allowing some to soak into cake before brushing with more. Cool cake completely. Can be made 1 day ahead. Cover and store at room temperature.

Strawberries: Toss all ingredients into a medium bowl. Let stand at room temperature until juices form, at least 1 hour and up to 3 hours. Serve over Lemon-Almond Buttermilk Loaf.

Serves 10 to 12

Cream Cheese Pound Cake

2 cups unsalted butter, room temperature
1 (8-ounce) package cream cheese, room temperature
3 cups sugar
6 eggs
3 cups cake flour
2 tablespoons vanilla extract (2 tablespoons is correct)

Preheat oven to 325 degrees. Cream butter and cream cheese together in a large mixer bowl. Gradually add sugar and beat until thoroughly dissolved. Add eggs, one at a time, until well mixed. Blend in flour gradually, then vanilla. Batter will be light in texture but very thick. Grease and flour a 10-inch tube pan and spoon batter into pan. Bake at 325 degrees for 1 hour to 1 hour and 15 minutes. Check cake after an hour and remove it, slightly underdone, as it continues to cook after being removed from oven. Let cake cool in pan for 10 minutes; invert over plate.

Serves 8 to 10

Mother's Fig Cake

Cake:
2 cups all-purpose flour
1 teaspoon salt
1 teaspoon baking soda
1 1/2 cups sugar
1 teaspoon ground cloves
1 teaspoon ground cinnamon
1 teaspoon ground nutmeg
1 cup vegetable oil
3 eggs
1 teaspoon vanilla
1 cup buttermilk
1 cup fig preserves
1 cup chopped pecans

Glaze:
1 cup sugar
1 teaspoon light corn syrup
1/2 cup buttermilk
1/2 teaspoon baking soda
1 stick butter
1 teaspoon vanilla extract

Cake: Preheat oven to 325 degrees. Sift flour, salt, baking soda, sugar, cloves, cinnamon and nutmeg into a large mixer bowl. Add oil, eggs, vanilla and buttermilk and mix. Stir in preserves and pecans.
Pour into a greased 10-inch bundt pan and bake for 1 hour.

Glaze: In a medium saucepan, add sugar, corn syrup, buttermilk, baking soda, butter and vanilla. Cook 10 minutes. Pour over cake immediately and let set 1 hour.

Serves 10 to 12

Betty Mitchell Sims

Desserts 235

Sour Cream Pound Cake

1 cup unsalted butter, room temperature
1/2 cup solid vegetable shortening
3 cups sugar
5 eggs
3 cups all-purpose flour
1/2 teaspoon baking soda
8 ounces sour cream
1/4 cup milk
1 teaspoon vanilla extract

Preheat oven to 325 degrees. Cream butter and shortening with an electric mixer on low speed until light and fluffy. Gradually add sugar, beating on medium speed until light and fluffy. Add eggs, one at a time, beating after each addition. Combine flour and baking soda in separate bowl, stirring well with a fork. Combine sour cream and milk in separate bowl. Add 1/3 of flour to butter mixture with half of the sour cream mixture. Mix with an electric mixer on medium speed until blended. Add another 1/3 of the flour mixture and mix until blended. Add remaining flour mixture, remaining sour cream mixture and vanilla. Mix until blended. Pour batter into a heavily greased and floured 10-inch tube pan. Bake for 1 hour and 10 minutes to 1 hour and 15 minutes, or until a cake tester, inserted in center, comes out clean. Cool in pan 10 minutes; turn out on a rack and cool completely.

Serves 12

Cake Flour

Cake flour contains less gluten than regular flour, which is why it produces lighter cakes. If a recipe calls for cake flour and you don't have any, substitute 1 cup stirred all-purpose flour minus 2 tablespoons for 1 cup cake flour.

Sweet Cream Pound Cake

2 sticks unsalted butter, room temperature
3 cups sugar, divided
6 eggs, separated and yolks beaten
3 cups cake flour, sifted 3 times before measuring
1 cup whipping cream
1 teaspoon vanilla extract

Do not preheat oven. Have all ingredients at room temperature. Grease and flour a deep 10-inch tube pan. In mixer bowl, cream butter well; add 2 cups sugar and cream more until light and fluffy. Add beaten egg yolks and mix well. Alternate cake flour and whipping cream (beginning and ending with flour) and add to mixture, beating well after each addition. Add vanilla and mix well. Beat egg whites until soft peaks form. Gradually add remaining 1 cup sugar to egg whites to make a stiff meringue. Fold egg whites into batter. Pour batter into greased and floured tube pan. Put pan into a cold oven and set temperature at 325 degrees. Bake 1 1/2 hours or until cake is golden brown and a cake tester inserted in center comes out clean. Let cake stand in pan 15 minutes. Loosen sides with a knife and invert pan over a cake rack. Allow to cool completely before slicing.

Serves 10 to 12

Walnut Pound Cake with Glaze

You'll surely notice the huge difference sifting the flour 6 times makes in the wonderful texture of this cake.
This was a special recipe of my sister, Carol Buckins.

Cake:
3 cups sugar
2 sticks margarine, room temperature
1/2 cup shortening
5 eggs, room temperature
1 teaspoon vanilla extract
1 teaspoon coconut extract
3 cups plain flour, sifted 6 times
3/4 to 1 cup milk
3/4 cup chopped walnuts

Glaze:
1/2 cup sugar
1/4 cup water
1/2 teaspoon almond extract

Cake: Preheat oven to 350 degrees. In mixer bowl, cream sugar, margarine and shortening until sugar is completely dissolved. Add eggs, one at a time. Add flavorings. Add flour and milk alternately, beginning and ending with flour. Fold in walnuts. Bake in a greased and floured 10 x 4-inch tube pan for 1 hour and 20 minutes or until tester inserted in center comes out clean.

   Glaze: Heat sugar, water and almond extract until sugar dissolves. Brush on cake while cake is hot.

Serves 10 to 12

Birthday Cake Frosting

Use with your favorite layer cake. This frosting works well in a pastry bag for decorating cakes. Very good with Perfect Chocolate Cake (page 217)

12 tablespoons (1 1/2 sticks) unsalted butter, room temperature
5 cups confectioners' sugar
5 to 7 tablespoons milk
2 teaspoons vanilla extract

In a large bowl, using electric mixer at medium speed, beat butter for 30 seconds. Gradually beat in 2 1/2 cups confectioners' sugar. Beat in 5 tablespoons of milk and vanilla.

Gradually beat in the remaining 2 1/2 cups confectioners' sugar. Continue to beat for about 2 minutes, or until frosting is light and fluffy and of spreadable consistency, adding up to 2 or more tablespoons of milk if necessary.

Frosts a 2-layer cake

Caramel Icing

Marion Cross has given away hundreds of cakes, and many of them were covered with this icing. Use on any white or yellow cake layer.

2 1/2 cups sugar
1 1/4 sticks margarine, room temperature
3/4 cup evaporated milk
1/3 cup confectioners' sugar
1 teaspoon vanilla extract

Brown 1/2 cup sugar in heavy skillet. Add margarine and 1 cup sugar. Mix well. Add evaporated milk and bring to a boil. Add remaining cup sugar and boil until mixture reaches soft-ball stage in cold water, or 234 degrees. Remove from heat and beat well. Add confectioners' sugar and vanilla. Mix well and spread on cake.

Makes icing for two 9-inch layers

Mary's Pineapple Filling

Mary Roberson, much-loved retired home economics teacher and caterer used this filling in her delicious wedding cakes. Now, Cathy Flory, another talented caterer, bakes up more wedding cakes than one could ever imagine and continues the tradition!

5 tablespoons flour
2 cups sugar
1 (20-ounce) can crushed pineapple
1 stick margarine, cut in chunks
1 teaspoon vanilla extract

Mix flour and sugar in saucepan. Purée pineapple in blender. Mix into flour and sugar mixture. Add 1 stick margarine and stir until thick on medium heat. Add vanilla.

Makes 3 1/2 cups filling

Chocolate Frosting for Brownies

2 1/2 cups confectioners' sugar
2 tablespoons (heaping) cocoa
1 stick butter, room temperature
3 tablespoons brewed black coffee
1 teaspoon vanilla or almond extract

Mix sugar and cocoa until no lumps remain. Add butter, coffee and vanilla; cream together well. More sugar or milk can be added if adjustments are needed.

Note: Recipe will frost a 9 x 13 x 2-inch dish of brownies, etc. If you're feeling on the lazy side, use Betty Crocker Original Supreme Brownie mix (with syrup pouch). Let cool and frost. Cut in 1/2-inch by 2-inch bars. Cuts better after being refrigerated.

Mary Ann Speake

Cooked White Frosting

Many prefer using this mystery frosting on Red Velvet Cakes instead of Cream Cheese Frosting. If you ever have trouble identifying it, refer to it as "Noxzema Frosting"—instant recognition!

1 cup milk
3 tablespoons flour
1 cup sugar
1/2 cup butter, room temperature
1/2 cup shortening
1 teaspoon vanilla extract
1/4 teaspoon salt

In pan, cook milk and flour until thick, stirring constantly. Remove from heat and chill.

In large mixer bowl, beat sugar, butter and shortening until fluffy (of whipping cream consistency). Blend in vanilla and salt. Mix well with flour mixture.

Note: This frosting can be used any time a white frosting is needed. It is especially good as a filling for chocolate cake.

Makes frosting for a 2-layer cake

Syble Murphy

Chocolate Ganache

Ganache has two textures—the creamy whipped undercoat which covers and smoothes the baked layers of a cake and the thin, shiny ganache which can be poured over an entire stacked cake and smoothed to perfection with a small metal spatula.

1 pound semisweet chocolate, cut into bits
2 cups heavy cream

Melt chocolate with cream in a heavy saucepan and cook over very low heat until the mixture is smooth and glossy.

Place half the mixture in a mixing bowl and beat until it becomes thick. Use this mixture as the undercoat for the cake layers. Pour the shiny, thin other half of ganache over the entire stacked cake, smoothing with a metal spatula. The mixture must be relatively liquid to do this, but if it is too thin, gently stir over ice thickening it slightly. Chill iced cake before serving.

Note: When doubled, this recipe will ice a 4-layer cake.

Makes 3 cups ganache

Royal Icing

2 large egg whites
3 1/2 cups sifted confectioners' sugar
Juice of 1 lemon
2 drops glycerin, optional
Food coloring, optional

In mixer bowl, beat egg whites until stiff but not dry. Add sugar, lemon juice and glycerin. Beat 1 minute. If icing is too thick, add water; if too thin, add sugar.

Divide icing into smaller bowls. Tint with small amounts of paste or liquid food coloring; mix well for an even color.

Note: Glycerin is available in pharmacies and baking-supply stores. It keeps the icing soft a little longer and adds a slight sparkle. If using food coloring, use a toothpick and add to icing one dab at the time.

Makes about 2 cups icing

Caramel Brownie Cheesecake

1 3/4 cups vanilla wafer crumbs
1/4 cup plus 1 tablespoon melted butter
1 (14-ounce) package caramels
1 (5-ounce) can evaporated milk
2 cups coarsely crumbled brownies (own recipe or purchased)
3 (8-ounce) packages cream cheese, room temperature
1 cup firmly packed light brown sugar
3 large eggs
1 (8-ounce) carton sour cream
2 teaspoons vanilla

Preheat oven to 350 degrees. Combine vanilla wafers and butter, stirring well. Press mixture firmly in bottom and 2 inches up sides of a 9-inch springform pan. Bake for 5 minutes. Let cool completely.

Combine caramels and milk in heavy saucepan. Cook over low heat, stirring often, until caramels melt. Pour caramel mixture over crust. Sprinkle brownies over caramel.

In mixer bowl, beat cream cheese at medium speed for 2 minutes or until light and fluffy. Gradually add sugar, mix well. Add eggs, one at a time, beating just until blended. Stir in sour cream and vanilla. Pour batter into prepared crust and bake for 50 to 60 minutes. Cool to room temperature, then cover and chill at least 4 hours. Remove from springform pan.

Serves 12

Bobbi Shelton

Cheesecake Squares

A very pleasant, refreshing taste.

1/4 cup melted butter
1 cup graham cracker crumbs
1 (3-ounce) package lemon gelatin
1 cup boiling water
8 ounces cream cheese, room temperature
1 cup sugar
1 (14-ounce) can evaporated milk, well chilled

Preheat oven to 375 degrees. Mix butter and crumbs. Press into a 9 x 9-inch square pan. Bake crust for 8 minutes and set aside. Dissolve gelatin in boiling water. Chill until it begins to thicken. In mixer bowl, mix cream cheese and sugar until creamy. Whip evaporated milk until it has the consistency of whipped cream. Mix gelatin, cream cheese mixture and whipped milk together until it is well blended and creamy. Pour into crumb crust and refrigerate for at least 1 hour before serving.

Serves 8 to 9

Cheesecake with Strawberry Topping

Vary the topping to create seasonal favorites with this sweet classic.

Crust:
20 whole graham crackers (10 ounces), broken
3/4 cup (1 1/2 sticks) chilled unsalted butter, diced
1/2 cup light brown sugar, firmly packed

Filling:
4 (8-ounce) packages cream cheese, room temperature
1 3/4 cups sugar
3 tablespoons fresh lemon juice
2 1/2 teaspoons vanilla extract
Pinch of salt
3 tablespoons all-purpose flour
5 large eggs

244   *Desserts*

Topping:
2 cups sour cream
3 tablespoons sugar
1/2 teaspoon vanilla extract
2 (16-ounce) baskets strawberries, hulled
1 (18-ounce) jar raspberry jelly

Crust: Position rack in center of oven and preheat to 350 degrees. Wrap foil around outside of 10-inch springform pan with 3-inch-high sides. Combine graham crackers, butter and sugar in processor. Pulse until crumbs begin to stick together. Press crumbs onto bottom and 2 3/4 inches up sides of springform pan.

Bake 10 minutes. Transfer to rack and let cool while preparing filling. Maintain oven temperature.

Filling: Beat cream cheese, sugar, lemon juice, vanilla and salt in large bowl until very smooth. Beat in flour; add eggs and beat just until blended, stopping occasionally to scrape down sides of bowl. Pour batter into crust.

Bake until outer 2-inch edge of cake is puffed and slightly cracked, center is just set and top is brown in spots, about 55 minutes. Transfer cake to rack. Cool 10 minutes.

Maintain oven temperature.

Topping: Whisk sour cream, sugar and vanilla in medium bowl to blend. Spoon topping over cake, spreading to edge of pan. Bake until topping is just set, about 5 minutes. Remove from oven. Run knife between side crust and pan. Cool hot cake in pan on rack. Chill overnight.

Assemble: Release pan sides from cheesecake. Arrange whole berries, points facing up, atop cheesecake; cover top completely. Stir jelly in heavy, small saucepan over medium-low heat until melted. Cool to barely lukewarm, about 5 minutes. Brush enough jelly over berries to glaze generously, allowing some to drip between berries. Cover and refrigerate.

Note: Cake and glaze can be prepared 6 hours ahead, but wait closer to serving time to glaze.

Serves 12

Apple Dumplings

Classical Fruits offers 160 acres of fruits ranging from May strawberries to December apples and pears, with peaches, grapes, raspberries and plums throughout the year.

5 apples, cut in half crosswise and cored
10 biscuits, homemade or refrigerated
Ground cinnamon
1 1/2 cups sugar
1 1/2 cups apple cider
2 sticks butter, melted

Preheat oven to 350 degrees. Roll each biscuit into a 6-inch circle. Wrap 1 biscuit around each apple half.

Place the apples, seam side down, in a greased 9 x 13 x 2-inch baking dish and sprinkle with cinnamon. Pour sugar, cider and butter over apples.

Bake for 45 minutes or until brown.

Serves 10

Frannie Adair
Classical Fruits
Moulton, AL

Blueberry Crumble

3 cups fresh blueberries
1/3 cup sugar
Juice of 1 lemon

Topping:
1/4 cup butter, room temperature
1/3 cup sugar
2/3 cup flour

Preheat oven to 350 degrees. Place fresh blueberries in shallow 1 to 1 1/2 quart baking dish. Sprinkle with 1/3 cup sugar and lemon juice.

Blend butter, sugar and flour. Sprinkle over berries. Bake for 45 minutes or longer, until brown. Serve warm with a topping of ice cream.

Variation: Try a mixed berry crumble. Mix a variety of your favorite berries in place of blueberries.

Serves 4 or 5

Natalie Ann Adair
Classical Fruits
Moulton, AL

Peach Cobbler Supreme

Cobbler:
8 cups fresh peaches, peeled and sliced
2 cups sugar
2 to 4 tablespoons all-purpose flour
1/2 teaspoon ground nutmeg
1 teaspoon almond or vanilla extract
1/3 cup butter or margarine

Double-Crust Pastry:
2 cups all-purpose flour
1 teaspoon salt
2/3 cup plus 2 tablespoons shortening
4 to 5 tablespoons cold water

Cobbler: Combine peaches, sugar, flour and nutmeg in a Dutch oven; set aside until syrup forms (about 30 minutes). Bring peach mixture to a boil; reduce heat to low, and cook 10 minutes or until tender. Remove from heat; add almond extract and butter, stirring until butter melts.

Double-Crust Pastry: Combine flour and salt; cut in shortening with pastry cutter until mixture resembles coarse meal. Sprinkle cold water (1 tablespoon at a time) evenly over surface; stir with a fork until dry ingredients are moistened. Shape into a ball; chill and divide in half.

Assemble: Preheat oven to 425 degrees. Roll half of pastry to 1/8-inch thickness on a lightly floured surface; cut into an 8-inch square. Spoon half of peaches into a lightly buttered 8-inch square baking dish; top with a pastry square. Bake for 14 minutes or until lightly browned. Spoon remaining peaches over baked pastry square.

Roll remaining pastry to 1/8-inch thickness, and cut into 1-inch strips; arrange in lattice design over peaches. Bake for 15 to 18 minutes or until brown.

Note: Commercial crusts may be used.

Serves 8

Ice Cream for Dessert?

If your dessert calls for a scoop of ice cream, scoop ice cream ahead-of-time into paper muffin cups. Place in freezer. Bring out at last minute—no time-consuming dipping and messes at serving time.

Quick Peach Cobbler

1 stick unsalted butter
1 cup self-rising flour
1 cup sugar
3/4 cup milk
1 (28-ounce) can sliced peaches in heavy syrup

Preheat oven to 350 degrees. Melt butter in a 2 to 2 1/2 quart dish. Mix flour, sugar and milk and add to the warm butter. Do not stir!
Place peaches with syrup on top of batter. Bake for 35 minutes or until brown.

Note: Wonderful with ice cream!

Serves 8

Laura Lee Latham

Creamy Apple Pie

2 unbaked (10-inch) pie shells
5 pounds tart apples, peeled
1 cup sugar
2 tablespoons cornstarch
1 tablespoon flour
1 cup milk or cream
Butter
Cinnamon

Preheat oven to 400 degrees. Line a 10-inch pie pan with pie shell. Core and cut apples in 1/4-inch wedges and lay them in pie shell, slightly overlapping.

Mix sugar, cornstarch and flour. Sift over apples. Pour milk over apples; dot with butter and sprinkle with cinnamon. Top pie with remaining pie shell, flute edges together and cut three long steam vents in top. Bake for 15 minutes and reduce heat to 350 degrees and bake for 35 minutes.

Note: Best when served warm.

Serves 6

Chocolate Chess Pie

*This pie is as smooth as velvet. When you dream of chocolate
pie, it most likely will be this one. Make an extra one and freeze it.*

1 unbaked (9-inch) pie shell
1 1/2 cups sugar
3 tablespoons cocoa
1/4 cup melted margarine
 2 eggs, slightly beaten
1/8 teaspoon salt
1 (5-ounce) can evaporated milk
1 teaspoon vanilla extract

Preheat oven to 350 degrees. In mixer bowl, mix sugar, cocoa and margarine. Stir well. Add eggs and beat at medium-high speed with electric mixer for 2 1/2 minutes. Add salt, milk and vanilla and mix to blend. Pour filling into pie shell. Bake for 40 to 45 minutes. Let stand to cool completely before serving (3 to 4 hours).

Serves 6 to 8

Lynn Littrell

Chocolate Cream Pie

1 baked (9-inch) pie shell

Pie Filling:
3 tablespoons Nestlé Quik (or cocoa)
1 1/3 cups sugar
1/2 cup flour
2 2/3 cups milk
4 eggs, divided
1/4 teaspoon salt
1 tablespoon butter
2 teaspoons vanilla extract

Meringue:
4 egg whites
1/2 cup sugar

Pie Filling: Mix Nestlé Quik, sugar and flour in medium saucepan. Add milk and egg yolks, slightly beaten, and salt. Mix well. Cook over medium heat, stirring constantly, until thick, about 5 minutes. Remove from heat and add butter and vanilla. Pour into baked pastry shell.

Meringue: Preheat oven to 325 degrees. Beat egg whites and sugar until stiff, adding sugar slowly. Cover top of pie with meringue and brown in oven.

Serves 6

Patsy Terry

Chocolate Pecan Pie

Crust:
1 stick butter
1 (3-ounce) package cream cheese
1 cup flour

Filling:
1 cup sugar
1/2 cup all-purpose flour
1/2 cup melted butter
2 eggs, beaten
1 teaspoon vanilla extract
1 cup chopped pecans
6 ounces semisweet chocolate mini-chips

Crust: Preheat oven to 325 degrees. Allow butter and cream cheese to soften in a mixer bowl. Cream together and gradually add flour. Wrap in wax paper and refrigerate about 1 hour. Roll out a 9-inch crust on a floured board. Place in an oiled 9-inch pie plate. Prebake for 10 to 12 minutes before filling.
   Filling: Preheat oven to 350 degrees. In mixer bowl, combine sugar and flour, mixing well. Stir in melted butter, beaten eggs and vanilla extract. Fold in chopped pecans and mini-chips.
   Pour into crust and bake for 45 minutes. Let cool before serving.

Note: Top with vanilla ice cream and hot fudge sauce!

Serves 6

Blind Baking

When pie shells are prebaked without filling it is referred to as blind baking. To bake pie shell, pierce with fork tines to prevent puffing during baking.

Preheat oven to 375 degrees. Line pie shell with aluminum foil, extending edges of foil to cover edge of pie shell. Fill with baking weights, rice or dried beans. Bake 15 to 20 minutes. Remove foil and weights and bake another 12 minutes or until crust is golden brown. Let cool on wire rack. Produces a crisp pie shell.

Southern Pecan Pie

3/4 cup sugar
3 eggs, beaten
3/4 cup light corn syrup
1/4 cup dark corn syrup
3 tablespoons melted butter
1 teaspoon vanilla
1 cup chopped pecans
1 unbaked (9-inch) pie shell

Preheat oven to 350 degrees. In mixer bowl, mix sugar and eggs until blended. Add corn syrup, butter, vanilla and nuts. Pour into pie shell and bake 45 minutes. Let stand before slicing.

Serves 6

Coconut Cream Pie

This recipe is my best attempt at duplicating a pie served at a wonderful restaurant in Seattle, WA. This version makes me happy.

Crust:
1 1/4 cups unsifted all-purpose flour
1/4 cup confectioners' sugar
1/4 teaspoon salt
1/2 cup (1 stick) cold unsalted butter, cut into small pieces
1 large egg yolk
1 tablespoon ice water

Filling:
2/3 cup sugar
1/4 cup cornstarch
1/4 teaspoon salt
2 1/2 cups whole milk
5 large egg yolks
2 to 3 tablespoons unsalted butter, cut into pieces
1 tablespoon vanilla extract
1 1/3 cups shredded coconut, fresh or frozen (reserve 1/3 cup for topping)

254 *Desserts*

Whipped Cream Topping:
1 pint whipping cream, chilled
5 tablespoons confectioners' sugar, sifted
1 tablespoon vanilla extract
White Chocolate Curls and Coconut shavings for garnish

Crust: In food processor, combine flour, confectioners' sugar and salt. Process until blended. Add butter; process with on-and-off pulses until coarse crumbs form. In small cup, beat together yolk and water with fork; add to processor. Process until dough comes together. With fingers, press dough into 9-inch pie pan with removable bottom. Place in freezer 15 minutes. Use blind baking process (page 253).

Filling: In a medium saucepan over low heat, whisk sugar, cornstarch and salt until well blended. Gradually whisk in milk. Vigorously whisk in egg yolks until no yellow streaks remain. Stirring constantly with a wooden spoon, bring the mixture barely to a simmer over medium heat.

Remove from heat and scrape sides and corners of pan; whisk until smooth. Return to heat and whisking constantly, bring to a simmer and cook for 1 minute.

Remove from heat; whisk in butter, vanilla and 1 cup shredded coconut. Spoon filling into a prepared crust and immediately press a sheet of plastic wrap directly over pie surface. Refrigerate for a least 3 hours before slicing.

Topping: Shortly before serving pie, remove plastic wrap and cover pie with whipped cream topping.

Use cold bowl and beaters (put in freezer 15 minutes before beating). Whip cream at medium-high speed. When it begins to thicken, add sugar and flavoring. Continue to beat until soft peaks form. Spread over pie filling. Add remaining coconut and garnish with white chocolate curls (page 323) and coconut shavings (page 324).

Serves 6

Desserts   255

Key Lime Pie

Key Lime Pie is a famous dessert originating in the Florida Keys, dating back to 1830. Debate over the original recipe continues today: pastry shell or graham cracker crust? Whipping cream or meringue? Whichever, this version is delicious! The recipe makes 2 pies but may be halved.

Filling:
8 large eggs, lightly beaten
2 cups sugar
2/3 cup Key lime juice, or to taste, (freshly squeezed or bottled Key lime juice)
1/4 cup grated lime rind (grate lime before juicing)
Dash of salt
1 cup unsalted butter, room temperature

Crusts:
2 1/2 cups graham cracker crumbs
1/2 cup firmly packed light brown sugar
2/3 cup unsalted melted butter

Topping:
2 cups whipping cream
1/4 cup confectioners' sugar, sifted
2 teaspoons almond or vanilla extract
Garnish: lime twist and mint sprigs, along with a few blueberries

Filling: Preheat oven to 300 degrees. Combine eggs, sugar, Key lime juice and lime rind in top of double boiler. Bring water to a boil. Reduce heat to low; cook, whisking constantly, until thickened. Add butter and salt; cook, whisking constantly, until butter melts and mixture thickens. Pour into graham cracker crusts. Bake for 20 minutes or until set. Cool completely. Cover and chill at least 8 hours.

Crusts: Preheat oven to 375 degrees. In bowl, combine all ingredients; press into two 9-inch pie plates. Bake for 6 to 8 minutes and cool.

Topping: Beat whipping cream at high speed with an electric mixer until foamy; gradually add confectioners' sugar, beating until soft peaks form. Stir in vanilla and spread over filling. Chill. Garnish just before serving, if desired.

Serves 12

Caryl Ward Littrell

Fresh Strawberry Pie

This pie is the perfect showcase for seasonal strawberries. Substitute fresh peaches and peach gelatin and you have another great dessert that is quick and delicious!

1 baked (8 or 9-inch) pie shell
Fresh small strawberries, enough to cover bottom of pie shell
1 cup water
1 cup sugar
3 tablespoons cornstarch
Pinch of salt
1/4 cup strawberry gelatin
2 cups heavy cream, whipped

In pan, mix water, sugar, cornstarch and salt together and cook until thick, about 5 minutes. Remove from heat and add gelatin. Cool slightly.

Place strawberries in pie shell and pour mixture over berries. Refrigerate. When ready to serve, top with whipped cream.

Serves 6

Mini-Cheesecake Fruit Tarts

Graham Cracker Crust (page 317)
3 (8-ounce) packages cream cheese, room temperature
1 cup sugar
5 eggs
1 1/2 teaspoons vanilla extract
Selected fruits (strawberries, kiwis, blueberries)
Fruit Glaze (page 313)

Preheat oven to 350 degrees. Prepare crust and press crumbs into bottom of paper 2-inch mini-muffin baking cups to make a 1/4-inch-thick crust. Place baking cups into muffin baking tins. Bake 5 to 8 minutes. Remove and cool before adding filling.

Filling: Reduce heat to 300 degrees. In mixer bowl, mix cream cheese and sugar well. Add eggs, one at a time; then add vanilla. Fill muffin baking cups 2/3 full and place in baking tins. Bake 20 to 25 minutes. Cool and refrigerate.

When tarts are cool, place selected fruits on top. Arrange according to a contrast of colors. Glaze with Fruit Glaze and refrigerate until ready to serve.

Note: Tarts may be frozen after baking and topped with fruit and glazed before serving. For bite-size tarts, use 1 1/2-inch paper muffin cups.

Makes fifty 2-inch tarts

Lime Tartlets

1 (15-ounce) package refrigerated pie shells (9 inch)
1/3 cup sugar
2 teaspoons cornstarch
1/3 cup whipping cream
1 teaspoon finely grated lime peel
2 tablespoons lime juice
1 tablespoon butter
1/4 cup sour cream
Green food coloring
Whipped cream (page 322)
Finely grated lime peel

Pie Shells: Preheat oven to 350 degrees. Roll 1 pie shell on a lightly floured surface to press out fold line. Cut into rounds with a 2 1/2-inch round cutter. Fit pastry rounds into miniature (1 3/4-inch) muffin pans. Repeat procedure with remaining pie shell. Bake until golden brown.

Filling: Combine sugar and cornstarch in a medium saucepan; stir in whipping cream, lime peel and lime juice. Bring to a boil over medium high heat, stirring constantly. Reduce heat; simmer for 1 minute, stirring constantly until thickened and smooth. Remove from heat. Stir in butter, sour cream and food coloring to make mixture pale green. Let mixture cool to room temperature. Spoon into tart shells. Cover and chill for 2 to 4 hours. To serve, spoon a small amount of whipped cream onto the center of each tartlet. Top with grated lime peel.

Note: Pie shells can be prepared ahead, baked and frozen. Filling can be refrigerated up to 2 days before filling tarts 1 to 2 hours before serving. Whipped cream topping should be added immediately before serving.

Makes 18 tartlets

Betty Mitchell Sims

Crème Fraîche

Crème fraîche has a nut-like, slightly sour taste and can replace sour cream in recipes. Sweeten it and fold into whipped cream to use with fresh berries or add to soups and sauces for extra thickness. It will keep refrigerated for up to 2 weeks.

Desserts

Baking in a Water Bath

Baking a dish in a water bath helps to keep the food moist. It is a method often used when cooking items such as puddings. To create a water bath, place the baking dish in a larger pan. Pour water into the larger pan until it reaches halfway up the side of the baking dish. Place the pans in the oven and bake as directed.

Toasty Southern Pecan Tarts

1 tablespoon butter or margarine
1 cup chopped pecans
1/8 teaspoon salt
1 (15-ounce) package refrigerated pie shells (9 inch)
1/2 cup butter or margarine
1 cup light corn syrup
1 cup sugar
1/4 teaspoon ground cinnamon
3 large eggs, beaten
1 teaspoon vanilla extract
1/2 teaspoon lemon juice

Preheat oven to 350 degrees. Place 1 tablespoon butter in a shallow baking pan; bake until melted. Add pecans, stirring to coat; bake 8 to 10 minutes or until toasted, stirring once. Remove from oven, and sprinkle evenly with salt; cool.

Roll 1 pie shell on a lightly floured surface to press out fold lines. Cut into rounds with a 2 1/2-inch round cutter. Fit pastry rounds into miniature 1 3/4-inch muffin pans; do not trim edges.

Repeat procedure with remaining pie shell. Sprinkle toasted pecans evenly into prepared tart shells and set aside.

Place 1/2 cup butter in a small heavy saucepan; cook over medium heat, stirring constantly, until light brown (do not burn). Remove from heat; cool 10 minutes.

Add corn syrup and next 5 ingredients to butter, stirring well; spoon evenly over pecans.

Bake for 35 to 40 minutes or until set. Cool in pans 5 minutes. Remove from pans and cool completely on wire racks.

Makes 4 1/2 dozen tarts

Betty Mitchell Sims

Chocolate Crème Brûlée

With a crusty top and silky-smooth interior, Chocolate Crème Brûlée offers the most satisfying texture contrasts.

1 1/4 cups heavy or whipping cream
1 1/4 cups crème fraîche (page 311)
1 vanilla bean
4 ounces bittersweet chocolate, broken into squares
4 egg yolks
1 tablespoon honey
6 tablespoons raw sugar, for topping

In a large heatproof bowl, mix cream and crème fraîche; add vanilla bean. Place bowl over saucepan of barely simmering water and stir about 10 minutes. Do not let bowl touch water.

Remove the vanilla bean and stir in the chocolate, a few pieces at a time, until melted. When mixture is completely smooth, remove bowl but leave pan of water over heat.

In second heatproof bowl, whisk egg yolks and honey, then gradually pour in chocolate cream, whisking constantly. Place over the pan of simmering water and stir constantly until custard thickens enough to coat back of wooden spoon.

Remove from heat; spoon custard into 6 ovenproof ramekins. Cool, then chill until set.

Preheat broiler to high, sprinkle 1 tablespoon raw sugar evenly over each dessert and spray lightly with a little water. Broil briefly, as close to heat as possible, until sugar melts and caramelizes.

Chill desserts once more before serving.

Note: This can be prepared up to 2 days in advance. Make caramelized sugar topping several hours before serving so desserts can chill.

Serves 6

Vanilla Bean

Split vanilla bean lengthwise, using a paring knife. Using knife blade, scrape tiny seeds from split bean into custard mixture, etc., before cooking. Discard vanilla pods from cooked mixture, etc., when cooking is finished.

Caramelized Pumpkin Custards

6 egg yolks
1/3 cup sugar
2 cups heavy cream
1 cup pumpkin, packed
1 (5-ounce) can evaporated milk
1/4 cup sugar
1/2 teaspoon ground cinnamon
1/4 teaspoon ground ginger
1/8 teaspoon ground cloves
1/2 cup packed brown sugar

Preheat oven to 300 degrees. In top of double boiler, whisk together egg yolks and 1/3 cup sugar. Cook over simmering water, whisking until thickened. In a medium saucepan, bring cream to a boil. Slowly add cream to egg yolks, whisking constantly. Continue cooking in double boiler until mixture is smooth and thickened. In a large mixing bowl, combine pumpkin, evaporated milk, 1/4 cup sugar, cinnamon, ginger and cloves. Pour hot custard mixture into pumpkin mixture and stir until smooth. Pour into eight 6-ounce custard cups and place in a large baking dish. Pour hot water 1 inch deep around custard cups and place in oven. Bake until custard is set in center, about 50 minutes. Remove from oven and allow to cool for 30 minutes before removing from water. Cover and chill for 2 to 24 hours.

Preheat broiler. Force brown sugar through a sieve using the back of a spoon. Sprinkle 1 tablespoon sugar evenly over each custard and place on a baking sheet. Broil until sugar melts and caramelizes, 2 to 4 minutes. Serve immediately.

Serves 8

Syble Murphy

262 *Desserts*

Vanilla Crème Brûlée

1 cup half-and-half
1 vanilla bean
1/2 teaspoon vanilla extract
8 egg yolks
1 whole egg
5/8 cup plus 1 tablespoon sugar (5 ounces)
3 cups heavy cream
1 cup fine sugar, as needed

In pan, heat half-and-half with vanilla bean and extract. In a bowl whisk together yolks, egg and sugar. Pour a small amount of hot half-and-half into the egg mixture to temper the eggs. Add the remaining half-and-half. When cooled, add in cream and mix. Cool completely. Remove vanilla bean. Preheat oven to 325 degrees. Fill ramekins with mixture and place in baking dish. Fill baking dish with hot water half way up, cover tightly with foil and bake for 35 minutes. Cool well. Sprinkle sugar over surface of crème. Place under broiler and broil until nicely browned and caramelized.

Serves 8

Banana Pudding with Meringue

Banana pudding has to be the original American trifle. It always reminds us of home and family reunions! A true comfort food.

3/4 cup plus 6 tablespoons sugar
5 tablespoons all-purpose flour
2 cups milk
4 large eggs, separated
2 teaspoons vanilla extract
1/4 teaspoon cream of tartar
1 cup heavy cream
2 cups vanilla wafers
3 to 4 ripe bananas, sliced

Pudding: Whisk together 3/4 cup sugar and flour in a heavy-bottom 2-or 3-quart saucepan. Add 1/2 cup milk and egg yolks and whisk until smooth. Add remaining 1 1/2 cups milk and blend. Cook, stirring constantly with a wooden spoon, over low heat about 15 minutes, or until custard is thickened. Remove from heat and stir in vanilla. Let cool to room temperature.
Meringue: Preheat oven to 350 degrees. Beat egg whites in a medium-size bowl until frothy. Add cream of tartar and beat just to soft peaks. Gradually add remaining 6 tablespoons sugar and beat to stiff peaks. Set aside.
Whip cream to stiff peaks in a medium-size bowl. Gently fold whipped cream into cooled custard.
Arrange 1 cup vanilla wafers in bottom of a 2-quart ovenproof bowl. Top with half of the bananas and half of custard. Repeat process again for second layer. Spoon meringue on top of custard, spreading to cover the entire surface and sealing the edges.
Bake in center of oven for 15 minutes or until meringue is turning light brown.
Serve immediately or cool to room temperature and chill.

Variation: Substitute 16 ounces or 2 cups fresh or frozen strawberries in place of bananas for another treat.

Serves 8

If whipped cream has begun to liquefy, rewhip to thicken.

Selma's Chocolate Pudding

Selma Terry supplied this recipe for the deli in Ott's Foodland Supermarket. She and the other hard working ladies were great cooks. This pudding was a weekly menu specialty and pans and pans were served. Use it, if you'd like, as a pie filling, or serve it as it was served in the deli with a vanilla wafer crust and a meringue topping.

Filling:
1 cup sugar
1/2 cup all-purpose flour
1 tablespoon cocoa
2 eggs, divided (slightly beat egg yolks)
2 cups milk
2 tablespoons butter
1 teaspoon vanilla extract

Meringue:
2 egg whites
1/4 cup sugar
1/4 teaspoon salt

Filling: In a medium saucepan, mix sugar, flour and cocoa. Add eggs and milk and mix until blended. Cook over medium heat, stirring constantly until thickened. Do not let it stick. Remove from heat and add butter and vanilla extract. Stir until smooth and velvety. Pour into a baked (9-inch) pie shell or a deep dish, if serving as pudding.

    Meringue: Preheat oven to 400 degrees. Beat egg whites, gradually adding sugar and salt, until stiff peaks form. Top pie with meringue. Bake for 5 to 7 minutes.

Serves 6

Selma Terry

Strawberry Meringue Roulade

4 large egg whites
1 1/4 cups sugar
1 1/4 cups whipping cream, chilled
2 teaspoons vanilla extract
2 1/2 cups fresh sliced strawberries
1/2 cup strawberry preserves
Confectioners' sugar
Whole strawberries with stems for garnish

Position rack in center of oven and preheat to 400 degrees. Line 15 x 10 x 1-inch baking sheet with wax paper, extending 2 inches over ends of pan. Butter wax paper.

Beat egg whites in large bowl until soft peaks form. Gradually add sugar, beating until meringue is stiff and shiny.

Spread meringue evenly on prepared baking sheet. Bake until pale golden in color, about 8 minutes. Reduce oven temperature to 325 degrees. Bake until meringue is slightly firm to the touch on top but soft inside, about 8 minutes longer.

Remove baking sheet from oven. Run knife around pan sides to loosen meringue. Turn onto a sheet of wax paper. Carefully peel off wax paper. Cool meringue 25 minutes.

Whip cream and vanilla in medium bowl until stiff peaks form. Mix sliced strawberries and preserves in another medium bowl. Spoon strawberry mixture onto meringue, leaving a 1-inch border on all sides. Spread whipped cream over strawberry mixture.

Starting at 1 long side, gently roll up meringue jelly-roll style, enclosing filling. Place roulade, seam side down, on platter. Refrigerate at least 1 hour and up to 4 hours.

Dust roulade with confectioners' sugar. Cut into slices when ready to serve and transfer to platter. Garnish with whole strawberries. Serve chilled.

Serves 10

Chocolate Amaretto Trifle

1 (18.25-ounce) box Devil's Food cake mix, baked according to directions
1/2 cup amaretto or 1/2 cup water mixed with 1 teaspoon almond flavoring
6 (1.4-ounce) Heath or Skor bars, crushed
1 1/2 cans Hershey's chocolate syrup
1 (12-ounce) container whipped topping

Bake devil's food cake in a 13 x 9 x 2-inch pan. Punch holes in the cake and pour either amaretto or almond water over the entire cake. Let sit overnight. Divide the cake into thirds. Crumble 1/3 in bottom of bowl. Crush 2 Heath or Skor bars and crumble over cake. Pour 1/2 can chocolate syrup over candy and cake. Top with 1 cup whipped topping. Repeat layers twice, ending with a top layer of whipped topping. Garnish with chocolate curls.

Serves 12

Verna White

Pastry Cream

2 cups milk
2/3 cup sugar
1/4 cup cornstarch
6 egg yolks
2 tablespoons butter
2 teaspoons vanilla extract

Bring 1 1/2 cups of milk and sugar to a boil in a 2-quart saucepan. Meanwhile, whisk together remaining milk and cornstarch in a 2-quart bowl until smooth. Whisk in yolks. Whisk 1/3 of the boiling milk into the yolk mixture. Return the remaining milk to a boil and whisk in the tempered yolk mixture. Whisk constantly until pastry cream thickens and returns to a boil. Beat in the butter and vanilla. Pour into a bowl and press plastic wrap against surface; refrigerate.

Makes filling for 1 cake layer

To prevent a skin from forming on dessert sauces or custards, cover the mixture with plastic wrap. Press wrap directly onto the sauce's surface to seal completely.

Desserts

Strawberry Trifle

This trifle is exceptional with the sponge cake layer called for, but a 9-inch white or yellow cake layer (or 4 cups ladyfingers) can be successfully substituted.

Cake Layer:
One 9-inch layer sponge cake (page 226) or substitution

Pastry Cream:
2 cups milk
2/3 cup sugar
1/4 cup cornstarch
6 egg yolks
2 tablespoons butter
2 teaspoons vanilla extract

Whipped Cream:
1 1/2 cups heavy whipping cream
2 tablespoons sugar
1 teaspoon vanilla extract

Strawberries:
2 pints fresh strawberries
1/2 cup sugar

3/4 cup sliced almonds, toasted
2/3 cup strawberry preserves

Cake: Cut the cooled sponge layer into vertical slices, about 1/4-inch thick. Set aside, covered, at room temperature.

Pastry Cream: Bring 1 1/2 cups of milk and sugar to a boil in a 2-quart saucepan. Meanwhile, whisk together the remaining milk and the cornstarch in a 2-quart bowl until smooth. Whisk in the yolks. Whisk 1/3 of the boiling milk into the yolk mixture. Return the remaining milk to a boil and whisk in the tempered yolk mixture. Whisk constantly until the pastry cream thickens and returns to a boil. Beat in butter. Pour the pastry cream into a bowl and press plastic wrap against the surface; refrigerate until cold.

Whipping Cream: Combine the cream with the sugar and whip on medium speed until it holds its shape, but is not too stiff. Add vanilla extract. Cover and refrigerate.

Strawberries: Reserve the 6 best-looking strawberries in the refrigerator for decoration. Rinse, hull and slice the remaining strawberries into a bowl. Sprinkle with sugar, cover and refrigerate.

Pastry Cream: Remove pastry cream from refrigerator and gently stir in vanilla. Fold in about 1/3 of the whipped cream.

Assemble: Make a layer of the cake slices or ladyfingers in the bottom of a 3 to

3 1/2-quart glass bowl. Sprinkle with 1/4 of the almonds and 1/3 of the preserves and strawberries; spread with 1/3 of the filling. Repeat for 2 more layers. Top with a last layer of cake. Spread with remaining whipped cream for topping.

Halve the reserved strawberries, leaving the hull intact and cutting through the berry. Arrange, cut side up, around the inside edge of bowl. Scatter remaining almonds in center. Loosely cover with plastic wrap and refrigerate several hours.

Note: Trifle can be made the day before, tightly covered with plastic wrap and refrigerated. Finish top with whipped cream, strawberries and almonds before serving.

Serves 12

Lemon Meringue Nests

Meringue Nests:
1/2 cup egg whites
1/8 teaspoon salt
3/4 cup sugar
1/2 teaspoon vanilla extract

Lemon Filling:
3 egg yolks, beaten
2/3 cup sugar
1/4 cup lemon juice
Zest of 1 lemon
2 cups whipping cream, whipped
Mint leaves (optional)

Meringue Nests: Preheat oven to 300 degrees. Combine egg whites and salt; beat with electric mixer at high speed until stiff. Add sugar, 1 tablespoon at a time, beating well after each addition. Stir in vanilla.

Grease cookie sheet or line with heavy brown paper. Spoon meringue onto cookie sheet in 6 equal mounds. Make a deep well in the center of each mound, building up the sides with the back of a spoon, forming a nest. Bake until shells are a delicate golden color, 12 to 15 minutes. Lower heat to 250 degrees, continue baking until dry and light brown in color, 30 to 40 minutes. Turn off heat; leave shells in oven with door closed, 1 to 2 hours.

Remove from oven to cool completely; fill with Lemon Filling.

Shells may be refrigerated, uncovered, for 2 hours or unfilled shells may be frozen in an airtight container. Return unfilled shells to the oven to crisp before filling.

Lemon Filling: Combine egg yolks, sugar, lemon juice and zest in top of double boiler. Stir well. Cook over boiling water until thick. Cool. Remove 1/2 cup whipped cream and set aside for garnish. Fold remaining whipped cream into cooled lemon mixture. Fill shells. Garnish with whipped cream and mint leaves.

Serves 6

Pears En Croûte

2 (15-ounce) packages refrigerated pie shells
6 firm ripe pears, unpeeled (Bartlett pears work well)
1 egg yolk
1 tablespoon water
Caramel Sauce
Fresh mint for garnish, optional

Caramel Sauce:
1 (12-ounce) jar caramel ice cream topping
1 (14-ounce) can sweetened condensed milk
2 tablespoons lemon juice.
1/4 cup Cointreau, Grand Marnier or other orange-flavored liqueur (optional)

Pears: Preheat oven to 350 degrees. Unfold pie shells, one at a time; place on a lightly floured surface and roll each into a 10 inch-square. Cut each square into 1-inch strips. Starting at bottom of pear, carefully begin wrapping with 1 pastry strip, overlapping strips 1/4 inch as you cover pear. Continue wrapping by moistening ends of strips with water and joining to previous strip until pear is completely covered. Repeat procedure with remaining pears and pastry strips.

Place pears on a baking sheet. Combine egg yolk and water; brush evenly on pastry. Bake for 1 hour or until tender.

Caramel Sauce: Combine caramel topping and milk in top of a double boiler; bring water to a boil. Reduce heat to low; cook, stirring constantly, until smooth. Stir in lemon juice and liqueur (if used).

Spoon 2 to 3 tablespoons caramel sauce onto each dessert plate; top with a pear. Garnish with mint leaves, if desired, by sticking leaf into top of pear near stem.

Note: To make ahead, wrap pears in pastry; cover tightly with plastic wrap, and chill 8 hours. Remove plastic wrap; brush with egg yolk mixture and bake as directed.

Serves 6

Syble Murphy

Poached Pears in Chocolate Sauce

3 cups water
1 1/2 cups sugar
4 tablespoons raspberry vinegar (can use 1 vanilla bean instead)
4 pears (ripe, but firm)

Chocolate Sauce:
4 ounces semisweet chocolate
1/2 cup butter
3/4 cup sugar
Pinch of salt
1 teaspoon vanilla extract

In bowl, combine water and sugar in saucepan. Cook until sugar dissolves. Reduce heat to low simmer, and add raspberry vinegar. Peel and core pears and immediately place in hot sugar mixture. Simmer from 10 to 30 minutes, depending upon ripeness of pears. Let cool in syrup. Serve cold or reheat and serve with chocolate sauce.

    Chocolate Sauce: Melt chocolate and butter in saucepan, stirring often. Add sugar, salt and vanilla. Serve on dessert plate drizzled under pears.

Serves 4

Ice Cream Tortoni

1/3 cup almonds, chopped and toasted
3 tablespoons melted butter
1 cup crushed vanilla wafers
1 teaspoon almond extract
3 pints vanilla ice cream, slightly softened
12 ounces apricot preserves

Mix almonds, butter, wafers and extract. Reserve 1/4 cup of mixture for topping. Sprinkle 1/2 mixture over the bottom of an 8-inch pan which has been sprayed with Pam. Spoon 1/2 of the ice cream over the crumb mixture and press down with a large spoon. Drizzle with 1/2 of the apricot preserves. Repeat this procedure. Add remaining crumbs on top. Freeze. Just before serving, set out about 5 minutes to soften. Cut into small squares as this is very rich.

Makes nine 2 1/2-inch squares

Carol F. Thompson

Frozen Peach Dessert

1st layer:
7 1/2 ounces vanilla wafers, crushed
1 stick margarine, melted

In bowl, mix well and press into 9 x 13 x 2-inch Pyrex dish.
Bake at 325 degrees 8 to 10 minutes. Let cool completely.

2nd layer:
1 stick margarine, room temperature
1 (16-ounce) box confectioners' sugar
2 eggs

In bowl, mix well and spread over first layer.

3rd layer:
6 cups fresh peaches, peeled and sliced (Sprinkle with small amount of lemon juice. Do not sweeten.)

4th layer:
1 (8-ounce) container of whipped topping

Assemble, cover well and freeze. To serve, let thaw at least 30 minutes to make cutting easier.
Variation: Can use other fresh fruit —strawberries, blueberries, bananas, etc. A combination is good.

Serves 12

Virginia Johnson

Vanilla Wafer Dessert

1 (12-ounce) box vanilla wafers, crushed
1 cup chopped pecans
3/4 cup melted margarine
1/2 gallon vanilla ice cream
Hot fudge sauce

In bowl, combine first 3 ingredients and spread half of mixture in a 9 x 13 x 2-inch pan. Spread 1/2 gallon ice cream on top, and sprinkle remaining crumbs over ice cream. Cover securely and freeze. Serve with hot fudge sauce.

Serves 12

Jeanette McKelvey

Butterfinger Ice Cream

1/2 gallon chocolate milk
1 (14-ounce) can sweetened condensed milk
1/2 cup sugar
16 ounces whipped topping
6 (2.1 ounce) Butterfinger candy bars, crushed

In bowl, mix chocolate milk, sweetened condensed milk and sugar; put in ice cream freezer. Place whipped topping on top of milk mixture. Put Butterfingers on top of whipped topping. Freeze in ice cream freezer.

Variation: To make chocolate ice cream, leave out sugar and Butterfingers. The chocolate variation makes 1 gallon.

Makes 1 1/2 gallons ice cream

Jane McCullough

Crème de Menthe Ice Cream

This silky ice cream is perfect crowned with fresh mint leaves,
chocolate curls and a generous amount of hot fudge sauce.

2 eggs
1/2 cup sugar
Dash of salt
2 cups half-and-half
2 cups whipping cream
1/4 cup light corn syrup
1/3 cup crème de menthe
1 teaspoon vanilla extract
4 ounces semisweet chocolate, for curls or shavings

Beat eggs, sugar and salt with electric mixer until thick and cream colored. Add half-and-half, whipping cream, corn syrup, crème de menthe and vanilla. Mix well. Freeze according to manufacturer's directions. Top each serving with chocolate curls.

Variation: Make a parfait of crumbled brownies, chocolate curls, crème de menthe ice cream and hot fudge sauce. Top with mint leaf.

Makes about 1 quart ice cream

Peach Ice Cream

3 cups very ripe peaches
2 1/2 cups sugar
6 eggs
1 pint half-and-half
1/2 gallon whole milk
1 (14-ounce) can sweetened condensed milk
2 tablespoons vanilla extract
1 pint heavy whipping cream

Peel peaches, chop and mash with potato masher until very smooth or purée in food processor. Mix with 1 cup sugar and set aside.

In mixer bowl, beat eggs until very foamy. Beat in remaining sugar, half-and-half and 1 quart of whole milk. Add sweetened condensed milk, beating well. Place in heavy saucepan over low heat and cook until thick as custard, stirring constantly. Remove from heat and add vanilla. Let cool thoroughly. Stir in whipping cream and remaining milk. Fold in peaches. Place in freezer can and add enough milk to fill to proper level. Freeze in electric freezer according to freezer directions.

Makes 1 1/2 gallons ice cream

Syble Murphy

Amaretto Brownies

Bottom Layer:
1 (19-ounce) box Duncan Hines Brownie Mix, plain
1/4 cup vegetable oil
3 eggs
1 cup chopped nuts
6 tablespoons amaretto

Filling:
1/2 cup butter, room temperature
2 cups confectioners' sugar
3 tablespoons amaretto

Topping:
6 ounces chocolate chips
4 tablespoons butter

Bottom Layer: Preheat oven to 350 degrees. In mixer bowl, prepare brownie mix with oil, eggs, nuts and amaretto. Spread in a greased 9 x 13 x 2-inch pan. Bake for 25 to 30 minutes.

Filling: Remove from oven and sprinkle with 3 tablespoons amaretto (by hand). Let cool completely. Spread filling over cold brownies. Chill 1 hour or overnight.

Topping: In pan, melt chocolate chips and butter for topping and spread quickly over filling. Chill again. Cut into small squares. Keep refrigerated.

Makes 24 squares

Karen Little

Chess Bars

Crust:
1(18.5-ounce) box Duncan Hines Butter Recipe cake mix
1 stick melted butter
1 cup chopped pecans
1 egg, slightly beaten

Filling:
1 (8-ounce) package cream cheese, room temperature
16 ounces confectioners' sugar
3 eggs
1 teaspoon vanilla extract

Crust: Preheat oven to 325 degrees. In mixer bowl, mix all ingredients and press into a 9 x 13 x 2-inch greased glass baking dish.
Filling: In bowl, mix all ingredients with electric mixer until smooth and pour onto the crust. Bake 1 hour, cool and cut into small squares.

Note: Can be frozen.

Makes 2 dozen bars

Karen Little

German Chocolate Chess Squares

1 (18.25 ounce) package German chocolate cake mix with pudding
1 large egg, lightly beaten
1/2 cup butter or margarine, melted
1 cup chopped pecans
1 (8-ounce) package cream cheese, room temperature
2 large eggs
1 (16-ounce) package confectioners' sugar, sifted

Preheat oven to 350 degrees. Combine first four ingredients in a large bowl, stirring until dry ingredients are moistened. Press into bottom of a greased 9 x 13 x 2-inch baking dish; set aside.

In mixer bowl, combine cream cheese, 2 eggs and 1 cup sifted confectioners' sugar. Beat at medium speed with an electric mixer until blended well. Gradually add remaining confectioners' sugar, beating well. Pour over chocolate layer and spread evenly.

Bake for 30 minutes. Cool in pan on wire rack and cut into squares.

Makes forty-eight 1-inch squares

Syble Murphy

Fudgy Chocolate-Raspberry Bars

Cake:
10 ounces bittersweet (not unsweetened) or semisweet chocolate, chopped
3/4 cup (1 1/2 sticks) unsalted butter, cut into small pieces
1/3 cup seedless raspberry jam
1 cup sugar
5 large eggs
1/3 cup all-purpose flour
1 teaspoon baking powder

Glaze:
1/4 cup whipping cream
1/4 cup seedless raspberry jam
6 ounces bittersweet (not unsweetened) or semisweet chocolate, chopped

Two 6-ounce baskets fresh raspberries

Cake: Preheat oven to 350 degrees. Line 9x9x2-inch baking pan with foil. Butter foil; dust with flour. Stir chocolate and butter in heavy medium saucepan over low heat until melted and smooth. Add jam and whisk until melted. Cool slightly.

Using electric mixer, beat sugar and eggs in large bowl until mixture thickens, about 6 minutes. Sift flour and baking powder over egg mixture and fold in. Gradually fold in chocolate mixture.

Pour batter into pan. Bake until top of cake is slightly crusty, begins to crack and tester inserted into center comes out with moist crumbs attached, about 45 minutes. Cool 5 minutes. Gently press down any raised edges of cake to even. Cool in pan. Invert cake onto platter. Peel off foil. Trim 1/2 inch off each edge of cake.

Glaze: Stir cream and jam in heavy small saucepan over medium heat until jam melts; bring to boil. Remove from heat. Add chocolate and stir until melted. Let stand until cool but still spreadable, about 15 minutes. Spread over cake layer and place raspberries on top.

Makes twenty-four 1-inch squares

Lemon Bars

1 cup all-purpose flour
1/4 cup confectioners' sugar
1/2 cup butter, room temperature
Pinch salt
2 eggs
1 cup sugar
1 tablespoon flour
2 tablespoons lemon juice

Preheat oven to 350 degrees. In mixer bowl, mix 1 cup flour, confectioners' sugar, butter and salt together. (It will be crumbly.) Pat this mixture into a greased 8 x 8-inch pan and bake for 15 minutes.
   Mix eggs, sugar, flour and lemon juice. Pour over the baked crust while hot. Return to oven and bake 25 minutes more. Remove from oven. Sprinkle with confectioners' sugar. Cool 15 minutes. Cut into squares.

Makes fifty 1-inch squares

Basic Cookie Dough

Take this basic dough and make 5 delicious cookie treats: Peanut Butter,
Pecan Refrigerator, Chocolate Chip, Sugar or Cinnamon.

2 eggs
1 1/2 cups sugar
2/3 cup butter
2/3 cup shortening
3 1/2 cups self-rising flour
2 teaspoons vanilla extract

Preheat oven to 375 degrees. Beat eggs slightly in large mixer bowl. Add remaining ingredients. Blend on low speed about 30 seconds and on medium speed until well- blended and has come together. Form into a ball and cut in half. Use any of the following recipes for your cookie choice.

Peanut Butter Cookies

1/2 Basic Cookie Dough
2/3 cup peanut butter

In mixer bowl, use 1/2 Basic Cookie Dough mixed with peanut butter. Mix thoroughly and roll into 1-inch balls. Place about 2 inches apart on an ungreased cookie sheet. Flatten with a fork. Bake 12 minutes or until set but not hard.

Pecan Refrigerator Cookies

1/2 Basic Cookie Dough
1 cup chopped pecans
Confectioners' sugar

In mixer bowl, use 1/2 Basic Cookie Dough mixed with pecans. Mix thoroughly and shape into two 7-inch rolls. Wrap in wax paper. Chill 2 hours or until firm enough to slice. Bake 10 minutes or until slightly brown. Roll in confectioners' sugar while warm.

Chocolate Chip Cookies

1/2 Basic Cookie Dough
2/3 cup light brown sugar
2 tablespoons water
1 (6-ounce) package semisweet chocolate pieces
1 cup chopped pecans

In mixer bowl, use 1/2 Basic Cookie Dough mixed with brown sugar, water, chocolate and pecans. Mix well. Drop dough by teaspoons onto ungreased baking sheet. Bake 8 to 10 minutes or until delicately brown.

Cinnamon Balls

1/2 Basic Cookie Dough
1/3 cup finely chopped pecans
2 tablespoons sugar
2 tablespoons ground cinnamon

In mixer bowl, use 1/2 Basic Cookie Dough mixed with pecans, sugar and cinnamon. Roll dough into 1-inch balls and roll the balls in the pecan, sugar and cinnamon mixture. Place 2 inches apart on an ungreased baking sheet. Bake 8 to 10 minutes.

Sugar Cookies

1/2 Basic Cookie Dough
Decorator's sugar, if desired

In mixer bowl, use 1/2 Basic Cookie Dough and roll dough 1/8-inch thick on a floured surface. Cut dough with a 2-to3-inch cutter. Place cookies on an ungreased baking sheet. Sprinkle with sugar or decorator's sugar. Bake 8 to 10 minutes. Cookies can also be frosted after baking.

Note: If dough seems too soft to cut out cookies, flatten dough ball into a flat disc, wrap and refrigerate at least 1 hour. Proceed with recipe.

Makes 3 dozen cookies

Carol Rollins

Favorite Chocolate Chip Cookies

1 cup (2 sticks) butter, room temperature
1 cup sugar
1 cup brown sugar
2 eggs, lightly beaten
2 teaspoons vanilla extract
2 cups all-purpose flour
2 cups oatmeal, processed in a food processor to a fine powder
1/2 teaspoon salt
1 teaspoon baking powder
1 teaspoon baking soda
1/4 teaspoon ground cinnamon
Freshly grated nutmeg
1 1/2 cups semisweet chocolate chips
1/2 cup grated bittersweet chocolate (not unsweetened)
2 cups chopped walnuts
3/4 cup shredded coconut, lightly toasted in a 350-degree oven for 5 minutes (optional)

Preheat the oven to 375 degrees. Lightly coat 2 baking sheets with nonstick spray. Set aside.

In a heavy-duty mixer combine the butter and the sugars. Beat until light and fluffy, about 2 minutes. Add the eggs and vanilla and mix well.

On a piece of wax paper, sift together the flour, processed oatmeal, salt, baking powder, baking soda, cinnamon and nutmeg to taste. Add to the butter-egg mixture and mix until all ingredients are moistened. Stir in the semisweet chocolate chips, grated chocolate and chopped walnuts. Add the toasted coconut if desired.

Shape mixture into balls of 1 to 1 1/2 tablespoons each. Place about 2 inches apart on the prepared baking sheets. Bake for 12 to 14 minutes, or until the cookies are golden brown. Remove from the oven and let sit on baking sheet a couple of minutes. Carefully transfer the cookies to a wire rack to cool completely.

Note: Store in airtight container for 1 week, or freeze for up to 3 months.

Makes about 4 dozen cookies

Chocolate Heart Cookies

These are great for wedding festivities!

Cookies:
3/4 pound (3 sticks) unsalted butter
1 3/4 cups sugar
2 eggs, lightly beaten
3 cups all-purpose flour
1 1/2 cups cocoa
1/4 teaspoon salt
1/3 teaspoon freshly ground black pepper
Pinch of cayenne pepper
1 teaspoon ground cinnamon

Icing:
Approximately 1 cup sifted confectioners' sugar
1 egg white
1/4 teaspoon freshly squeezed lemon juice

Cookies: Cream the butter and sugar together with an electric mixer in a large bowl until light and fluffy. Add the eggs and beat well.

Sift the dry ingredients together and stir by hand into the butter mixture until thoroughly incorporated. (You may need to add more flour if the dough seems too soft.) Divide the dough into three flat rounds, wrap in plastic wrap and chill for at least 1 hour.

Preheat the oven to 375 degrees. Lightly butter a baking sheet, or cover it with parchment paper.

On a well-floured board, roll out the dough to a thickness of slightly more than 1/8 inch. Cut the dough into 3-inch hearts, and place on the prepared baking sheet. Bake for 8 to 10 minutes, just until the cookies are crisp but not darkened. Let cool on wire racks.

Icing: To make the icing, mix the sugar, egg white and lemon juice in a bowl until very smooth and creamy. It should be the consistency of heavy cream; add more confectioners' sugar if necessary. When the cookies have cooled completely, dip one half into the icing, gently shake off the excess and place on a rack until the icing hardens. Store in an airtight container or freeze.

Note: May add the very smallest amount of red food color to make pale pink icing.

Makes 3 dozen 3-inch cookies

Christmas Cookies with Royal Icing

A really tasty sugar cookie that is good for Christmas cookies and little children. Use Royal Icing as it hardens when dry. Don't forget to save some for the children.

2 cups sifted all-purpose flour
1/4 teaspoon salt
1/2 teaspoon baking powder
8 tablespoons (1 stick) unsalted butter, room temperature
1 cup sugar
1 large egg
1 teaspoon vanilla extract or 1 teaspoon fresh lemon juice and zest of 1 lemon
Royal Icing (page 242)

In a large bowl, sift together flour, salt and baking powder. Set aside.

In the bowl of an electric mixer fitted with the paddle attachment, cream together butter and sugar until fluffy. Beat in egg. Add flour mixture and mix on low speed until thoroughly combined. Stir in vanilla or lemon juice and zest. Do not roll dough into a ball. Instead, roll and pat into a flat disc, wrap in plastic and chill for 30 minutes to an hour.

Preheat oven to 325 degrees. On a well-floured board, roll out dough to 1/8 inch. Cut into desired shapes. Place on ungreased baking sheet and chill until firm, about 15 minutes. Bake for 8 to 10 minutes, or until edges start to brown lightly. Cool on wire racks.

Makes about 4 dozen 3-inch cookies

Jane McCullough

Crescents

1 stick margarine, room temperature
1/2 cup vegetable shortening
1 cup pecan pieces
5 tablespoons confectioners' sugar
3 cups cake flour
1 tablespoon water
1 tablespoon vanilla extract

Preheat oven to 325 degrees. In mixer bowl, cream margarine and shortening. Add nuts and sugar. Add flour gradually, alternating with water and vanilla. Mix and shape into half moons (pinch off ball the size of marble). Bake on ungreased sheet for 20 minutes. Cover with confectioners' sugar after baking.

Makes 60 cookies

Desserts

Fruitcake Cookies

Make this cookie dough after Thanksgiving and bake as needed until Christmas. The dough may be refrigerated in an airtight container for up to 6 weeks!

16 ounces butter, melted and set aside
1 pound dark brown sugar
4 1/2 cups self-rising flour
1 tablespoon baking soda
3 quarts pecans, chopped
3 eggs, slightly beaten
3 tablespoons milk
1 teaspoon sherry or vanilla extract
1 (16-ounce) jar pineapple preserves
1 pound candied cherries, chopped
2 pounds dates, chopped

Preheat oven to 345 to 350 degrees. In very large bowl, mix sugar, flour and soda. Add pecans and mix. Add melted butter, eggs, milk and vanilla. Mix well. Add preserves, cherries and dates. Batter will be stiff. Drop by a rounded teaspoonfuls onto cookie sheet and bake for 12 to 15 minutes or until slightly brown. Works best if cooked as needed. Cookies tend to soften if stored.

Makes 500 cookies

Caryl Ward Littrell

Lemon Slices

Using half confectioners' sugar and half granulated sugar gives these cookies a melt-in-your-mouth texture.

2 cups all-purpose flour
1/4 teaspoon baking powder
1/4 teaspoon salt
2 to 3 large lemons
3/4 cup butter or margarine (1 1/2 sticks), room temperature
1/2 cup plus 2 tablespoons granulated sugar
1/2 cup confectioners' sugar
1/2 teaspoon vanilla extract

On sheet of wax paper, stir together flour, baking powder and salt. From lemons, grate 1 tablespoon peel and squeeze 2 tablespoons juice.

In large bowl, with mixer at medium speed, beat butter, 1/2 cup granulated sugar and confectioners' sugar until creamy. Beat in vanilla, lemon peel and juice until blended. Reduce speed to low and beat in flour mixture just until combined.

Divide dough in half. Shape each half into a 6-inch long log. Wrap each log in wax paper and refrigerate dough overnight. (If using margarine, freeze dough overnight.)

Preheat oven to 350 degrees. Keeping remaining log refrigerated, cut 1 log into scant 1/4-inch thick slices. Place slices, 1 1/2 inches apart, on ungreased large cookie sheet. Sprinkle lightly with some of remaining granulated sugar. Bake 12 minutes, or until lightly browned at edges. Cool on cookie sheet on wire rack 2 minutes. With wide spatula, transfer to wire rack to cool completely.

Repeat with remaining dough and sugar.

Note: The cookies will be 2 to 2 1/2 inches in diameter. If you prefer a smaller cookie, roll the dough into a thinner roll.

Makes 5 dozen cookies

Key Lime–White Chocolate Cookies

1/2 cup margarine or butter, room temperature
3/4 cup packed light brown sugar
2 tablespoons sugar
1 egg
1 1/2 teaspoons vanilla extract
2 1/3 cups Bisquick baking mix
6 ounces white chocolate (white baking bars) cut into chunks
1 tablespoon grated lime peel

Preheat oven to 350 degrees. Beat margarine, sugars, egg and vanilla in large bowl until well mixed. Stir in baking mix. Stir in white chocolate chunks and lime peel.

Drop dough by rounded teaspoonfuls onto greased cookie sheet.

Bake 8 to 10 minutes or until set, but not brown. Cool 1 minute before removing from cookie sheet. Cool on wire rack.

Makes about 3 1/2 dozen cookies

Syble Murphy

Marion's Dish Pan Cookies

4 cups all-purpose flour
2 cups light brown sugar
2 cups sugar
2 teaspoons baking soda
1/2 teaspoon salt
2 cups Quick Quaker Oats
4 cups cornflakes, uncrushed
2 cups golden raisins
2 cups flaked coconut
1 cup chopped nuts
2 cups canola oil
4 eggs
1 tablespoon vanilla extract

Preheat oven to 350 degrees. In large bowl, mix all dry ingredients together. Add oil, eggs and vanilla. Mix well. Roll into small balls and place on ungreased cookie sheet. Bake for 10 to 12 minutes or until light brown.

Makes about 5 to 6 dozen cookies

Marion Cross

Orange Shortbread

3 sticks (1 1/2 cups) butter or margarine, room temperature
1 cup plus 2 tablespoons sifted confectioners' sugar
1 tablespoon grated orange zest
3 cups all-purpose flour
Sugar for sprinkling

Preheat oven to 325 degrees. Beat butter at medium speed with an electric mixer until creamy; gradually add confectioners' sugar, beating until light and fluffy. Add orange zest. Gradually add flour, beating just until blended.

Press dough firmly into a lightly greased 15x10-inch jellyroll pan; pierce dough with a fork at 2-inch intervals. Sprinkle with sugar.

Bake for 30 to 35 minutes or until golden. Cut immediately into 2 1/2 x 1-inch bars.

Cool in pan on a wire rack.

Makes 2 dozen bars

Soft-Ball Stage

The soft-ball stage is reached when the mixture being cooked measures a temperature of 234 to 240 degrees. This is best determined using a candy thermometer. If no thermometer is available, the cold water test may be used. Use a fresh cup cold water for each test. Drop a small amount of the mixture into the cup. It will form a soft ball that flattens of its own accord when removed from the water.

Praline Thumbprint Cookies

1 cup unsalted butter, room temperature
1 cup sifted confectioners' sugar
2 cups all-purpose flour
1 cup finely chopped pecans
1 tablespoon vanilla extract

Praline Filling:
1/2 cup butter
1 cup firmly packed light brown sugar
Dash of salt
1/2 cup evaporated milk
2 cups sifted confectioners' sugar
1/2 teaspoon vanilla extract

Cookie: Preheat oven to 375 degrees. Cream butter; gradually add confectioners' sugar, beating well in electric mixer at medium speed. Add flour, mixing well. Stir in pecans and vanilla.

Shape dough into 1-inch balls; place about 2 inches apart on ungreased cookie sheet. Press thumb in center of each cookie to make an indentation. Bake for 10 to 13 minutes, until lightly brown. Cool on wire racks. Spoon about 1/2 teaspoon Praline Filling into each cookie indentation.

Praline Filling: Melt butter in saucepan. Add brown sugar and salt; bring to a boil. Boil 2 minutes, stirring constantly. Do not use highest heat. Remove from heat; stir in milk. Bring to a boil and let boil 2 minutes or until it reaches 232 degrees or near the soft-ball stage.

Remove praline mixture from heat. Let cool to lukewarm. Stir in confectioners' sugar and vanilla; beat with a wooden spoon until mixture is smooth.

Note: Make all cookies before preparing filling. The 1 1/2 cups filling is enough for 2 cookie recipes.

Makes 36 cookies

Judy Richardson

290 *Desserts*

The Ultimate Sugar Cookie

3 1/2 cups all-purpose flour
1 teaspoon baking powder
1/2 teaspoon salt
1 cup unsalted butter, room temperature (no substitute)
1 1/2 cups granulated sugar
2 eggs
2 teaspoons vanilla extract
Confectioners' sugar

Sift together flour, baking powder and salt. In a large bowl, using electric mixer, cream butter and sugar. Beat in eggs and vanilla. Gradually add dry ingredients and combine. Chill for at least 1 hour.

Preheat oven to 400 degrees. Remove half of dough from refrigerator and let stand at room temperature for 15 minutes. Lightly dust work surface with confectioners' sugar. Roll out dough to 1/4-inch thickness.

Cut with cookie cutters and place on greased baking sheets. Gather up scraps and chill. Repeat process using other half of dough. Combine scraps from both batches and repeat process. Bake until edges are lightly browned, 8 to 10 minutes. Cool on a wire rack.

Makes 3 dozen cookies

Syble Murphy

Cookie Baking

The most common mistake made when baking cookies is overbaking them. Cookies cook in a short time, usually at 350 to 375 degrees. A few degrees and a few extra minutes can make a difference. Often cookies look undercooked when they are actually perfectly done. Watch for browning on the edges which indicates that cookies are baked.

White Chocolate-Chunk Macadamia Cookies

2/3 cup butter or margarine (10 tablespoons plus 2 teaspoons) at room temperature
1/2 cup granulated sugar
1/2 cup packed dark brown sugar
1 large egg
1 teaspoon vanilla extract
1 1/2 cups all-purpose flour
1 (3-ounce) jar macadamia nuts, coarsely chopped (about 3/4 cup)
2 (3-ounce) bars white chocolate, chopped in 1/2-inch pieces

Heat oven to 325 degrees. Lightly grease two 17 x 14-inch cookie sheets. In large bowl of electric mixer beat butter, sugars, egg and vanilla at medium-high speed until fluffy. Reduce mixer speed to low, add flour, increase mixer speed gradually and beat just until blended. Stir in nuts and chocolate. Drop heaping tablespoonfuls of dough 2 1/2 inches apart onto prepared cookie sheets. Bake 1 sheet at a time 17 minutes or until edges of cookies are lightly browned and tops look dry. Cool on sheet on wire rack 5 minutes. Remove to rack to cool completely.

Makes 24 cookies

Chocolate Chews

Wrap up these minibites of chocolate for a gift. They're easy to make!

16 squares (16-ounces) semisweet chocolate
21 large marshmallows, cut into halves
1/2 cup walnuts or pecans, chopped
8 red candied cherries, cut into halves

Line an 8 x 8-inch baking pan with foil; grease foil. In top of double boiler placed over simmering water, melt chocolate stirring occasionally
    Scatter marshmallows in bottom of prepared pan, then nuts and cherries. Pour melted chocolate on top, spreading evenly. Refrigerate until firm, one hour. Cut into 1-inch squares.

Makes 64 squares

Chocolate-Toffee Crunch

1 1/2 packages saltine crackers, about 50 (uncrushed)
1/2 cup unsalted butter, no substitute
1/2 cup packed light brown sugar
1 (6-ounce) package semisweet chocolate chips

Preheat oven to 350 degrees. Spray a 13 x 17 1/2 x 1-inch cookie sheet (with sides) with cooking spray. Line with aluminum foil and spray again. Line bottom of cookie sheet with crackers.

Add butter and brown sugar to a small saucepan and boil for exactly 3 minutes, stirring constantly. Pour over crackers and spread. Bake in oven for 5 minutes.

Remove from oven and sprinkle chocolate chips over layer and spread with spoon to cover as chips melt. Put in refrigerator to harden, about 1 hour. Remove and break into pieces.

Belinda Elliott
Libby Smith

Divinity Candy

This candy is a perfect holiday candy. It's best to make it on a dry, sunny day.

3 cups sugar
1/2 cup white corn syrup
2/3 cup water
1 egg white
1/4 teaspoon salt
1 tablespoon vanilla extract
1 1/2 cups chopped pecans

In a heavy saucepan, heat the sugar, corn syrup and water over low heat until sugar is dissolved. Continue cooking to the hard-ball stage, 260 degrees. In a mixer bowl, using electric mixer, beat the egg white with salt until stiff peaks form. Pour the hot sugar syrup slowly into the egg white in a steady stream, whipping constantly. Add vanilla extract and beat until mixture holds its shape and loses its glossy sheen, about 10 minutes. Fold in chopped nuts. Drop the candy by tablespoons onto wax paper-covered racks and let dry at room temperature. Store in an airtight container. Best used within 48 hours.

Makes about 30 candies

Marion Cross

Desserts

White Chocolate Salties

1 pound white chocolate
2 tablespoons shortening
3 cups pretzel sticks
1 cup salted Spanish peanuts (can use dry roasted peanuts, unsalted)

Combine chocolate and shortening in top of double boiler; bring water to a boil. Reduce heat to low; cook until chocolate melts. Pour chocolate mixture into large mixing bowl. Stir in pretzels and peanuts; spread into a buttered 15 x 10 x 1-inch jelly roll pan (can use a cookie sheet). Chill 20 minutes or until firm; break into pieces. Store in airtight container.

Makes 1 1/2 pounds

Earline Berryman

Chocolate Sauce

3 squares semisweet chocolate
2 squares unsweetened chocolate
1/2 cup margarine
1 cup evaporated milk
1/3 cup milk
3 cups confectioners' sugar
1 1/2 teaspoons vanilla extract

In pan, melt chocolate and margarine. Add milk and sugar. Stir until boiling. Remove from heat and add vanilla.

Makes 2 cups sauce

Marlynn Rhyne

Hot Fudge Sauce

This is the kind of hot fudge sauce that becomes firm and sticky-chewy when ribboned over ice cream. Be sure your ice cream is frozen hard.

1/2 cup sugar
1/4 cup unsweetened cocoa
1/4 teaspoon salt
1/2 cup water
1 cup heavy cream
1 cup light corn syrup
1/4 teaspoon vinegar
4 ounces semisweet or bittersweet chocolate (2 ounces coarsely chopped and 2 ounces finely chopped)
4 tablespoons (1/2 stick) unsalted butter, room temperature
1 tablespoon vanilla extract

Whisk together in large, heavy saucepan, until blended, sugar, cocoa and salt. Whisk in 1/2 cup water until well blended. Bring this to a simmer over medium-high heat. Remove the pan from the heat and whisk in the heavy cream, corn syrup, vinegar and 2 ounces chocolate, coarsely chopped.
  Return to medium-high heat and, whisking frequently, boil until the bubbles become small and the syrup is thick and sticky, about 225 degrees on a candy thermometer. This will take 5 to 8 minutes. Remove from heat and add 2 ounces chocolate, finely chopped, butter and vanilla. Whisk until smooth. Serve at once, or let cool; cover and refrigerate for up to 2 weeks. Reheat in a heavy saucepan over low heat.

Makes 2 1/2 cups sauce

Freezing Egg Whites

Egg whites will keep in the freezer for up to a year. When fully thawed, they should beat up to the same volume as fresh egg whites, so you'll be able to use them in any other recipes that call for egg whites.

To freeze egg whites, carefully separate the eggs, making sure no bits of yoke remain in the whites. Transfer the egg whites to a container. They can be frozen unseparated in one container or frozen singly in ice cube trays and then turned out and sealed in a plastic bag—that saves you from having to measure the whites for future recipes. When you are ready to use the whites, allow them to thaw overnight in the refrigerator. If necessary, measure 2 tablespoons of thawed egg whites for each fresh egg white in the recipe. Egg whites that are covered tightly will also keep in the refrigerator for up to 4 days.

Desserts

Raspberry Sauce

1 (10-ounce) package frozen raspberries, thawed
1 tablespoon lemon juice
1/2 cup hot water
1/3 cup sugar
1 tablespoon cornstarch
1/4 teaspoon salt

Drain raspberries, reserving juice. In pan, combine reserved juice with all other ingredients except raspberries. Bring to a boil; reduce heat to medium and cook until mixture thickens, stirring constantly. Add raspberries and cook for 3 minutes. Let cool before serving.

Makes about 2 1/2 cups sauce

Strawberry Glaze

1 cup crushed strawberries
3/4 cup sugar
1 1/2 tablespoons cornstarch
1/4 cup cold water
Dash of salt
1 tablespoon butter

Combine in a saucepan the sugar, cornstarch, cold water and salt. Boil, stirring constantly, until thick and clear. Add butter and refrigerate. When cooled, add the crushed strawberries and serve over cheesecake, pound cake or ice cream.

Note: Any fresh fruit can be substituted.

Chocolate Dipped Strawberries

3 ounces semisweet chocolate, coarsely chopped
6 tablespoons butter or margarine
1/2 cup water
3 tablespoons safflower oil
3/4 cup cocoa
1/2 cup plus 2 tablespoons sugar
36 whole strawberries, unhulled (about two 1-pint baskets)

Combine the chocolate, butter, water and safflower oil in double boiler. Heat over simmering water until chocolate and butter melt, stirring to mix well; remove from heat.

Add the cocoa and sugar; mix until the sugar dissolves and the glaze is smooth. Chill until slightly thickened and completely cooled.

Dip the strawberries into the glaze, refrigerate and let stand until set.

Note: For easy cleanup, line cookie sheet with wax paper and place chocolate-dipped strawberries to set.

Makes 36 strawberries

Blueberry Sauce

In sauce pan, cook 1 pint fresh blueberries, 1/2 to 3/4 cup sugar, 1 teaspoon lemon juice and 1/4 cup water over low heat for 15 minutes.

Makes 1 1/2 pints sauce

Notes

Condiments and Basics/Charts

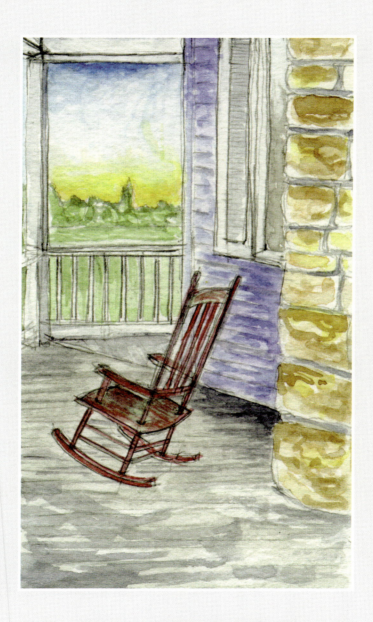

The Jesse Owens Memorial Park and Museum
Built 1896 - Restored 1995
Oakville, Alabama

*Condiments
Basics/Charts*

Cranberry and Apricot Chutney

This seasonal chutney has more than one thing in its favor: it can be made 4 days ahead and will probably show up on more menus than just as a turkey sidekick.

1 1/4 cups sugar
1/2 cup water
1 (12-ounce) package fresh cranberries (3 cups)
3/4 cup snipped dried apricots
3 tablespoons cider vinegar
3 tablespoons light brown sugar
1 tablespoon minced fresh ginger

In a 3-quart heavy saucepan combine sugar and water. Cook and stir over medium-high heat until sugar is dissolved. Bring to boiling without stirring.

Stir in cranberries, apricots, vinegar, brown sugar and ginger. Reduce heat. Simmer, uncovered, for 5 minutes or until berries have popped and mixture starts to thicken, stirring occasionally. Remove from heat and allow to cool. Cover; refrigerate up to 4 days. Bring to room temperature 30 minutes before serving.

Makes 3 1/2 cups chutney

Mexican Cranberries

1 (16-ounce) can whole-berry cranberry sauce
1 (10 1/2-ounce) jar jalapeño pepper jelly
2 tablespoons chopped fresh cilantro
Limes, optional

Combine first 3 ingredients in a small saucepan; cook over low heat until the jelly melts, stirring often. Cool and refrigerate.

Note: Remove pulp from lime halves and fill with Mexican Cranberries for a great garnish, or serve cranberries in a bowl.

Makes 2 1/2 cups sauce

Cherry Butter

This butter keeps in an airtight container, refrigerated, for several weeks. Serve it on hot biscuits! Yum!

1 stick butter, room temperature
1 (8-ounce) package cream cheese, room temperature
1/3 cup confectioners' sugar
1 (5-ounce) jar cherry preserves
Zest of 1 orange, finely grated

Process the butter, cream cheese and confectioners' sugar in a food processor to blend well. Stir in the preserves and zest by hand. Chill well before serving.

Makes 2 cups butter

Honey-Orange Butter

1/2 cup butter, room temperature
3/4 cup honey
1/2 teaspoon grated orange rind

In bowl, cream butter with electric mixer until light and fluffy. Slowly add honey and beat well. Add orange rind and mix well. Cover and refrigerate several hours.

Note: Serve with biscuits, waffles or pancakes.

Makes 1 1/3 cups butter

Betty Mitchell Sims

Apricot-Orange Jam

12 ounces dried apricots
1 cup sugar
Juice of 1 lemon
2 oranges, peeled and cut into sections (no white pulp)
2 to 3 tablespoons orange or lemon zest

Combine the apricots with enough water to cover in a saucepan. Bring to boil over high heat; reduce heat to low. Simmer until apricots are plump and tender, stirring occasionally. Add the sugar, stirring until dissolved. Cook for 10 minutes, stirring frequently. Remove from heat. Add the juice of 1 lemon and pulse in food processor until desired consistency.

Transfer apricot mixture to a bowl and pulse the peeled orange sections and the lemon zest until just broken up. Make sure there is no white pulp in the mixture, straining if necessary before adding to apricot mixture. Refrigerate and use within several days.

Makes 2 cups jam

Blackberry Jam

2 cups fresh blackberries
1 1/2 cups sugar

Combine blackberries and sugar in a pan. Cook over low heat until sugar is completely dissolved. Bring to a rolling boil, stirring frequently to prevent sticking. Boil until a small amount of the mixture dropped on a plate will stay in place. Spoon hot mixture into a jar.

Note: If jam is not to be used shortly, sterilize and seal the jars (page 306).

Makes 1 pint jam

Betty Mitchell Sims

Orange Marmalade Spread

1 tablespoon grated orange zest
1 (8-ounce) package cream cheese, room temperature
1/2 cup orange marmalade
2 tablespoons orange juice
1/2 cup chopped pecans

Place orange zest and cream cheese into food processor or blender. Process until smooth. Add marmalade, orange juice and nuts. Process until blended.

Makes 1 cup spread

Betty Mitchell Sims

Seasoned Mayonnaise

Our family loves leftover smoked turkey sandwiches as much as the Thanksgiving meal itself. An oversized yeast roll makes a great bun with this mayonnaise and crisp lettuce.

1 quart mayonnaise
1 teaspoon salt
2 teaspoons pepper
2 tablespoons prepared mustard
1/4 cup chopped parsley
1/4 cup chopped celery tops
1/4 cup chopped onion

Blend all ingredients together in a blender or food processor until thoroughly mixed. Refrigerate.

Makes 1 quart mayonnaise

Garlic Pickles

1/4 cup whole black peppercorns
3 or 4 cinnamon sticks
1/4 cup mustard seeds
5 pounds sugar
1 head garlic
1 gallon sour pickles

In bowl, mix peppercorns, cinnamon sticks, mustard seeds and sugar together. Set aside. Drain pickles and cut into 3 to 4-inch slices. Place the pickle slices in a large nonreactive container. Add the garlic head which has been separated into cloves and peeled. Add sugar mixture and mix well. Let the pickles cure for 3 weeks, stirring daily.

Makes 4 quarts pickles

Bobbi Shelton

Sweet Dill Pickles

My family calls these pickles "Grandmother's pickles" because she has made gallons and gallons and always has them on hand. Actually, the recipe was given to me by a dear neighbor, the late Patti Terry. Patti was from Hawaii. She and Bill named their children: Penny Alohi, Paige Au'Lihi, Piper Ahulani, Paula Aolani and Billy Powell, Jr. Good neighbors and good pickles!

Unpeeled cucumbers (length to stand up in a quart fruit jar)
2 garlic cloves per quart jar
2 fresh dill sprigs per quart jar
2 hot pepper pods per quart jar
2 cups apple cider vinegar
2 heaping teaspoons salt
1 1/2 cups sugar
1 cup water

Prepare large cucumbers by cutting into quarters lengthwise. Have 4 quart jars sterilized and tightly pack each jar with as many pickles as you can. To each jar, add 2 garlic cloves, 2 dill sprigs and 2 hot pepper pods.

In pan, mix vinegar, salt, sugar and water. Bring to a boil and add to the filled jars. Seal jars and put into water bath (with water to neck of jars). Boil for 10 minutes.

Makes 4 quarts pickles

Rubye Little

To Sterilize Jars and Glasses For Pickling and Preserving

Wash jars in hot suds and rinse in scalding water. Put jars in a kettle and cover with hot water. Bring water to a boil, cover, and boil jars for 15 minutes from time that steam emerges from kettle. Turn off heat and let jars stand in the hot water. Just before they are to be filled, invert jars onto a kitchen towel to dry. (The jars should be filled while they are still hot.) Sterilize jar lids for 5 minutes, or according to the manufacturer's instructions.

Quick Spiced Peaches

These spiced peaches are very good as an accompaniment for pork or poultry. They also make an attractive garnish.

1 (29-ounce) can cling peach halves, drained (reserve syrup)
1/2 cup light corn syrup
1/2 cup cider vinegar
1 tablespoon mixed pickling spice

Drain peaches, reserving syrup. In a sauce pan, mix reserved syrup, corn syrup, vinegar and pickling spice. Boil for 10 minutes. Add peaches and simmer gently for 5 minutes. Remove from heat and chill in refrigerator several hours or overnight.

Roasted Pepper and Black Olive Relish

2 roasted red bell peppers, peeled, seeded and diced
2 roasted green bell peppers, peeled, seeded and diced
1 cup pitted and coarsely chopped black olives
2 cloves garlic, finely chopped
1 tablespoon fresh thyme leaves
1/4 cup coarsely chopped parsley
1/4 cup sherry vinegar
1 tablespoon honey
Salt and freshly ground pepper

Combine all ingredients in a medium bowl and season with salt and pepper to taste. Serve at room temperature.

Note: Serve with Garlic and Oregano Marinated Chicken (page 143).

Tartar Sauce

1 cup mayonnaise
1 sweet pickle, chopped
Juice of 1/2 lemon
1 tablespoon grated yellow onion
1/2 teaspoon dried tarragon
Hot sauce, (Tabasco)

In bowl, mix together mayonnaise, sweet pickle, lemon juice, onion and tarragon. Add hot sauce to taste. Cover and refrigerate for at least 2 hours. Keeps 1 week.

Makes 1 cup sauce

Cilantro Tartar Sauce

1 cup mayonnaise
2 tablespoons chopped pitted olives
1 tablespoon freshly squeezed lemon juice
2 tablespoons capers, drained
1/4 cup chopped fresh cilantro
1 teaspoon Dijon mustard

In bowl, mix all ingredients well and season with salt and pepper.

Makes 1 1/4 cups

Caryl Ward Littrell

Water Bath Processing

Immerse sealed jars in actively boiling water, making sure jars do not touch each other. Water must cover jars by 1 to 2 inches. Cover and return to boil over high heat. If product contains vinegar, jars should be processed 10 minutes. Without vinegar, half-pints and pints should be processed for 15 minutes and quarts for 20 minutes. Jars are properly sealed if, after contents have cooled, lids have "popped down". Store in a cool, dry place.

Note: Preserves, pickles, relishes and chutneys should be processed in a water bath. Jellies, however, do not need water bath processing.

Roasted Corn and Tomato Tartar Sauce

1 (15-ounce) can niblet corn, drained
1/4 cup mayonnaise
2 Roma tomatoes, peeled, seeded and diced
2 green onions, minced (include green tops)
1/2 teaspoon Creole Seasoning (page 318)
1/4 teaspoon salt
Freshly ground black pepper

Preheat oven to 350 degrees. Place corn in single layer on a baking sheet and roast in oven 15 minutes. In bowl, combine corn, mayonnaise, tomatoes, onions, Creole seasoning and salt. Season with pepper. Cover and refrigerate until ready to use. Use same day.

Makes 2 cups sauce

Chili Glaze

1/2 cup champagne vinegar
1 to 2 tablespoons red chili flakes
1 tablespoon minced garlic
2 tablespoons minced red onion
2 cups packed light brown sugar
1/2 cup soy sauce or to taste
1 teaspoon salt
2 tablespoons tomato paste
1/2 to 1 stick butter, cut into chunks

In pan, simmer vinegar, chili flakes, garlic and onion until reduced 50%. Add brown sugar, soy sauce, salt and tomato paste and simmer for 3 minutes. Remove from heat and whisk in butter chunks, one at a time.

Note: Serve as a sauce with pork, lamb or game. Glaze will keep 2 weeks refrigerated.

Makes 2 cups glaze

Tim Littrell

Clueless Barbecue Sauce

Those who reckon that college football is merely another sporting event should go to an Auburn-Alabama game. The atmosphere is like that of no other game, and the spirit and heritage of one's alma mater becomes a big deal! Count the generations of family members who are Auburn or Alabama graduates, and there are grounds for even more bragging rights!

Whenever games are played in Tuscaloosa, lots of folks crowd to Dreamland, known far and wide for its ribs. The sauce is a major secret and we don't have a clue, but this sauce is good!

1 (14-ounce) can tomato purée
1 1/2 cups water
1/4 cup yellow mustard
3/4 cup cider vinegar
1/8 cup dark corn syrup
1 tablespoon lemon juice
1 tablespoon sugar
1 tablespoon chili powder
1 tablespoon brown sugar
1 1/2 teaspoons dry mustard
1 1/2 teaspoons paprika
1 teaspoon ground red pepper
1 teaspoon onion powder
1/2 teaspoon salt
1/2 teaspoon ground black pepper
1/4 teaspoon garlic powder

Mix tomato purée, water and 1/4 cup mustard together in saucepan. Add remaining ingredients and stir. Bring to boil, reduce heat and simmer 30 minutes.

Note: Use this on ribs the last 30 minutes of cooking. This is not a basting sauce.

Makes 1 quart

Quick-Cleaning the Blender

Fill dirty blender bowl half-full with hot water and add a couple of drops of liquid detergent. With top firmly in place, turn blender on high for 30 seconds. A much easier clean up!

Hot Cocktail Sauce

Good with boiled shrimp or raw oysters.

2 cups chili sauce
2 cups ketchup
1/2 cup prepared horseradish
1 teaspoon hot mustard
2 tablespoons Worcestershire sauce
1/4 cup lemon juice
1/2 teaspoon Tabasco sauce
1/2 teaspoon salt
2 tablespoons finely chopped parsley
1/2 cup minced onion
3 stalks celery, finely chopped

Combine all ingredients in blender and blend well.

Makes 4 cups sauce

Batter for Deep Frying

For the finest onion rings, fish and shrimp, it is virtually impossible to find a more delicious, yet simple-to-make, batter than the classic beer batter. Two simple rules: use exactly the same proportions of plain flour and beer and blend well, and allow the batter to stand at room temperature no less than 3 hours. The alcohol in the beer quickly disappears when heated, and what's left is a delightful taste.

Bouquet Garni

8 sprigs fresh thyme or 1 teaspoon dried
1 bay leaf
2 to 3 celery leaves
Small bunch parsley

Wrap bouquet garni in a 4 x 4-inch piece of cheesecloth and tie with a string or omit the cheesecloth and tie the herbs with string.

Refrigerate in tightly covered container until ready to use.

Crème Fraîche

1 cup heavy cream
1 cup sour cream

Whisk heavy cream and sour cream together in a bowl. Cover and let stand in a warm place overnight or until thickened.

Stir well, cover and refrigerate for at least 4 hours.

Will keep in refrigerator for up to 2 weeks.

Makes 2 cups crème fraîche

Buttered Bread Crumbs

6 slices stale white bread (pulse in food processor until a coarse size)
2 tablespoons butter

Melt butter in skillet over medium heat. Pour bread crumbs into skillet and toss until golden brown. Set aside. Top desired dish and bake 10 to 15 minutes at 375 degrees.
Variation: For seasoned bread crumbs, add 1 teaspoon salt, pepper and 1/2 teaspoon herb of choice (dried chives, tarragon or rosemary). Also, 3 tablespoons Parmesan cheese can be added.

Makes 3 cups crumbs

Cracker Crumb Topping

1 sleeve saltine crackers, crushed
1/2 cup butter, melted

Preheat oven to 375 degrees. Mix crushed crackers (may be done in food processor) and melted butter together. Sprinkle over dish and bake for 15 minutes.

Makes 1 1/2 cups topping

Croutons

6 tablespoons butter
1/2 teaspoon seasoned salt
1 cup bread cubes

In skillet, melt butter. Add seasoned salt and sauté bread cubes until lightly browned on all sides. Drain on paper towels.

Baked Croutons

6 (1-inch) slices crusty white bread, cut into 3/4-inch cubes
3 tablespoons olive oil
1 teaspoon minced garlic
1 tablespoon fresh parsley, minced
Coarse salt to taste

Heat oven to 350 degrees. In a medium-size bowl, toss bread cubes with olive oil, garlic and parsley; season with salt. On a parchment-lined baking sheet, toast croutons until golden brown, 10 to 15 minutes.

Makes 96 croutons

Roasted Garlic

3 to 4 garlic heads

Preheat oven to 425 degrees. Place garlic heads in a baking dish. Bake until soft, approximately 30 minutes. Let garlic cool; then squeeze out the pulp.

Makes 1/2 cup purée

Fruit Glazes

Fruit preserve glazes add taste and give a glistening sheen to fresh fruit toppings used on fruit tarts.

Red Currant Glaze:
Place 3 to 4 tablespoons red currant jelly and 2 to 3 teaspoons water into a small pan and let stand over low heat until the jelly has melted and is completely clear. Let cool until slightly thickened but use while still warm. This glaze covers a 9-inch fruit tart.

Apricot Glaze:
Place 1 cup apricot jam and 3 tablespoons water into a small pan and let stand over low heat until the jam has melted. Pour into a sieve over a small bowl and press through with a wooden spoon. Keeps in the refrigerator, in a sterilized screw-top jar, for 2 weeks. Warm before use.

Makes about 1 cup glaze

Condiments and Basics/Charts

Honey Glaze for Baked Ham

1/3 cup sugar
2/3 cup light brown sugar, firmly packed
1 1/2 teaspoons ground nutmeg
1 teaspoon ground cloves
1/2 teaspoon ground cinnamon
1/2 cup honey

In bowl, combine sugar and spices, mixing well. Brush baked ham generously with honey. Pat brown-sugar mixture over honey, coating ham thoroughly. Return ham to oven after glazing, and bake 30 to 45 minutes for sugar to melt.

Makes glaze for 1/2 ham

Mayonnaise

1 tablespoon lemon juice
2 egg yolks
1/2 teaspoon Dijon mustard
1/2 teaspoon salt
Freshly ground black pepper
2 teaspoons white wine vinegar
1 1/2 cups vegetable oil

Add ingredients except oil to bowl of a food processor and pulse until well blended. With machine on, drizzle the first 1/4 cup of oil very slowly into mixture until emulsion starts to form. With machine still running, add rest of oil more quickly.

Makes 2 cups mayonnaise

Meringue

4 large egg whites
1/4 teaspoon cream of tartar
6 tablespoons sugar

Preheat oven to 350 degrees. Beat egg whites in a medium-size bowl until frothy. Add cream of tartar; gradually add sugar and beat until stiff peaks form.

Spoon meringue on top of dessert, spreading to cover the entire surface and sealing edges well. Bake in center of oven 15 to 20 minutes or until meringue is golden brown.

Makes meringue for 9-inch dessert

Sky-High Meringue

Make any pie a show-stopper with this meringue. Be sure to adjust oven racks for the extra height!

1 cup sugar
1/2 cup water
8 egg whites
1 teaspoon cream of tartar

Preheat oven to 350 degrees. Combine sugar and water in saucepan; bring to boil. Cook, without stirring, until candy thermometer registers 240 degrees. In large mixing bowl, beat egg whites and cream of tartar at high speed of mixer until foamy. Pour hot sugar syrup in a thin stream over egg white mixture; beat at high speed until stiff peaks form. Spread meringue over filling; seal to edge of crust. Bake for 15 minutes or until lightly browned.

Meringue for 1 pie

Pastry Dough

1 1/3 cups all-purpose flour
1/4 cup cold butter, diced
1/3 cup vegetable shortening
1/4 teaspoon salt
3 to 4 tablespoons ice water

In a bowl with a pastry cutter or in a food processor, blend or pulse flour, butter, shortening and salt until mixture resembles coarse meal. Add ice water, 1 tablespoon at a time, over flour mixture until pastry begins to hold together. On a work surface, knead dough in 3 or 4 forward motions with heel of hand. Form dough into a ball and flatten into a disc. Wrap dough in plastic and refrigerate 1 hour or overnight.

Adjust rack to lowest 1/3 of oven. Preheat oven to 425 degrees. On a floured surface, roll pastry with floured rolling pin to a 13-inch circle. Place pastry into a 9-inch pie plate, gently pressing pastry along bottom and side of pie plate. Trim edge and flute. Freeze 15 minutes. Line pie shell with foil. Fill with dried beans or rice. Bake 12 to 14 minutes until edge of crust is set and lightly colored. Remove foil with beans and bake crust 10 to 12 minutes, until bottom and sides are golden brown. Cool completely on a wire rack.

Makes one 9-inch pie shell

Sweet Pie Pastry Dough

1 1/4 cups all-purpose flour
1/4 teaspoon salt
1/2 cup confectioners' sugar
1 teaspoon finely grated lemon zest
6 tablespoons chilled butter, cut into pieces
1 egg yolk, lightly beaten
1 tablespoon ice water

Sift the flour, salt and sugar into the bowl of the food processor. Add the lemon zest and the chilled butter pieces and blend in short bursts for 10 to 15 seconds, or until it has formed a fine crumblike mixture. Do not allow the crumbs to form into large lumps as this will overwork the mixture.

Mix the egg yolk with water. With the motor running, quickly pour the liquid into the bowl and blend a few seconds until mixture has formed a compact ball. Turn the pastry out on a lightly floured surface, knead briefly and gently until smooth, then cover tightly with plastic wrap and chill for at least 1 hour before using, but overnight is best. Allow pastry to come back to room temperature; then knead briefly before using. To bake, preheat oven to 375 degrees. Roll out dough and place into pie plate. Refrigerate crust 20 minutes and bake until edges are lightly brown, about 20 minutes.

Note: Pastry will keep in the refrigerator for 4 to 5 days, tightly covered in plastic wrap.

Makes one 9-inch pie shell

Graham Cracker Crust

20 whole graham crackers, (10 ounces) broken
1 1/2 sticks chilled unsalted butter, diced
1/2 cup packed light brown sugar

Preheat oven to 350 degrees. Combine graham crackers, butter and sugar in processor. Pulse until crumbs begin to stick together. Press crumbs into pie plate. Bake 10 minutes.

Variation: Vanilla wafer crumbs can be substituted.

Makes one 9 to 10-inch pie shell

Four-Season Citrus Salt

This homemade seasoned salt is excellent on fish or chicken. It's also a nice alternative to creamy butter sauces.

1/2 cup of your favorite salt
Grated rind of 1 orange
Grated rind of 1 lemon
Grated rind of 2 limes
Handful of chopped fresh tarragon

In bowl, mix all of the above ingredients well. Sprinkle over food just before cooking.

Caryl Ward Littrell

Creole Seasoning

3 tablespoons salt
3 tablespoons paprika
2 1/2 tablespoons cayenne pepper
2 tablespoons black pepper
2 tablespoons garlic powder
1 1/2 tablespoons onion powder
1 tablespoon powdered thyme
1 tablespoon oregano

Mix well and store in a glass jar. Keeps indefinitely. Use to spice shrimp, fish and chicken.

Beef Stock

3 pounds beef shank bones, cut into 2-inch pieces
4 lean short ribs of beef
4 celery ribs
2 whole carrots
1 large yellow onion, halved
2 bay leaves
1 sprig fresh thyme
2 whole scallions
1 whole head of garlic
1/2 teaspoon whole black peppercorns

Preheat oven to 400 degrees. Place all ingredients in an 8-quart Dutch oven. Add 2 cups water and roast in oven 30 minutes.

Remove pot from oven and add water to cover. Simmer on top of stove for 3 to 4 hours. Add water as needed keeping bones and meat pieces covered. When done, let stock cool, and strain. Refrigerate for up to 5 days or freeze.

Makes 3 cups stock

Chicken Stock

4 pounds chicken pieces (backs, necks, drumsticks and wings)
1 large onion, quartered
1 large carrot, quartered
1 rib celery, quartered
1 bouquet garni (page 311)
6 whole peppercorns

Put chicken, vegetables and seasoning into a 6-quart pot and add cold water to cover. Bring to a simmer and cook gently for 1 1/2 hours, occasionally skimming with a spoon. Do not let stock boil. As broth cooks, keep adding enough water to cover meat pieces. Strain broth. Let cool and refrigerate for up to 5 days or freeze.

Makes 2 quarts stock

Condiments and Basics/Charts   319

Quick Chicken Broth

3 (14-ounce) cans chicken broth
Chicken giblets, trimmings or bones (optional)
1 bouquet garni, no need to wrap, (page 311)
1 small onion
1 carrot
1 celery rib
1 garlic clove (optional)

Combine broth, chicken trimmings and bouquet garni in heavy saucepan.

Cut onion, carrot, celery and garlic into 1-inch pieces and pulse in a food processor until finely chopped; add to broth. Bring almost to a boil, reduce heat and simmer for 30 minutes. Strain, cool and refrigerate.

Makes 4 cups broth

Turkey Stock

Gizzard, neck and liver from turkey cavity or turkey carcass
    and accompanying bits of meat from leftover Thanksgiving turkey
1 large onion, quartered
3 ribs celery, chopped
3 tablespoons butter
2 tablespoons paprika
1 tablespoon black pepper
1 teaspoon sage
1 teaspoon Tabasco

Place all ingredients in a large pot. Cover with water and cook on medium heat for 1 1/2 hours. Do not boil. Add water to keep meat and bone pieces covered.

Simple Syrup

1/2 cup water
1 cup sugar

Place water and sugar in heavy-bottomed pan. Cook over low heat, stirring constantly, until sugar has completely dissolved and liquid is clear. Bring to a rolling boil and immediately remove pan from heat. Leave syrup until absolutely cold. Pour into jar and seal. Keep refrigerated until needed.

Note: This syrup is used to moisten and flavor cake layers. Two teaspoons vanilla extract or other flavorings may also be added to the syrup.

Lots of Simple Syrup

5 pounds sugar
Hot water

Put 5 pounds sugar in a gallon jug and fill the remainder of the jug with water. Stir until sugar dissolves and syrup is clear. (Hot water speeds up the process.) Cool completely. Can be refrigerated for up to 1 month.

Makes 1 gallon syrup

Toast Cups

12 slices white bread, crust removed
1/4 cup butter, melted

Preheat oven to 340 degrees. Cut bread into 2-inch squares. Press gently into miniature muffin tins and brush each with butter. Toast until tips are brown, about 8 minutes. These can be made ahead and frozen.

Note: Toast cups do not absorb the moisture of chicken salad as pastry shells do.

Makes 24 toast cups

Toast Points

12 thin slices of sandwich bread, crust removed

Cut bread slices in half on the diagonal. Preheat oven to 300 degrees. Arrange on baking sheet. Bake, turning once, until dry and lightly toasted, 5 to 7 minutes per side. Transfer to wire rack to cool. Store in airtight container in refrigerator for up to a week or freeze for up to 6 months.

Note: Use for the simplest hors d'oeuvres. For more substantial accompaniments, such as salsas and heavy dips, grill the bread.

Makes 24 toast points

Magic Whipped Cream Frosting

Most whipped cream frostings don't hold up well, so use a bit of dissolved unflavored gelatin to give the whipped cream some stiffness and staying power.

1 teaspoon unflavored gelatin
2 cups heavy cream
1/4 cup confectioners' sugar
1/2 teaspoon vanilla extract

Chill bowl and beaters of an electric mixer in the freezer for at least 10 minutes.
　　　Sprinkle gelatin over 2 tablespoons water in a small saucepan. Let dissolve for 4 minutes. Over very low heat, melt gelatin mixture, about 3 minutes.
　　　Place heavy cream and melted gelatin into the chilled bowl. Beat on low speed for 30 seconds until dissolved gelatin is thoroughly mixed into cream. Increase speed to high and beat until cream starts to take shape. Add sugar and vanilla and beat until stiff.

Note: Makes enough to frost the top and sides of an 8 or 9-inch cake.

Sweetened Whipped Cream

1 cup whipping cream
1/4 cup confectioners' sugar
1 teaspoon vanilla extract

Chill whipping cream, bowl and beaters before whipping the cream. Beat all ingredients at medium speed with electric mixer until soft peaks form. Add confectioners' sugar and vanilla extract. Mix well.

Makes 2 cups cream

Chocolate Brittle for Garnish

11 ounces semisweet chocolate chips
Confectioners' sugar

Melt the semisweet chocolate chips in a stainless steel bowl set over simmering water. Stir until chocolate has melted and is smooth.

Line a baking sheet with parchment or wax paper. Pour the chocolate onto the baking sheet and spread evenly. Let cool; then chill until it sets. Break the chocolate into pieces, like brittle. Mound the pieces on top of cake, sticking them in at various angles. Sprinkle with confectioners' sugar.

Chocolate Curls

A chocolate garnish adds to the presentation of a dessert. Piled atop a dessert, curls make a festive crown. A curl can also dress individual servings. The type of curl created will be determined largely by the temperature of the chocolate when you begin scraping. How you scrape chocolate from the pan also affects the curls. Practice makes perfect!

Melt 2 ounces finely broken chocolate (semisweet or white chocolate) in microwave, stirring chocolate at 1 minute intervals. When it is just melted, spread it in a thin layer on the bottom of an inverted glass baking dish or baking sheet. You may need to refrigerate for a minute or two.

Chocolate is ready for curlmaking when it's firm but not hard. A lightly pressed finger leaves a slight print on room temperature chocolate. These conditions produce big, loose curls if a pastry scraper is held at a 45-degree angle and pushed straight forward. Colder chocolate produces tighter curls or thatch. Chill or freeze curls until needed.

Makes 6 to 8 curls

How to Melt Chocolate

Double Boiler Method: Break chocolate into small pieces and place in top pan of double boiler over hot, but not boiling water. Allow chocolate to melt, stirring occasionally.

Microwave Method: Using a microwave-safe container, place chocolate in microwave at medium power (50%) for 1 to 1 1/2 minutes. Remove and stir. If not melted, return to microwave and repeat, stirring every 30 seconds to avoid scorching. If small lumps remain, remove and continue to stir to complete melting.

Preparing Fresh Coconut

1 heavy coconut without cracks and containing liquid with a distinct sloshing

Preheat oven to 400 degrees. Pierce the 3 eyes of the coconut with an ice pick or metal skewer; drain and reserve liquid.
     Bake coconut in oven for 15 minutes. With a hammer, break shell and remove flesh carefully with point of a strong knife. Remove brown membrane with a sharp paring knife or vegetable peeler.

To grate coconut:
Chop coconut and in a blender or food processor fitted with metal blade, grate in batches.

To shred coconut:
In food processor fitted with fine shredding blade, shred coconut meat from 1 coconut in batches or shred by hand on fine shredding side (small tear-shaped holes) of a 4-sided grater.

To shave coconut:
With a vegetable peeler, shave edges of coconut meat pieces.

Note: Coconut may be prepared 1 day ahead and chilled in a sealable plastic bag.

Makes about 2 1/2 cups coconut

Just Right Egg Whites

Egg whites won't expand to their greatest volume if even a speck of yolk is in them. Separate eggs carefully (and perhaps individually).

Use eggs that are room temperature, not cold from the refrigerator. (Cold eggs are easier to separate, though; so divide and then bring to room temperature.)

Water and fat weigh down whites. Make sure your bowl and beater are clean, dry and grease-free.

Mix egg whites at medium speed of an electric mixer until soft peaks form (about 1 minute). At the soft-peak stage, egg whites mound but don't form sharp tips. At this stage, begin adding sugar, 1 tablespoon at a time, and increase mixer speed to high.

At the stiff-peak stage, sharp tips form when the beaters are lifted.

Over-beaten egg whites look dry, dull and curdled.

Condiments and Basics/Charts

Edible Flowers

Colorful flower garnishes add sparkle to desserts, but not all flowers are edible. Even with edible flowers, avoid those sprayed with chemicals or pesticides.

Listed are common names of flowers which you can safely use:

Chives	Forget-me-Not
Lavender	Squash blossoms
Nasturtium	Pansy
Rose	Snapdragon
Violet	Lemon-Gem Marigold
Bee balm	

The Best Mashed Potatoes

Follow this chart to whip up the perfect batch of fluffy spuds for any size gathering

Servings	Potatoes	Butter/Marg.	Hot Milk	Salt	Pepper	Makes
8	2 Lbs.	3 Tbs.	3/4 cup	1/4 tsp.	1/8 tsp.	4 cups
16	4 Lbs.	6 Tbs.	1 1/2 cups	1/2 tsp.	1/4 tsp.	8 cups
24	6 Lbs.	1/2 Cup	2 to 2 1/4 cups	3/4 tsp.	1/2 tsp.	12 cups

Method:

Peel and cut potatoes into 1 1/2-inch chunks. Bring potatoes with enough cold water to cover to boil in large saucepan or Dutch oven. Reduce heat to medium and cook 16 to 18 minutes until fork-tender. Drain in colander. Return potatoes to pan; cook over medium heat, stirring, 1 minute to dry.

Add softened butter, milk, salt and pepper. Combine on low speed. Beat at high speed 2 minutes until light and fluffy.

Meat Roasting Guide

Thermometer reading of meat's internal temperature is as follows:

Pork   160 to 165 degrees (sit 10 minutes before serving)

Lamb   Rare-130 to 140 degrees

Medium-150 to 160 degrees

Well Done-165 to 170 degrees

Beef   Rare-135 to 140 degrees

Medium-155 to 160 degrees

Well Done-165 to 170 degrees

Poultry   170 degrees

Approximate Total Cooking Times For Grilled And Broiled Steaks

Consult the chart below for cooking times for your steaks. Turn them once just past the halfway point in the cooking time.

Steak Type	Thickness	Rare	Medium-Rare	Medium
Tenderloin, filet flank or skirt steak	1 inch	6 to 8 minutes	8 to 10 minutes	10 to 12 minutes
	2 inches	12 to 14 minutes	14 to 18 minutes	18 to 20 minutes
Boneless top loin, rib sirloin, top round or chuck steak	1 inch	6 to 8 minutes	8 to 10 minutes	10 to 12 minutes
	2 inches	16 to 18 minutes	18 to 20 minutes	20 to 22 minutes
Bone-in T-bone, porterhouse, rib top loin or sirloin steak	1 inch	10 to 12 minutes	12 to 16 minutes	16 to 18 minutes
	2 inches	18 to 20 minutes	20 to 24 minutes	24 to 28 minutes

To Core A Fresh Pineapple

Cut off leaves at base. Slice off bottom rind, and stand pineapple on its base. Cut off the rind from the sides, being sure to remove as many eyes as possible. For rings, the fruit can be sliced crosswise and the core of each slice cut out with a small knife.

If not using rings, cut the pineapple lengthwise into quarters or thirds. Cut away the core; then slice the quarters or thirds into chunks or wedges if needed.

Toasting Seeds and Nuts

Toasting nuts and seeds brings out their fullest flavors.

Place nuts in single layer on rimmed baking sheet in 350-degree oven. Shake midway. Here's a more precise chart:

Pecan halves	7 to 13 minutes
Pecans, chopped	3 to 5 minutes
Almonds, whole	5 to 10 minutes
Almonds, sliced	4 to 7 minutes
Pine nuts	about 4 minutes
Pumpkin seeds	30 minutes at 250 degrees (dry overnight after removing from pumpkin) Sesame seeds 2 to 3 minutes in an ungreased skillet over medium high heat

Season A Cast-Iron Skillet

Wash and dry a new skillet. Rub all over, inside and out, with vegetable shortening and place on a baking sheet in a 300-degree oven to "cure" for at least an hour. (It should develop a shiny and smooth glaze.) Turn oven off and let skillet remain in oven overnight. In the morning, wipe skillet with a barely dampened cloth. Thereafter, clean skillet after each use by rinsing in hot water, scrubbing if necessary with a wire brush and drying well. Never use soap, never let soak and always dry thoroughly to prevent rust.

If rust does develop, pour salt over the area, scour, wipe off and reseason the skillet.

If you have 1 skillet earmarked for "cornbread only," you probably can just wipe the skillet and avoid washing altogether.

Blanching Vegetables

Many vegetables used for crudités benefit from a quick immersion in rapidly boiling water for blanching. Blanching maximizes their flavor and color and makes them tender, yet crispy. Vegetables are best blanched no longer than 6 hours before using.

Vegetables require varying amounts of blanching time depending upon size. Consider also if the vegetable is to be cooked a second time as in a sauté.

Asparagus   3 to 6 minutes, depending on thickness of stalk

Green Beans   2 to 5 minutes, depending on freshness and size

Broccoli   3 to 6 minutes to tenderize and brighten color

Brussels Sprouts   About 8 minutes to tenderize

Carrots   3 to 6 minutes to brighten color

Cauliflower   5 to 6 minutes

Snow Peas   1 minute

Sugar Snap Peas   4 minutes

Measurement Equivalents

Liquid Measures

1 gallon =	4 quarts =	8 pints =	16 cups =	128 fluid ounces
1/2 gallon =	2 quarts =	4 pints =	8 cups =	64 fluid ounces
1/4 gallon =	1 quart =	2 pints =	4 cups =	32 fluid ounces
	1/2 quart =	1 pint =	2 cups =	16 fluid ounces
	1/4 quart =	1/2 pint =	1 cup =	8 fluid ounces

Dry Measures

1 cup =	8 fluid ounces =	16 tablespoons =	48 teaspoons
3/4 cup =	6 fluid ounces =	12 tablespoons =	36 teaspoons
2/3 cup =	5 1/3 fluid ounces =	10 2/3 tablespoons =	32 teaspoons
1/2 cup =	4 fluid ounces =	8 tablespoons =	24 teaspoons
1/3 cup =	2 2/3 fluid ounces =	5 1/3 tablespoons =	16 teaspoons
1/4 cup =	2 fluid ounces =	4 tablespoons =	12 teaspoons
1/8 cup =	1 fluid ounce =	2 tablespoons =	6 teaspoons
		1 tablespoon =	3 teaspoons

Condiments and Basics/Charts   331

Substitution Savvy

When you're in the middle of a recipe and discover an ingredient is missing, the solution may be on your pantry shelf.

Baking Products:

Needed Ingredient:	*Substitute:*
1 cup confectioners' sugar	1 cup sugar plus 1 tablespoon cornstarch (processed in food processor)
1 cup honey	1 1/4 cups sugar plus 1/4 cup water
1 cup chopped pecans	1 cup regular oats, toasted (in baked products)
1 cup light corn syrup	1 cup sugar plus 1/4 cup water

Dairy Products:

Needed Ingredient: *Substitute:*

1 cup milk

1/2 cup evaporated milk plus 1/2 cup water

1 cup whipping cream

3/4 cup milk plus 1/3 cup melted butter (for baking only; will not whip)

1 cup plain yogurt

1 cup buttermilk

1 cup sour cream

1 cup yogurt plus 3 tablespoons melted butter or 1 cup yogurt plus 1 tablespoon cornstarch

1 cup buttermilk

1 tablespoon white vinegar or lemon juice plus milk to equal 1 cup

Vegetable products:

Needed Ingredient: *Substitute:*

1 pound fresh mushrooms, sliced

1 (8-ounce) can sliced mushrooms, drained, or 3 ounces dried mushrooms

3 tablespoons chopped red bell pepper

2 tablespoons chopped pimiento

3 tablespoons chopped shallots

2 tablespoons chopped onion plus 1 tablespoon minced garlic

Seasoning products:

Needed Ingredient:	Substitute:
1 tablespoon grated fresh horseradish	2 tablespoons prepared horseradish
1 tablespoon dried orange peel	1 1/2 teaspoons orange extract or 1 tablespoon grated fresh orange rind
1 tablespoon crystallized ginger	1/8 teaspoon ground ginger
1 (1-inch) vanilla bean	1 teaspoon vanilla extract
1 teaspoon garlic salt	1/8 teaspoon garlic powder plus 7/8 teaspoon salt
1 teaspoon dry mustard	1 tablespoon prepared mustard

Miscellaneous products:

Needed Ingredient:	Substitute:
1/2 cup balsamic vinegar	1/2 cup red wine vinegar (slight flavor difference)
1 cup tomato juice	1/2 cup tomato sauce plus 1/2 cup water
2 cups tomato sauce	3/4 tomato paste plus 1 cup water

Substitutions for Herbs and Spices

Herbs and spices each have their own flavor and aroma. The following substitutions are only recommended for emergencies and may change the intended flavor of the recipe. They are only intended for a tablespoon or two. Recipes calling for large amounts of fresh herbs should only use fresh herbs.

1 tablespoon fresh herbs =   1 teaspoon dried herbs

1 teaspoon allspice =   1 teaspoon equal parts
cinnamon, nutmeg, and cloves

anise =   fennel

1 teaspoon basil =   1 teaspoon oregano

bay leaf =   thyme

capers =   chopped gherkins

1 teaspoon caraway =   1 teaspoon anise

cardamon =   coriander

1 teaspoon cayenne =   1 teaspoon chili pepper

1 teaspoon chervil =   1 teaspoon parsley or tarragon

chives =	scallion
cinnamon =	ground cloves
cloves =	ground cinnamon
coriander =	basil
cumin =	caraway seeds
dill =	caraway
1 teaspoon fennel =	1 teaspoon anise, tarragon or dill
1 small garlic clove =	1/8 teaspoon garlic powder or 1 teaspoon garlic salt (reduce salt by 1/2 teaspoon)
1 tablespoon fresh ginger =	1 teaspoon powdered or candied ginger with sugar washed off
1 tablespoon mustard =	1 teaspoon dried mustard

1 teaspoon nutmeg =	1 teaspoon mace
1 small fresh onion =	1 tablespoon dehydrated minced onion
1 medium fresh onion =	1 tablespoon onion powder
1 teaspoon oregano =	1 teaspoon marjoram, sweet basil
paprika =	ground red pepper (1/8 of amount)
rosemary =	oregano or sweet basil leaves
1 teaspoon sage =	1 teaspoon thyme
dash cayenne or red pepper =	few drops hot pepper sauce
thyme leaves =	young sage leaves
turmeric =	curry powder

| fines herbs = | equal parts of parsley, chives, tarragon and chervil |
| bouquet garni (herbs wrapped in cheese cloth); classic = | 2 sprigs parsley, 1/2 bay leaf, 1 sprig thyme or 1/8 teaspoon dried thyme |

With	*Use*
Lamb	rosemary, parsley and celery
Veal	parsley, thyme and lemon rind
Beef	basil, parsley, bay leaf and clove
Poultry	sage, tarragon and thyme
Pork	thyme, allspice, cloves, sage

Alcohol Substitution Chart

Liqueurs, spirits and wines add a special flavor to desserts that is difficult to replace. But should you choose to make a substitution for the alcohol in any of the recipes, here's what is suggested. Note, however, that the flavor will change, and it takes some experimenting to find what works best for your particular taste preferences.

If the recipes call for:	Substitute:
2 tablespoons Grand Marnier or other orange-flavored liqueur	2 tablespoons unsweetened orange juice concentrate or 2 tablespoons orange juice and 1/2 teaspoon orange extract
2 tablespoons rum or brandy	1/2 to 1 teaspoon rum or brandy extract for recipes in which liquid amount is not crucial. Add water, white grape juice or apple juice, if necessary, to get the specified amount of liquid
2 tablespoons amaretto	1/4 to 1/2 teaspoon almond extract *
2 tablespoons sherry or bourbon	1 to 2 teaspoons vanilla extract *
2 tablespoons Kahlúa or coffee-or chocolate-flavored liqueur	1/2 to 1 teaspoon chocolate extract plus 1/2 to 1 teaspoon instant coffee in 2 tablespoons water
1/4 cup or more port wine, sweet sherry, rum, brandy or fruit-flavored liqueur	Equal measure of unsweetened orange juice or apple juice plus 1 teaspoon or corresponding flavored extract or vanilla extract
1/4 cup or more white wine	Equal measure of white grape juice or apple juice
1/4 cup or more red wine	Equal measure of red grape juice or cranberry juice

*Add water, white grape juice or apple juice to get the specified amount of liquid (when the liquid amount is crucial).

About the Author

Annette Sanderson majored in Home Economics at Auburn University, and her career has been in interior design, owning Sanderson Interiors in Moulton, Alabama, and living in Moulton with her husband Ott. Her family includes Scott Sanderson, Cathy and Laura Lee and Bart Sanderson and Kate.

GOOD TASTE

GOOD TASTE goes beyond recipes. Hopefully, this book captures other aspects typically Southern: bits of architecture, food celebrations, customs and traditions. It also offers suggestions for using garnishes to make food a feast for the senses, for we know food is always enhanced by its presentation.

Not only will you gain insights into the tastes and traditions that make the South a place of gracious hospitality and good food, but you will also detect our Southern accent in the way we revere our past savoring our grandmother's teacakes, our mother's blackberry cobbler or those buttermilk biscuits.

You will find simple comfort foods, foods for special occasions and some old recipes that are eternal favorites. At the same time, we are great food tinkerers, always open to adopting flavors from all over the country.

Many hints, how-to's and helpful charts are included to make *GOOD TASTE* recipes easy and fun to use.

- More than 400 tested recipes

- Countless tips for solving many culinary problems

- Basic recipes and charts allow *GOOD TASTE* to be used without searching elsewhere for additional recipes or information.

- Original watercolor works exhibit a glimpse of architectural history of North Alabama and the City of Moulton, which Peter Jenkins describes in his book "Walk Across America" as "sleepy."

- Enjoy *GOOD TASTE* !

Index

A

Appetizers
Apricot-Pecan Tea Sandwich Spread 31
Baked Mexican Spinach Dip 26
Black Bean Salsa 23
Black-Eyed Pea Dip 21
Blue Cheese Ball 16
Buckaroo Bean and Bacon Salsa 24
Cheddar Cheese Ring 17
Cheese Ball 16
Cheese Rolls 17
Cheese Straws 18
Cherry Tomato Tea Sandwich 29
Citrus-Shrimp Salad 15
Cream Cheese-Olive Spread 31
Crunchy Chicken Wings 13
Cucumber Sandwiches 27
Fabulous Pimento Cheese Spread 18
Fillings for Yeast Rolls 32
Hot Bean Dip 19
Hot Crab Dip 14
Magnificent Mushrooms 14
Marinated Vidalia Onions 20
Mississippi Sin 20
Party Cucumber Sandwiches 28
Peanuty Dip 22
Pecan Chicken Salad in Toast Cups 12
Pineapple-Cream Cheese Spread 32
Seviche 25
Spinach Dip 26
Texas Caviar 19
Toasted Pecans 27
Tomato-Basil Sandwiches 29
Turkey Tea Sandwiches 30
Vidalia Onion Soufflé 21

Apples
Apple and Cheese Bake 211
Apple Julep 33
Stove Top Apples 211

Apricots
Apricot-Pecan Tea Sandwich Spread 31

Asparagus
English Pea and Asparagus Casserole 190
Marinated Asparagus 176
Steamed Asparagus with Lemon Butter 176

B

Bacon
Buckaroo Bean and Bacon Salsa 24
Do-Ahead Broiled Bacon for a Crowd 126
Peppered Ranch Bacon 125
Sugared Bacon Twist 126

Basics
Baked Croutons 313
Batter for Deep Frying 311
Beef Stock 319
Bouquet Garni 311
Buttered Bread Crumbs 312
Chicken Stock 319
Chocolate Brittle for Garnish 323
Chocolate Curls 323
Cracker Crumb Topping 312
Crème Fraîche 311
Creole Seasoning 318
Croutons 312
Four-Season Citrus Salt 318
Fruit Glazes 313
Graham Cracker Crust 317
Honey Glaze for Baked Ham 314
How to Melt Chocolate 324
Just Right Egg Whites 325
Lots of Simple Syrup 321
Magic Whipped Cream Frosting 322
Mayonnaise 314
Meringue 314
Pastry Dough 316
Preparing Fresh Coconut 324
Quick Chicken Broth 320
Roasted Garlic 313
Simple Syrup 321
Sky-High Meringue 315
Sweet Pie Pastry Dough 317
Sweetened Whipped Cream 323
Toast Cups 321
Toast Points 322
Turkey Stock 320

Beans
Best Baked Beans 177
Black Bean Salsa 23
Black-Eyed Pea Dip 21
Buckaroo Bean and Bacon Salsa 24
Butterbeans and Peas 182
English Pea and Asparagus Casserole 190
Green Beans and Red Bell Pepper 178
Green Beans, Southern Style 179
Green Beans with Bacon Dressing 177
Hot Bean Dip 19
Jalapeño Black-Eyed Peas 189
Mean Beans 44
Tomato and White Bean Soup 58

Beef
Beef and Vegetable Stir-Fry 132
Beef Tenderloin Filling 32
Celebration Roast with Horseradish-Peppercorn Cream 130

342 Index

Cheesy Beef Enchiladas 133
Chutney Beef Tenderloin 128
Filet with Red Onion Confit 128
July 4th Hamburgers 138
Marinated Eye of Round Roast 130
Mustard-Topped Steak With Caramelized Onions 135
Onion-Stuffed Burgers 137
Sunday Pot Roast With Vegetables 136
You'll Never Believe It Rib Roast 131

Beverages
Apple Julep 33
Auburn Lemonade 38
Boiled Custard 34
Brandy Slush 33
Cathy's Party Punch 34
French Mint Tea 35
Frozen Ice Rounds 36
Fruited Ice Ring 36
Grape Juice Punch 36
Hot Chocolate 39
Hot White Chocolate 40
Icy Tea Punch 37
Just 1 Lemonade 38
Mock Champagne Punch 35
Quick Iced Tea 39
Raspberry Sherbet Punch 37
Rosy Wassail 41
Spiced Tea 40

Biscuits
Angel Biscuits 90
Angel Biscuits II 91
Cream Biscuits 92
Genuine Southern Biscuits 93
Mama Berlin's 3-Day Biscuits 91
Peppery White Cheddar Biscuit Squares 92
Quick and Easy Biscuits 95
Sweet Potato Biscuits 94

Breads
Advent Bazaar Rolls 96
Angel Biscuits 90
Angel Biscuits II 91
Blackberry Coffee Cake 100
Cheddar Dill Scones 98
Cinnamon Rolls 106
Corn Muffins 89
Cream Biscuits 92
Destin Trip Rolls 97
French Toast with Strawberries 124
Genuine Southern Biscuits 93
Hawaiian Banana Nut Bread 101
Hush Puppies 89
Mama Berlin's 3-Day Biscuits 91
Mexican Cornbread 88
Orange Rolls 107
Overnight Baked French Toast 123
Parmesan Toast 99
Pecan Mini-Muffins 104
Peppery White Cheddar Biscuit Squares 92
Quick and Easy Biscuits 95

Rough-Cut Breadsticks 98
Short and Sweet Caramel Bubble Ring 102
Simple Orange Rolls 108
Skillet Coffee Cake 103
Skillet Cornbread 88
Sweet Potato Biscuits 94
Sweet Potato Muffins 105
Zucchini Bread 109

Breakfasts & Brunches
Asparagus Quiche 112
Best Breakfast Waffles 125
Buttermilk Pancakes 122
Canadian Egg Casserole 110
Cook and Hold Scrambled Eggs 111
Country Ham with Red-Eye Gravy 126
Creamy Grits 119
Creamy Grits with Mushroom Sauce 120
Creamy Scrambled Eggs with Chives 112
Creole Grits 121
French Toast with Strawberries 124
Grits Soufflé 121
Overnight Baked French Toast 123
Sausage and Egg Casserole 111
Sugared Bacon Twist 126
Wonderful Waffles 125

Broccoli
Broccoli Cheese Soufflé 180
Broccoli Cheese Soup 50
Broccoli Salad 72

Brussels Sprouts
Charred Brussels Sprouts, Carrots, Onions and Garlic 181
Pecan-Glazed Brussels Sprouts 181

C

Cakes
Apple Cake 230
Carrot Cake 216
Chocolate Grand Marnier Torte 218
Chocolate Pound Cake 232
Chocolate Torte With Strawberry Filling 220
Cream Cheese Pound Cake 234
Deep Chocolate Cake 231
European Cake with Ambrosia Icing 223
Fresh Peach Meringue Cake 225
Fresh Pineapple Upside-Down Cake 228
Italian Cream Cake 224
Lemon-Almond Buttermilk Loaf with Balsamic Strawberries 233
Mattie B's Fabulous Fresh Coconut Cake 222
Mother's Fig Cake 235
Perfect Chocolate Cake 217
Peter Paul Mounds Cake 227
Plain Sponge Cake 226
Sour Cream Pound Cake 236
Strawberry Cake 229
Sweet Cream Pound Cake 237
Swiss Chocolate Cake 221
Walnut Pound Cake with Glaze 238

Index 343

Candy
Chocolate Chews 292
Chocolate-Toffee Crunch 293
Divinity Candy 293
White Chocolate Salties 294

Carrots
Carrot-Pecan Casserole 183
Charred Brussels Sprouts, Carrots, Onions and Garlic 181
Ginger and Honey-Glazed Carrots 184

Charts
Alcohol Substitution 340
Approximate Total Cooking Times For Steaks 328
Blanching Vegetables 330
Dry Measures 331
Edible Flowers 326
Liquid Measures 331
Meat Roasting Guide 327
Season A Cast-Iron Skillet 329
Substitution Savy
    baking products 332
    Dairy Products 333
    Miscellaneous products 335
    Seasoning products: 334
    Vegetable products 333
Substitutions for Herbs and Spices 336
The Best Mashed Potatoes 326
To Core A Fresh Pineapple 328
Toasting Seeds and Nuts 329

Cheese
Betty's Famous Pimento Cheese Sandwiches 84
Blue Cheese Ball 16
Blue Cheese Coleslaw 79
Broccoli Cheese Soup 50
Cheddar Cheese Ring 17
Cheese Ball 16
Cheese Rolls 17
Cheese Straws 18
Cold-Weather Cheese Soup 51
Cream Cheese-Olive Spread 31
Everyday Macaroni and Cheese 186
Fabulous Pimento Cheese Spread 18
Hot French Cheese Sandwiches 83
Macaroni and Cheese 184
Pineapple-Cream Cheese Spread 32
The Ultimate Macaroni and Cheese 185

Cheesecakes
Caramel Brownie Cheesecake 243
Cheesecake Squares 244
Cheesecake with Strawberry Topping 244

Chicken
Barbecue Chicken 139
Best Chicken Divan 150
Cheesy Chicken Crescents 151
Chicken and Artichoke Casserole 149
Chicken and Dumplings 45
Chicken Milk Gravy 149
Chicken Salad and Artichokes 174
Chicken Salad with Currants 173
Chicken Stew 60

Chicken Stock 54
Chicken with Lime Butter 145
Cornish Game Hens 152
Crunchy Chicken Wings 13
Garlic and Oregano Marinated Chicken 143
Good Chicken Salad 173
Grilled Chicken with Balsamic Peaches 144
Grilled Lemon Chicken 145
Hoisin Chicken with Grilled Peppers and Onions 142
Luncheon Chicken 146
Pecan Chicken Salad in Toast Cups 12
Roast Chicken 147
Shrimp-Chicken Étouffé 158
Southern Fried Chicken 148

Chili
Ballgame Chili 44
Texas-Style Chili 46

Condiments
Apricot-Orange Jam 302
Blackberry Jam 302
Cherry Butter 301
Chili Glaze 308
Cilantro Tartar Sauce 307
Clueless Barbecue Sauce 309
Cranberry and Apricot Chutney 300
Garlic Pickles 304
Honey-Orange Butter 301
Hot Cocktail Sauce 310
Mexican Cranberries 300
Orange Marmalade Spread 303
Quick Spiced Peaches 306
Roasted Corn and Tomato Tartar Sauce 308
Roasted Pepper and Black Olive Relish 306
Seasoned Mayonnaise 303
Sweet Dill Pickles 305
Tartar Sauce 307

Cookies & Bars
Amaretto Brownies 276
Basic Cookie Dough 280
Chess Bars 277
Chocolate Chip Cookies 281
Chocolate Heart Cookies 284
Christmas Cookies with Royal Icing 285
Cinnamon Balls 282
Crescents 285
Favorite Chocolate Chip Cookies 283
Fruitcake Cookies 286
Fudgy Chocolate-Raspberry Bars 279
German Chocolate Chess Squares 278
Key Lime–White Chocolate Cookies 288
Lemon Bars 280
Lemon Slices 287
Marion's Dish Pan Cookies 289
Orange Shortbread 289
Peanut Butter Cookies 281
Pecan Refrigerator Cookies 281
Praline Thumbprint Cookies 290

Sugar Cookies 282
The Ultimate Sugar Cookie 291
White Chocolate-Chunk Macadamia Cookies 292

Corn
Corn on the Cob 186
Grilled Corn in Husks with Basil Butter 187
Shoe Peg Corn Casserole 188

Cranberries
Cranberry Mayonnaise 86
Cranberry Ring Mold and Old-Fashioned Mayonnaise 61

Cucumbers
Cold Cucumber Mint Gazpacho 47
Cucumber Sandwiches 27
Marinated Tomatoes and Cucumbers 75
Party Cucumber Sandwiches 28

D

Desserts
Amaretto Brownies 276
Apple Cake 230
Apple Dumplings 246
Banana Pudding with Meringue 264
Basic Cookie Dough 280
Blueberry Crumble 247
Blueberry Sauce 297
Butterfinger Ice Cream 273
Caramel Brownie Cheesecake 243
Caramelized Pumpkin Custards 262
Carrot Cake 216
Cheesecake Squares 244
Cheesecake with Strawberry Topping 244
Chess Bars 277
Chocolate Amaretto Trifle 267
Chocolate Chess Pie 251
Chocolate Chews 292
Chocolate Chip Cookies 281
Chocolate Cream Pie 252
Chocolate Crème Brûlée 261
Chocolate Dipped Strawberries 297
Chocolate Grand Marnier Torte 218
Chocolate Heart Cookies 284
Chocolate Pecan Pie 253
Chocolate Pound Cake 232
Chocolate Sauce 294
Chocolate Torte With Strawberry Filling 220
Chocolate-Toffee Crunch 293
Christmas Cookies with Royal Icing 285
Cinnamon Balls 282
Coconut Cream Pie 254
Cream Cheese Pound Cake 234
Creamy Apple Pie 250
Crème de Menthe Ice Cream 274
Crescents 285
Deep Chocolate Cake 231
Divinity Candy 293
European Cake with Ambrosia Icing 223
Favorite Chocolate Chip Cookies 283
Fresh Peach Meringue Cake 225

Fresh Pineapple Upside-Down Cake 228
Fresh Strawberry Pie 257
Frozen Peach Dessert 272
Fruitcake Cookies 286
Fudgy Chocolate-Raspberry Bars 279
German Chocolate Chess Squares 278
Hot Fudge Sauce 295
Ice Cream Tortoni 271
Italian Cream Cake 224
Key Lime Pie 256
Key Lime White Chocolate Cookies 288
Lemon Bars 280
Lemon Meringue Nests 269
Lemon Slices 287
Lemon-Almond Buttermilk Loaf with Balsamic Strawberries 233
Lime Tartlets 259
Marion's Dish Pan Cookies 289
Mattie B's Fabulous Fresh Coconut Cake 222
Mini-Cheesecake Fruit Tarts 258
Mother's Fig Cake 235
Orange Shortbread 289
Pastry Cream 267
Peach Cobbler Supreme 248
Peach Ice Cream 275
Peanut Butter Cookies 281
Pears En Croûte 270
Pecan Refrigerator Cookies 281
Perfect Chocolate Cake 217
Peter Paul Mounds Cake 227
Plain Sponge Cake 226
Poached Pears in Chocolate Sauce 271
Praline Thumbprint Cookies 290
Quick Peach Cobbler 249
Raspberry Sauce 296
Selma's Chocolate Pudding 265
Sour Cream Pound Cake 236
Southern Pecan Pie 254
Strawberry Cake 229
Strawberry Glaze 296
Strawberry Meringue Roulade 266
Strawberry Trifle 268
Sugar Cookies 282
Sweet Cream Pound Cake 237
Swiss Chocolate Cake 221
The Ultimate Sugar Cookie 291
Toasty Southern Pecan Tarts 260
Vanilla Crème Brûlée 263
Vanilla Wafer Dessert 273
Walnut Pound Cake with Glaze 238
White Chocolate Salties 294
White Chocolate-Chunk Macadamia Cookies 292

Dressings
Poppy Seed Dressing 70
Ranch Dressing 70
Roquefort Dressing 71
Thousand Island Dressing 71

Index 345

Dumplings
Apple Dumplings 246
Chicken and Dumplings 45

E

Eggplant
Eggplant Parmesan 134
Eggs
Asparagus Quiche 112
Best Stuffed Eggs 82
Canadian Egg Casserole 110
Cook and Hold Scrambled Eggs 111
Creamy Scrambled Eggs with Chives 112
Egg Salad Sandwiches 83
Sausage and Egg Casserole 111
Enchiladas
Cheesy Beef Enchiladas 133
Entrées
Baked Easter Ham 163
Baked Ham with Mustard-Apricot Glaze 164
Baked Plantation Country Ham 162
Barbecue Chicken 139
Barbecue Sandwiches 171
Barbecued Shrimp 160
Basic Shrimp Boil 161
Beef and Vegetable Stir-Fry 132
Best Chicken Divan 150
Celebration Roast with Horseradish-Peppercorn Cream 130
Cheesy Beef Enchiladas 133
Cheesy Chicken Crescents 151
Chicken and Artichoke Casserole 149
Chicken Salad and Artichokes 174
Chicken Salad with Currants 173
Chicken with Lime Butter 145
Chili-Crusted Salmon And Roasted Scalloped Potatoes 156
Chutney Beef Tenderloin 128
Coconut Shrimp with Mustard Sauce 157
Coleslaw 171
Cornish Game Hens 152
Deep-Fried Catfish 154
Eggplant Parmesan 134
Filet with Red Onion Confit 128
Fried Catfish with Sunflower Seed Crust 153
Garlic and Oregano Marinated Chicken 143
Good Chicken Salad 173
Grilled Chicken with Balsamic Peaches 144
Grilled Lemon Chicken 145
Grilled Pork Tenderloin 166
Hoisin Chicken with Grilled Peppers and Onions 142
July 4th Hamburgers 138
Leg of Lamb Roast With Lemon Or Saffron Sauce 165
Luncheon Chicken 146
Marinated Eye of Round Roast 130
Marinated Pork Tenderloin with Mustard Sauce 167
Mustard-Topped Steak With Caramelized Onions 135
Onion-Stuffed Burgers 137
Pork Roast With Peppers 168
Roast Chicken 147

Roast Turkey 172
Roasted Pork Boston Butt 169
Saucy Catfish Bake 155
Shrimp and Crab Supreme 159
Shrimp-Chicken Étouffé 158
Slow-Simmered Pork Roast 172
Southern Corn Bread Dressing with Giblet Gravy 140
Southern Fried Chicken 148
Sunday Pot Roast With Vegetables 136
You'll Never Believe It Rib Roast 131

F

Fish
Catfish Stew 59
Chili-Crusted Salmon 156
Deep-Fried Catfish 154
Fresh Salmon BLT Sandwich 86
Fried Catfish with Sunflower Seed Crust 153
Saucy Catfish Bake 155
Seviche 25
Frostings
Birthday Cake Frosting 239
Caramel Icing 239
Chocolate Frosting for Brownies 240
Chocolate Ganache 242
Cooked White Frosting 241
Magic Whipped Cream Frosting 322
Mary's Pineapple Filling 240
Royal Icing 242
Fruit
Ambrosia 113
Fresh Fruit Salad with Citrus Sauce 114
Fresh Fruit Tray with Dip 115
Hot Sherried Fruit 116
Instant Fruit Salad 115
Spiced Fruit in Light Syrup 117
Summer's Best Fruit Toss 118
Warm Berry Compote 118
Watermelon Quarters 119

G

Gravy
Basic Turkey Gravy 141
Chicken Milk Gravy 149
Giblet Gravy 141
Red-Eye Gravy 126
Grits
Creamy Grits 119
Creamy Grits with Mushroom Sauce 120
Creole Grits 121
Grits Soufflé 121
Gumbo
Lela Phillips' Seafood Gumbo Over Rice 49

H

Ham
Baked Easter Ham 163
Baked Ham with Mustard-Apricot Glaze 164
Baked Plantation Country Ham 162
Country Ham with Red-Eye Gravy 126

Hamburgers
July 4th Hamburgers 138
Onion-Stuffed Burgers 137

L

Lamb
Leg of Lamb Roast With Lemon Or Saffron Sauce 165

Lemonade
Auburn Lemonade 38
Just 1 Lemonade 38

M

Macaroni
Everyday Macaroni and Cheese 186
Macaroni and Cheese 184
The Ultimate Macaroni and Cheese 185

Measurement Equivalents
Dry Measures 331
Liquid Measures 331

Mushrooms
Magnificent Mushrooms 14

N

Nuts
Toasted Pecans 27

O

Onions
Marinated Vidalia Onions 20
Onion Soup 54
Roasted Sweet Onions 191
Vidalia Onion Soufflé 21

Oranges
Mandarin Orange Salad 67

P

Pancakes
Buttermilk Pancakes 122

Pasta
Oriental Pasta Salad 73

Peas
Black-Eyed Pea Dip 21
Butterbeans and Peas 182
English Pea and Asparagus Casserole 190
Jalapeño Black-Eyed Peas 189

Peppers
Sweet Pepper Gratin 192

Pies, Cobblers and Tarts
Chocolate Chess Pie 251
Chocolate Cream Pie 252
Chocolate Pecan Pie 253
Coconut Cream Pie 254
Creamy Apple Pie 250
Fresh Strawberry Pie 257
Key Lime Pie 256
Lime Tartlets 259
Mini-Cheesecake Fruit Tarts 258
Peach Cobbler Supreme 248
Quick Peach Cobbler 249
Southern Pecan Pie 254
Toasty Southern Pecan Tarts 260

Pork
Baked Easter Ham 163
Baked Ham with Mustard-Apricot Glaze 164
Baked Plantation Country Ham 162
Barbecue Sandwiches 171
Country Ham with Red-Eye Gravy 126
Grilled Pork Tenderloin 166
Marinated Pork Tenderloin with Mustard Sauce 167
Pork Roast With Peppers 168
Roasted Pepper and Pork Sandwich 85
Roasted Pork Boston Butt 169
Slow-Simmered Pork Roast 172

Potatoes
Baked Potato Soup 55
Boursin Mashed Potatoes 193
Candied Sweet Potatoes 202
Do-Ahead Stuffed Potatoes 196
Easy Potato Soup 56
French Fries 195
Garlic Mashed Potatoes 197
Glorified Potatoes 198
Mashed Potatoes With Butter 199
Oven-Fried Potatoes 200
Potatoes Romanoff 200
Roasted New Potato Salad 77
Roasted New Potatoes with Rosemary 201
Roasted Scalloped Potatoes 156
Summer Potato Salad 78
Sweet Potato Salad With Rosemary-Honey Vinaigrette 79
Sweet Potato-Praline Casserole with Marshmallows 203

R

Raspberries
Raspberry Sauce 296
Raspberry Sherbet Punch 37

Rice
Wild Rice Salad 82
Wild Rice with Dried Cranberries and Apricots 214
Wild Rice with Mushrooms 213

Index 347

S

Salads

Blue Cheese Coleslaw 79
Broccoli Salad 72
Clara's 3-Week Slaw 80
Coleslaw 171
Cranberry Ring Mold and Old-Fashioned Mayonnaise 61
Crunchy Cabbage Slaw 80
Delightful Green Salad with Poppy Seed Dressing 66
Fresh Fruit Salad with Citrus Sauce 114
Frozen Frosted Fruit Salad 62
Keb's Slaw 81
Magnolia Salad 63
Mandarin Orange Salad 67
Marinated Tomatoes and Cucumbers 75
Marinated Vegetable Salad With Dijon Dressing 76
Oriental Pasta Salad 73
Party Relish Tray 74
Roasted New Potato Salad 77
Spinach Dill Salad 68
Strawberry Pretzel Salad 64
Summer Potato Salad 78
Summer Tomato Toss 75
Sweet Potato Salad With Rosemary-Honey Vinaigrette 79
Toasted Walnut Salad 69
Waldorf Salad 65
Wild Rice Salad 82

Sandwiches

Apricot-Pecan Tea Sandwich Spread 31
Betty's Famous Pimento Cheese Sandwiches 84
Cherry Tomato Tea Sandwich 29
Cucumber Sandwiches 27
Egg Salad Sandwiches 83
Fresh Salmon BLT Sandwich 86
Hot French Cheese Sandwiches 83
Party Cucumber Sandwiches 28
Roasted Pepper and Pork Sandwich 85
Tomato-Basil Sandwiches 29
Turkey Tea Sandwiches 30
Whitlock Wedges 86

Sauces

Blueberry Sauce 297
Chocolate Sauce 294
Hot Fudge Sauce 295
Hotter Hot Sauce 170
Raspberry Sauce 296
Vinegar Hot Sauce 169
White Barbecue Sauce 170

Shrimp

Barbecued Shrimp 160
Basic Shrimp Boil 161
Citrus-Shrimp Salad 15
Coconut Shrimp with Mustard Sauce 157
Lela Phillips' Seafood Gumbo Over Rice 49
Shrimp and Crab Supreme 159
Shrimp-Chicken Étouffé 158

Side Dishes

Apple and Cheese Bake 211
Baked Tomatoes 206
Fettucini Alfredo 212
Fried Green Tomatoes 206
Pineapple Casserole 212
Sautéed Cherry Tomatoes 207
Stove Top Apples 211
Summer Squash and Green Tomatoes 207
Wild Rice with Dried Cranberries and Apricots 214
Wild Rice with Mushrooms 213

Sidebars

Baking in a Water Bath 260
Blanching Tips 178
Blind Baking 253
Cake Flour 236
Chicken Stock 54
Cold, clear pitchers of lemonade 38
Cookie Baking 291
Crème Fraîche 259
Cube Art 37
Cut a kiwi fruit in half 115
Cutting Into Julienne 173
Deglazing 191
Dividing a Cake Layer 228
Do you Know How To Boil An Egg? 190
Do-Ahead Broiled Bacon for a Crowd 126
Filé Powder 49
For an edible July 4th centerpiece, 119
Freezing Egg Whites 295
Fresh Asparagus 177
Fresh Lettuce 65
Grilled corn is done when the husk begins to pull 187
Horseradish Sauce 161
How To Save Vidalia Onions 192
Ice Cream for Dessert? 248
Iced tea, like ice cubes, made with spring water 41
If Vidalias or other sweet onions are not available 193
If whipped cream has begun to liquefy 264
Is It Done? 155
Keep Parsley Fresh 154
Macerated Fruit 225
Okra 50
Peppered Ranch Bacon 125
Quick-Cleaning the Blender 310
Quick-rising yeast may be used interchangeably 90
Remove Bay Leaf 59
Scallions can be thought of as teenage onions 156
Serve homemade salsa in individual cabbage cups 23
Shallots 130
Soaking Dried Beans 188
Soft- Ball Stage 290
To get more juice from each lemon 39
To prevent a skin from forming on dessert sauces 267
To Quick-Soak Dried Beans 189
To Roast Peppers 194
To Sterilize Jars and Glasses 306
Tortes 219

Try Sweet Potato Biscuits with smoked ham 94
Unsweetened Chocolate 218
Vanilla Bean 261
Waffles 124
Water Bath Processing 307
Whole red chili peppers punctuate a platter of ham 139

Soups

Baked Potato Soup 55
Ballgame Chili 44
Broccoli Cheese Soup 50
Catfish Stew 59
Chicken and Dumplings 45
Chicken Stew 60
Chunky Italian Soup 53
Cold Cucumber Mint Gazpacho 47
Cold-Weather Cheese Soup 51
Dieter's Soup 52
Easy Potato Soup 56
Lela Phillips' Seafood Gumbo Over Rice 49
Mean Beans 44
Onion Soup 54
Santa Fe Soup 57
Texas-Style Chili 46
Tomato and White Bean Soup 58
White Gazpacho 48

Squash

Squash Dressing 205

Stir-Fry

Beef and Vegetable Stir-Fry 132

T

Tea

French Mint Tea 35
Icy Tea Punch 37
Quick Iced Tea 39
Spiced Tea 40

Tomatoes

Baked Tomatoes 206
Cherry Tomato Tea Sandwich 29
Fried Green Tomatoes 206
Marinated Tomatoes and Cucumbers 75
Sautéed Cherry Tomatoes 207
Summer Tomato Toss 75
Tomato and White Bean Soup 58
Tomato-Basil Sandwiches 29

Turkey

Basic Turkey Gravy 141
Roast Turkey 172
Turkey Filling 32
Turkey Tea Sandwiches 30

V

Vegetables

Boursin Mashed Potatoes 193
Broccoli Cheese Soufflé 180
Butterbeans and Peas 182
Candied Sweet Potatoes 202

Carrot-Pecan Casserole 183
Charred Brussels Sprouts, Carrots, Onions and Garlic 181
Company Potatoes 194
Corn on the Cob 186
Do-Ahead Stuffed Potatoes 196
English Pea and Asparagus Casserole 190
French Fries 195
Fresh Turnip Greens 208
Garlic Mashed Potatoes 197
Ginger and Honey-Glazed Carrots 184
Glorified Potatoes 198
Greek Spinach Casserole 204
Green Beans and Red Bell Pepper 178
Green Beans, Southern Style 179
Green Beans with Bacon Dressing 177
Green Beans with Honey Cashew Sauce 178
Grilled Corn in Husks with Basil Butter 187
Jalapeño Black-Eyed Peas 189
Marinated Asparagus 176
Mashed Potatoes With Butter 199
Oven-Fried Potatoes 200
Pecan-Glazed Brussels Sprouts 181
Potatoes Romanoff 200
Roasted Autumn Vegetables 210
Roasted New Potatoes with Rosemary 201
Roasted Sweet Onions 191
Roasted Vegetable Assortment 210
Shoe Peg Corn Casserole 188
Spinach and Artichoke Casserole 204
Squash Dressing 205
Steamed Asparagus with Lemon Butter 176
Summer Squash and Green Tomatoes 207
Sweet Pepper Gratin 192
Sweet Potato-Praline Casserole with Marshmallows 203
Vegetable Sauté 209
Wilted Spinach with Cranberries 205

W

Waffles

Best Breakfast Waffles 125
Wonderful Waffles 125

Credits and Purpose

GOOD TASTE expresses gratitude and grateful appreciation to the friends listed below for their generous contributions toward this Second Edition.

Corporate Friends

Affordable Elegance Limousine Service, Inc., Madison, AL
Anonymous Donation
Anonymous Donation
Bank Independent, Moulton, AL
Big Ed's Cajun Grille, Moulton, AL
Barbara Carroll, Remax Valley Professionals, Moulton, AL
CBS Bank, Moulton, AL
Cash Register Systems, Inc., Montgomery, AL
The Citizens Bank, Moulton, AL
Decatur Coco-Cola Bottling Company, Decatur, AL
Design Interiors, Tampa, FL
Dr. Page Dunlap, Decatur, AL
Electrical Outlet, Moulton, AL
Ellis Embroidery Shop, Hartselle, AL
Endelman & Associates PLLC, Seattle, WA
Engineered Solutions, Inc., Huntsville, AL
First Realty Property Management, Auburn, AL
Fite Building Company, Inc., Decatur, AL
Flowers Foods, Tuscaloosa, AL
The Gift Room, Moulton, AL
Gobble-Fite Lumber Company, Decatur, AL
Golden Flake Snack Foods, Inc., Birmingham, AL
Grande Bazaar, Decatur, AL
Robert B. Hall, M.D., Moulton, AL
Hayes-Rasbury Insurance Agency, Decatur, AL
Brent Johnson, Farmers Insurance, Moulton, AL
Mike Johnson, State Farm Insurance, Moulton, AL
Law Firm of Caine & Proctor, Moulton, AL
Lawrence County Abstract Company, Moulton, AL
Littrell Lumber Mill, Decatur, AL
Timothy D. Littrell, Attorney at Law, Moulton, AL
The Loft, Decatur, AL

David L. Martin III, Attorney at Law, Moulton, AL
Memories, Antiques & Ideas, Moulton, AL
Millidine's Salon & Day Spa, Madison, AL
Billy C. Mitchell Jewelry, Moulton, AL
Harry Montgomery, Attorney at Law, Moulton, AL
The Moulton Advertiser, Moulton, AL
Naylor Plumbing, Moulton, AL
Ol' Dean Foods, Florence, AL
Ott's IGA Foods, Moulton, AL
The Paper Chase, Decatur, AL
Pepsi- Cola Bottling Company, Decatur, AL
ReMax Plus, Inc., Hartselle, AL
Sanderson Truck Sales, Decatur, AL
Joe Sartain Ford, Inc., Decatur, AL
Schoel, Godwin, Barnett, P.C. Decatur, AL
Scott's Guitars, Moulton, AL
Kenneth F. Seale, D.M.D., Moulton, AL
Selecflex, Inc., Decatur, AL
Southern Printing, Moulton, AL
Steve's Discount Drugs, Moulton, AL
Sunshine Mills, Inc., Red Bay, AL
H.L. Speake, Attorney at Law, Moulton, AL
Terry's Florist & Gifts, Inc., Moulton, AL
Thermal Insulation, Inc., Decatur, AL
Tucker, Scott & Wates LLC, Decatur, AL
Turtle Pond Estates, Hartselle, AL
Village West, Hartselle, AL
WALW FM, Moulton, AL
Western Auto, Moulton, AL
Western Sirloin Steakhouse, Moulton, AL
Witt's Flooring Center, Moulton, AL
WS Electrical & Air Conditioning, Inc., Decatur, AL

Individual Friends

Anonymous Donation
Anonymous Donation
Jeff & Amy Black, Hartselle, AL
Wes & Katie Black, Decatur, AL
Carol Buckins, Florence, AL
Florence M. Caudle, Decatur, AL
Tommie & Linda Dunlap, Decatur, AL
Katharine G. Holland, Moulton, AL
Anna Little, Auburn, AL
Farol & Karen Little, Decatur, AL
Zachry & Stephanie Littrell, Franklin, TN
Tommy Wayne & Jane McCullough, Moulton, AL
Bobby & Syble Murphy, Falkville, AL
Matt & Nanette Pride, Decatur, AL

Philip & Vikki Reich, Moulton, AL
Dr. & Mrs. Robert H. Rhyne, Jr., Moulton, AL
Bart Sanderson & Kate Kaehny, Seattle, WA
Grace & Jemma Sanderson, Seattle, WA
Helen Holland Sanderson, Decatur, AL
Arthur W. & Annette Sanderson, Moulton, AL
Scott & Cathy Sanderson, Moulton, AL
Tennis & Berlin Sanderson, Moulton, AL
David & Betty Sims, Hartselle, AL
Mitchell D. Sims, Huntsville, AL
Tony & Jan Stockton, Moulton, AL
Neil & Laura Lee Wood, Waukee, IA
Trevor & Christine Wright, Hartselle, AL
Mary Burch Wynn, Hartselle, AL

Foundation Fighting Blindness

PO Box 17279
Baltimore, MD 21203-7279
www.FightBlindness.org

The urgent mission of The Foundation Fighting Blindness is to drive the research that will provide preventions, treatments and cures for people affected by retinitis pigmentosa, macular degeneration, Usher syndrome, and the entire spectrum of retinal degenerative diseases.

Net profits from the sale of *GOOD TASTE* will benefit **The Foundation Fighting Blindness.**

Notes

GOOD TASTE
107 Woodland Terrace
Moulton, AL 35650
256-974-0311
anniels@bellsouth.net

Please send_____copies of *GOOD TASTE* @ $21.95 each $_____
Add postage and handling @ $3.05 each $_____
Alabama residents add sales tax @ $1.98 each $_____

Ship to: Total enclosed $_____

Name: _____

Address: _____

City: _____ State _____ Zip_____

Please make checks payable to: *GOOD TASTE*

— —

GOOD TASTE
107 Woodland Terrace
Moulton, AL 35650
256-974-0311
anniels@bellsouth.net

Please send_____copies of *GOOD TASTE* @ $21.95 each $_____
Add postage and handling @ $3.05 each $_____
Alabama residents add sales tax @ $1.98 each $_____

Ship to: Total enclosed $_____

Name: _____

Address: _____

City: _____ State _____ Zip_____

Please make checks payable to: *GOOD TASTE*

— —

GOOD TASTE
107 Woodland Terrace
Moulton, AL 35650
256-974-0311
anniels@bellsouth.net

Please send_____copies of *GOOD TASTE* @ $21.95 each $_____
Add postage and handling @ $3.05 each $_____
Alabama residents add sales tax @ $1.98 each $_____

Ship to: Total enclosed $_____

Name: _____

Address: _____

City: _____ State _____ Zip_____

Please make checks payable to: *GOOD TASTE*